This book is dedicated to my ancestors,

the Kennedys of Yonkers, New York.

Hardworking, generous, and honest folks.

Killing Kennedy

A Note to Readers

NOVEMBER 22, 1963
MINEOLA, NEW YORK
APPROXIMATELY 2:00 P.M.

The students in Brother Carmine Diodati's freshman Religion class were startled. Over the loudspeaker, a radio report crackled into the Chaminade High School classroom. President John F. Kennedy had been shot in Dallas, Texas, and taken to the hospital. A short time later we would all learn he was dead. No one knew what to say.

Most Americans born before 1953 remember exactly where they were when they heard the news that JFK had been assassinated. The days following that terrible Friday were filled with sadness and confusion. Why did it happen? Who really killed the president? What kind of country did we live in anyway?

The assassination of JFK was somewhat personal for me. My maternal grandmother was born Winifred Kennedy, and my Irish-Catholic family had deep emotional ties to the young president and his family. It felt as if someone in my own home had died violently. Like most kids on Long Island, I didn't care much about national politics. But I vividly remember pictures of JFK displayed in the homes of my relatives. To them, he was a saint. To me, he was a distant figure who died in a terrible way, his brain splattered all over the trunk of a car. The vision of his wife, Jacqueline, crawling onto the back of the limo in order to retrieve the president's shattered skull has stayed with me always.

■ ■ ■

Martin Dugard and I were well pleased that millions of people read and enjoyed *Killing Lincoln*. We want to make history accessible to everyone. We want to tell readers exactly what happened and why, using a style that is entertaining as well as informative. After chronicling the last days of Abraham Lincoln, the progression to John Kennedy was a natural.

It has been widely pointed out that the two men had much in common. In fact, the parallels are amazing:

- ✦ Lincoln was first elected in 1860, Kennedy in 1960.
- ✦ Both were assassinated on a Friday, in the presence of their wives.
- ✦ Their successors were both southerners named Johnson who had served in the Senate.
- ✦ Andrew Johnson was born in 1808, Lyndon Johnson in 1908.
- ✦ Lincoln was elected to Congress in 1846, while Kennedy was elected to the House in 1946.
- ✦ Both men suffered the death of children while in office.
- ✦ The assassin Booth shot inside a theater and fled into a storage facility, while the assassin Oswald shot from a storage facility and fled into a theater.

Back in 1963, few Americans understood how profoundly the assassination of JFK would change the country. These days, history is a difficult thing to impart, especially because of political agendas. In this book, we will try to cut through the fog and bring you the facts. Unfortunately, some of the facts are still not known. In our narrative, Martin Dugard and I go only as far as the evidence takes us. We are not conspiracy guys, although we do raise some questions about what is unknown and inconsistent.

However, before you proceed further, please know that this is a fact-based book and some of what you will read has never before been publicly stated.

The truth about President Kennedy is sometimes gallant, and sometimes disturbing. The truth about how and why he was murdered is simply atrocious. But all Americans should know the story.

It's all here in this book. It is my special privilege to bring it to you.

BILL O'REILLY
May 2012
Long Island, New York

MAY 29, 1917–NOVEMBER 22, 1963

Prologue

JANUARY 20, 1961
WASHINGTON, D.C.
12:51 P.M.

The man with fewer than three years to live has his left hand on the Bible.

Chief Justice Earl Warren stands before him reciting the Presidential Oath of Office. "Do you, John Fitzgerald Kennedy, do solemnly swear . . ."

"I, John Fitzgerald Kennedy, do solemnly swear," the new president repeats in a clipped Boston accent. His gaze is directed at the jurist whose name will one day be synonymous with Kennedy's own death.

The new president, born into wealth, has a refined manner of speaking that would seem to distance him from the electorate. But he is an enthusiastic and easily likeable man's man. He joked openly about his father's vast riches during the campaign, defusing that divisive issue with humor and candor so that average Americans would trust him when he spoke about making America better. "Poor men in West Virginia heard a man from Boston say he needed their help, and they gave it. In the alien corn of Nebraska, with a familiar chopping motion of his right hand, he explained that America can be 'great-ah,' and the farmers knew what he meant," one writer noted of Kennedy's broad appeal.

But not everyone loves JFK. He won the popular vote over Richard Nixon by a razor-thin margin, garnering just 49 percent of the tally. Those farmers might have known what Kennedy meant, but 62 percent of Nebraskans voted for Nixon.

"That you will faithfully execute the office of President of the United States."

"That I will faithfully execute the office of President of the United States . . ."

Eighty million Americans are watching the inauguration on television. Twenty thousand more are there in person. Eight inches of thick, wet snow have fallen on Washington, D.C., overnight. The army had to use flamethrowers to clear the roads. The sun now shines on the Capitol Building, but a brutal wind strafes the crowd. Spectators wrap their bodies in sleeping bags, blankets, thick sweaters, and winter coats—anything to stay warm.

But John Kennedy ignores the cold. He has even removed his overcoat. At age forty-three, JFK exudes fearlessness and vigor. His lack of coat, top hat, scarf, or gloves is an intentional ploy to burnish his athletic image. He is trim and just a shade over six feet tall, with greenish-gray eyes, a dazzling smile, and a deep tan, thanks to a recent vacation at his family's Palm Beach home. But while JFK looks like the picture of health, his medical history has been troubling. Kennedy has already been administered the last rites of the Roman Catholic Church on two separate occasions. His medical woes will continue to trouble him in the years to come.

"And will, to the best of your ability . . ."

"And will, to the best of my ability . . ."

In the sea of dignitaries and friends arrayed all around him, there are three people vital to Kennedy. The first is his younger brother and reluctant choice for attorney general, Bobby. The president values him more for his honesty as an adviser than for his legal ability. He knows Bobby will always tell him the truth, no matter how brutal it may be.

Behind the president is the new vice president, Lyndon Johnson. It can be said, and Johnson himself believes, that Kennedy won the presidency because of this tough, tall Texan. Without Johnson on the ticket, Kennedy might never have won the Lone Star State and its treasure trove of 24 electoral votes. As it was, the Kennedy-Johnson ticket won by the slender margin of 46,000 votes in Texas—a feat that must be replicated if Kennedy is to win a second term.

Finally, the new president spies his young wife just behind Justice Warren's left shoulder. Jackie Kennedy is radiant in her taupe suit and matching hat. Dark brown hair and a fur collar frame her unlined face. Her amber eyes sparkle with excitement; she is not showing a hint of fatigue despite having stayed up until 4:00 A.M. The booze flowed freely at preinaugural celebrations thrown by the likes of Frank Sinatra and Leonard Bernstein. Jackie returned to their house in Georgetown long before the parties wound down, but her husband did not accompany her. When Jack finally showed up, just before 4:00 A.M., he found his wife wide awake, too excited to sleep. As the snow continued to fall on the stranded motorists and the impromptu bonfires lining the streets of Washington, the young couple sat together in early-morning conversation. He told her about a late dinner organized by his father, and they talked with excitement about the inauguration ceremony. It would be an extraordinary day, with the promise of many more to come.

John F. Kennedy well understands that the public adores Jackie. Just last night, when crowds on the snowy Washington streets glimpsed the Kennedys driving past in their limousine, the president-elect asked that the inside lights be turned on so that the people might glimpse his wife. Jackie's glamour, sense of style, and beauty have captivated America. She speaks fluent French and Spanish, secretly chain-smokes filtered cigarettes, and prefers champagne to cocktails. Like her husband, Jackie has a dazzling smile, but she is the introvert to his extrovert. Her trust in outsiders is scant.

Despite her glamorous image, Jackie Kennedy has already known great tragedy during their seven years of marriage. She miscarried their first child, and the second was a stillborn baby girl. But she has also enjoyed the birth of two healthy children, Caroline and John Jr., and the stunning ascension of her dashing young husband from a Massachusetts politician to president of the United States.

The sadness is now behind her. The future looks limitless and bright. The Kennedy presidency seems destined to be, in the words of a new hit play that just opened at Broadway's Majestic Theater, much like the mythical Camelot, a place where "there's simply not a more congenial spot, for happily-ever-aftering."

■ ■ ■

"Preserve, protect and defend the Constitution of the United States . . ."

"Preserve, protect and defend the Constitution of the United States . . ."

Kennedy's predecessor, Dwight Eisenhower, stands next to Jackie. Behind Kennedy stand Lyndon Johnson, Richard Nixon, and Harry Truman.

Normally, having just one of these dignitaries at an event means heightened security. Having all of them at the inaugural, sitting so closely together, is a security nightmare.

The Secret Service is on high alert. Its job is to protect the president. The fifty-five-year-old career agent and leader of the service, Chief U. E. Baughman, has been in charge since Truman was president. He believes that Kennedy's athleticism and fondness for wading into crowds will make guarding him a challenge unlike any other in the Service's history. The lean Baughman, with his trademark crew cut, almost cleared the inaugural stand three times today out of concern for presidential safety. On one occasion, blue smoke poured from the lectern during the invocation, and there was fear that it was a bomb. Agents rushed to investigate. As it turned out, the smoke came from the motor that raised and lowered the lectern. Stopping the problem was as simple as turning off the motor. Now Baughman's agents scan the crowd, nervous about the close proximity of the vast audience. One well-trained zealot with a pistol could kill the new president, two former presidents, and a pair of vice presidents with five crisp shots.

Baughman is well aware of another chilling fact. Since 1840, every president elected in a twenty-year cycle has died in office: Harrison, Lincoln, Garfield, McKinley, Harding, and Roosevelt. Yet no president has been assassinated for almost sixty years, thanks to the expertise of the Secret Service. Just last month, agents foiled an attempt on Kennedy's life by a disgruntled former postal worker who planned to blow him up with dynamite. Nonetheless, Baughman is faced with a haunting question: Will the chain of presidential deaths be broken, or will Kennedy be its next link?

JFK laughs off suggestions that he might die in office. Just to prove that he isn't a believer in omens, the new president has chosen to sleep in the Lincoln Bedroom during his first few nights in the White House—the ghost of Abe apparently of no concern.

"So help you God."

". . . So help me God."

The oath complete, Kennedy shakes Chief Justice Warren's hand, then those of Johnson and Nixon. Finally, he stands toe to toe with Eisenhower. The two men smile cordially, but there is steel in their eyes. Eisenhower's condescending nickname for Kennedy is "Little Boy Blue." He thinks him callow and incapable of governing, and finds it galling that a man who was a mere lieutenant during the Second World War is taking over the presidency from the general who directed the D-Day invasion. For his part, Kennedy sees the old general as a man little interested in righting the wrongs of American society—a top priority for JFK.

Kennedy is the youngest president ever elected. Eisenhower is the oldest. The great divide in their ages also represents two very different generations of Americans—and two very different views of America. In just a moment, Kennedy will deliver an inaugural address that will make those differences clearer than ever.

The thirty-fifth president of the United States lets go of Eisenhower's hand. He pivots slowly to his left and stands at the podium bearing the presidential seal. Kennedy looks down at his speech, then lifts his eyes and gazes out at the thousands of frozen faces before him, knowing that the crowd is impatient. The ceremony started late, the invocation by Cardinal Richard Cushing was extremely long, and the eighty-six-year-old poet Robert Frost was so blinded by the sun that he was unable to read the special verses he'd written for the occasion. Nothing, it seems, has gone according to plan. What these freezing people long for is something redemptive. Some words that will signal a shift from the stagnant state of Washington politics. Words that will heal a nation divided by McCarthyism, terrified of the cold war, and still struggling with racial segregation and discrimination.

Kennedy is a Pulitzer Prize–winning historian, having received the award for his book *Profiles in Courage*. He knows the value of a great inaugural address. For months he has fussed over the words he is about to recite. Just last night, when the lights were turned on inside the car to make Jackie visible to onlookers, he reread Thomas Jefferson's inaugural address—and found his own lacking by comparison. This morning, he rose after just four hours of sleep and, pencil in hand, scrutinized his speech again and again and again.

His words resonate like a psalm. "Let the word go forth from this time and place, from friend and foe alike, that the torch has been passed to a new generation of Americans—born in this century, tempered by war, disciplined by a hard and bitter peace, proud of our ancient heritage . . ."

This is no ordinary inaugural address. This is a promise. America's best days are still to come, Kennedy is saying, but only if everyone pitches in to do his part. "Ask not what your country can do for you," he commands, his voice rising to deliver the defining sentence, "but what you can do for your country."

The address will be hailed as an instant classic. In less than 1,400 words, John Fitzgerald Kennedy defines his vision for the nation. He now sets the speech aside, knowing that the time has come to fulfill the great promise he has made to the American people. He must manage the issue with Cuba and its pro-Soviet leader, Fidel Castro. He must tackle problems in a faraway land known as Vietnam, where a small band of U.S. military advisers is struggling to bring stability to a region long rocked by war. And here at home, the power of the Mafia crime syndicates and the divisiveness of the civil rights movement are two crucial situations requiring immediate attention. And on a much more personal level, he must negotiate the animus between Attorney General Bobby Kennedy and Vice President Lyndon Johnson, who despise each other.

JFK surveys the adoring crowd, knowing that he has much work to do.

But not all those invited to the inauguration have turned up. The famous entertainers attending the previous night's parties were promised prime seats for this pivotal moment in American history, but owing to the cold and a 100-proof celebration that stretched into the wee small hours, singer Frank Sinatra, actor Peter Lawford, and composer Leonard Bernstein—along with a host of others—opted to sleep late and watch the event on television. "I'll see the president's second inaugural" is their common refrain.

But there will be no second inaugural. For John Fitzgerald Kennedy is on a collision course with evil.

■ ■ ■

Approximately 4,500 miles away, in the Soviet city of Minsk, an American who did not vote for John F. Kennedy is fed up. Lee Harvey Oswald, a former U.S. Marine Corps sharpshooter, has had enough of life in this Communist nation.

Oswald is a defector. In 1959, at age nineteen, the slightly built, somewhat handsome, enigmatic drifter decided to leave the United States of America, convinced that his socialist beliefs would be embraced in the Soviet Union. But things haven't gone according to plan. Oswald had hoped to attend Moscow University, even though he never graduated from high school. Instead, the Soviet government shipped him more than four hundred miles west, to Minsk, where he has been toiling in an electronics factory.

Oswald is fond of being on the move, but the Soviets have severely restricted his travel. Until now, his life has been chaotic and nomadic.

Lee Harvey Oswald at his application for Soviet citizenship in 1959. (Bettmann/ Corbis/AP Images)

Oswald's father died before he was born. His mother remarried and soon divorced. Marguerite Oswald had little money and moved young Lee frequently, traveling through Texas, New Orleans, and New York City. By the time he dropped out of high school to enlist in the marines, Oswald had lived at twenty-two different addresses and attended twelve different schools—including a reform institution. There, a court-ordered psychiatric evaluation found him to be withdrawn and socially malad-justed. He was diagnosed as having "a vivid fantasy life, turning around the topics of omnipotence and power, through which he tries to com-pensate for his present shortcomings and frustrations."

The Soviet Union in 1961 is hardly the place for a man in search of independence and power. For the first time in his life, Lee Harvey Oswald is stuck. He gets up every morning and trudges to the factory, where he labors hour after hour operating a lathe, surrounded by cowork-ers whose language he barely understands. His defection in 1959 was reported by American newspapers because it was extremely unusual for a U.S. Marine—even one so pro-Soviet that his fellow marines had nicknamed him "Oswaldskovich"—to violate the Semper Fi (Always Faithful) oath and go over to the enemy. But now he is anonymous, which he finds completely unacceptable. Defection doesn't seem like such a good idea anymore. Oswald confides to his journal that he is thoroughly disenchanted.

Lee Harvey Oswald has nothing against John Fitzgerald Kennedy. He doesn't know much about the new president or his policies. And while Oswald was a crack shot in the military, little in his past indicates that he would be a threat to anyone but himself.

As America celebrates Kennedy's inauguration, the defector writes to the U.S. embassy in Moscow. His note is short and to the point: Lee Harvey Oswald wants to come home.

PART I

Cheating Death

1

~

I t is February 1961. The new president has a coconut on his desk. He is lucky to be alive, having already cheated death three times in his short life, and the unusual paperweight is a reminder of the first time he came face-to-face with his own mortality. His staff makes sure to place the coconut in a prominent position when they move the new president into the Oval Office. They know their boss wants that very special coconut in his line of sight, because it is a reminder of a now-famous incident that tested his courage.

■ ■ ■

Eighteen years earlier, in 1943, on a balmy Pacific night, three American patrol torpedo boats cruise the Blackett Strait in the South Pacific, hunting Japanese warships near a hotly contested area known as The Slot. At eighty feet long, with hulls of two-inch-thick mahogany, and powered by three powerful Packard engines, these patrol torpedo (PT) boats are nimble vessels, capable of flitting in close to sink Japanese battleships with a battery of Mark VIII torpedoes.

The skipper of the boat bearing the number 109, a young second lieutenant, slouches in his cockpit, half alert and half asleep. He has shut down two of his engines to conceal PT-109 from Japanese spotter planes. The third engine idles softly, its deep propeller shaft leaving almost no wake in the iridescent water. He gazes across the ocean on this night without moon or starlight in the hope of locating the two other nearby PTs. But they are invisible in the darkness—just like 109.

The skipper doesn't see or hear the destroyer *Amagiri* until it's almost too late. She's part of the Tokyo Express, a bold Japanese experiment to transport troops and weapons in and out of the tactically vital Solomon Islands via ultrafast warships. The Express relies on speed and the cover of night to complete these missions. *Amagiri* has just dropped nine hundred soldiers at Vila, on nearby Kolombangara Island, and is racing back to the Japanese bastion at Rabaul, New Guinea, before dawn will allow American bombers to find and destroy her. She is longer than a football field but a mere thirty-four feet at the beam, her shape allowing *Amagiri* to knife through the sea at an astonishing forty-four miles per hour.

In the bow of PT-109, Ensign George "Barney" Ross of Highland Park, Illinois, also peers into the night. His previous boat was recently, accidentally, sunk by an American bomber, and he volunteered for this mission as an observer. Now Ross is stunned when, through his binoculars, he sees the *Amagiri* just 250 yards away, bearing down on 109 at full speed. He points into the darkness. The skipper sees the ship and spins the wheel hard, trying to turn his boat toward the rampaging destroyer to fire his torpedoes from point-blank range—either that, or the Americans will be destroyed.

PT-109 can't turn fast enough.

It takes just a single terrifying instant for *Amagiri* to slice through the mahogany hull. The diagonal incision begins on the right side, barely missing the cockpit. The skipper is almost crushed, at that moment thinking to himself, "This is how it feels to be killed." Two members of the thirteen-man crew die instantly. Two more are injured as PT-109

Lieutenant John Fitzgerald Kennedy in the cockpit of PT-109. (Photographer unknown, Papers of John F. Kennedy, Presidential Papers, President's Office Files, John F. Kennedy Presidential Library and Museum, Boston)

explodes and burns. The two nearby American boats, PT-162 and PT-169, know a fatal blast when they see one, and don't wait around to search for survivors. They gun their engines and race into the night, fearful that other Japanese warships are in the vicinity. *Amagiri* doesn't stop either, speeding on to Rabaul, even as her crew watches the small American craft burn in her wake.

The men of PT-109 are on their own.

The skipper, and the man responsible for allowing such an enormous vessel to sneak up on his boat, is Lieutenant John Fitzgerald Kennedy. He is twenty-six, rail thin, and deeply tanned, a Harvard-educated playboy whose father forced him to leave naval intelligence to seek a combat position when it was discovered that his son's Danish mistress was suspected of being a Nazi spy. Being second-born in a family where great things are expected from the oldest son, Kennedy has had the luxury of a frivolous life. He was a sickly child, grew into a young man fond of books and girls, and, with the exception of commanding a minor vessel such as PT-109, has shown no interest in pursuing a leadership position in politics—an ambition required of his older brother, Joe.

But none of that matters right now. Kennedy must find a way to get his men to safety. Later in life, when asked to describe the night's imminent turning point, he will shrug it off: "It was involuntary. They sunk my boat."

His words belie the fact that he might have been court-martialed for allowing his boat to be sunk and two of his men to be killed. But the sinking of PT-109 will be the making of John F. Kennedy—not because of what just happened, but because of what is about to happen next.

The back end of PT-109 is already on its way to the bottom of the Blackett, some 1,200 feet below. The forward section of the hull remains afloat, thanks to watertight compartments. Kennedy gathers the surviving crew members on this section to await help. *Amagiri*'s wake is sweeping the flames away from the wreckage of 109, allaying Kennedy's fears that the gasoline fires will ignite any remaining ammunition or fuel tanks. But as the hours pass—one, then two and three—and it becomes obvious that help is not coming, Kennedy knows he must devise a new plan. The Blackett Strait is bordered on all sides by small islands that are home to thousands of Japanese soldiers. It's certain that someone on land has seen the explosion.

"What do you want to do if the Japs come out?" Kennedy asks the crew. Completely responsible for the lives of his men, he is at a loss. The hull is beginning to sink, and the only weapons he and his men possess are a single machine gun and seven handguns. A firefight would be ludicrous.

The men can plainly see a Japanese camp less than a mile away, on

Gizo Island, and know that two other large bases exist on Kolombangara and Vella Lavella islands, each just five miles away.

"Anything you say, Mr. Kennedy. You're the boss," replies one crewman.

But Kennedy is not comfortable being the boss. In his months being skipper of the 109, his job has largely consisted of steering the boat. The men complain that he is more interested in chasing girls than commanding a ship. Kennedy is much more at ease in a supporting role. Growing up, he took orders from his domineering father and looked up to his charismatic older brother. His dad, Joseph P. Kennedy, is one of the wealthiest and most powerful men in America, and a former ambassador to Great Britain. His brother Joe, at twenty-eight years old, is a flamboyant naval aviator soon to see action flying antisubmarine missions against the Nazis in Europe.

The Kennedy family takes all its directives from their patriarch. John Kennedy will one day liken the relationship to that of puppets and their puppet master. Joseph P. Kennedy decides how his children will spend their lives, monitors their every action, attempts to sleep with his sons' and daughters' girlfriends, and even had one of his own daughters lobotomized. He has already pinpointed Joe as the family politician. Indeed, his father saw to it that his eldest was a delegate at the 1940 Democratic National Convention. Meanwhile, in those days before the war broke out, John spent his time writing and traveling. Many in the family still believe that writing might become his chosen profession.

Now, on this tragic Pacific night, there is no way for Joseph P. Kennedy to tell his son what to do. "There's nothing in the book about a situation like this," JFK tells the crew, stalling for time. "Seems we're not a military organization anymore. Let's just talk this over."

The men have been trained to follow orders, not discuss strategy. They argue, and yet Kennedy still won't play the role of commander. The men have been waiting for a ship to come looking for them, or a search plane. As morning turns to noon, and PT-109 sinks lower and lower into the water, remaining with the wreckage means either certain capture by Japanese troops or death by shark attack.

The Kennedy family at their Hyannis Port compound in 1931. (Photograph by Richard Sears, John F. Kennedy Presidential Library and Museum, Boston)

Finally, John F. Kennedy takes charge.

"We'll swim," he orders the men, pointing to a cluster of green islands three miles to the southeast. He explains that while these specks of land might be more distant than the island of Gizo, which appears close enough almost to touch, they're less likely to be inhabited by Japanese soldiers.

The men hang on to a piece of timber, using it as a flotation device as they kick their way to the distant islands. Kennedy, a member of the swim team at Harvard, tows a badly burned crew member by placing a strap from the man's life jacket between his own teeth and pulling him. During the five long hours it takes to reach the island, Kennedy swallows mouthful after mouthful of saltwater, yet his strength as a swimmer allows him to

Joseph Kennedy with sons Joseph Kennedy Jr. and John F. Kennedy in Palm Beach in 1931. Joseph Kennedy expected his eldest son would be the one to go into politics. (Photograph by E. F. Foley, John F. Kennedy Presidential Library and Museum, Boston)

reach the beach before the rest of the crew. He leaves the burned crewman in the shallows and staggers ashore to explore their new home. The island is not much: sand, a few palm trees, and the reef that surrounds it. From one side to another, it's just a hundred yards. But it's land. After more than fifteen hours in the ocean, there's no better place to be.

The rest of the crew finally arrives. They hide in the shallows as a Japanese barge passes within a few hundred yards. Kennedy is collapsed

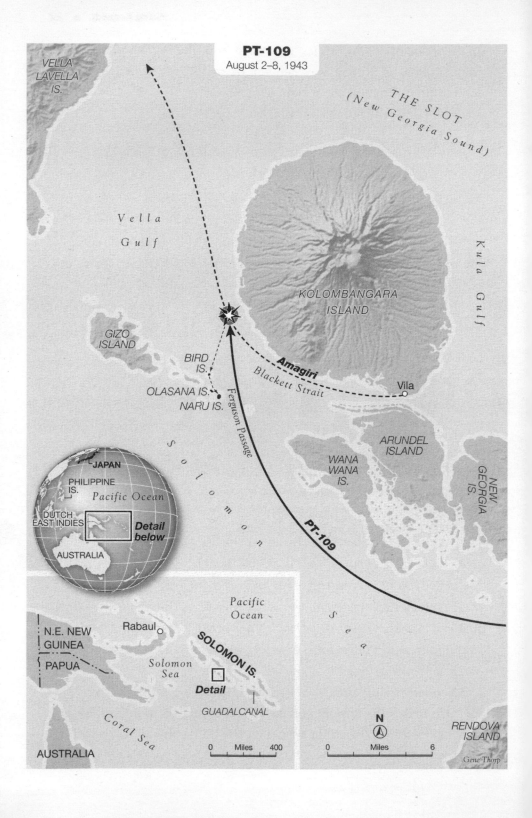

PT-109
August 2–8, 1943

VELLA
LAVELLA
IS.

THE SLOT
(New Georgia Sound)

Vella
Gulf

KOLOMBANGARA
ISLAND

Kula Gulf

GIZO
ISLAND

BIRD
IS.

Amagiri

Blackett Strait

OLASANA IS.

NARU IS.

Ferguson Passage

Vila

Solomon

ARUNDEL
ISLAND

WANA
WANA
IS.

NEW GEORGIA IS.

PT-109

JAPAN

PHILIPPINE
IS.

Pacific Ocean

DUTCH
EAST INDIES

Detail
below

AUSTRALIA

Sea

Pacific
Ocean

Rabaul

N.E. NEW
GUINEA

SOLOMON IS.

PAPUA

Solomon
Sea

Detail

GUADALCANAL

N

RENDOVA
ISLAND

AUSTRALIA

Coral Sea

| 0 | Miles | 400 |

| 0 | Miles | 6 |

Gene Thorp

in the shade of nearby bushes, exhausted from the swim and nauseated from swallowing all that seawater. Yet, despite his weakened condition, something is different about him. The man who once shied away from leadership has realized that only he can save his crew.

JFK rises to his feet and gets to work.

■ ■ ■

Kennedy looks toward the beach. The sand is off-white and slopes into the water. The men have sought shelter under low-hanging trees. With a sense of relief, he sees that nearby lies a large bundle wrapped in a kapok life vest, something the men salvaged from PT-109. Kennedy needs that package for what he is about to do next.

Inside the bundle is a ship's lantern. Kennedy staggers to his men and outlines a plan: he will swim to another nearby island, which is closer to a channel known as the Ferguson Passage, a popular route for the patrol torpedoes, and will use the lantern to signal any passing PT boats that might venture their way in the night. If Kennedy makes contact, he will signal to his crew with the lantern.

Kennedy prepares for the swim. He is still on the verge of vomiting, and is now also light-headed from dehydration and lack of food. He peels off his shirt and pants to save weight, and ties a .38-caliber pistol to a lanyard around his neck. He had stripped off his shoes and tied them around his neck before the long swim from PT-109, but now puts them back on to save his feet from being cut on the sharp reef. Finally, Kennedy hugs the kapok vest tightly around his naked body, knowing that the lantern wrapped inside it is the key to their rescue.

Kennedy steps back into the sea. He thinks of the giant barracuda that live in these waters, which are rumored to swim up out of the blackness and bite off the genitals of passing swimmers. Without pants, he is surely an inviting target.

Kennedy swims alone into the night until his shoes scrape against a reef. He makes his way along the sharpened surface, searching for that inevitable moment when the reef ends and the sandy beach begins. But the reef is endless. Even worse, the coral slices his hands and his legs time and again. Whenever Kennedy takes a misstep and plunges under-water into some unseen hole, his mind immediately races to thoughts of barracuda.

Kennedy never finds that sandy beach. So, tying his shoes to his life belt, he undertakes a courageous and slightly foolhardy alternate course of action: he swims out into open water, lantern held aloft, hoping to signal a passing PT.

But on this night, of all nights, the U.S. Navy is not sending patrol torpedo boats through the Ferguson Passage. Kennedy treads water in the utter blackness, waiting in vain for the sound of muffled propellers.

He finally gives up. But when he tries swimming back to his men, the currents work against him. He is swept far out into the Blackett Strait, frantically lighting the lamp to signal his men as he drifts past. They argue among themselves as to whether the lights they're seeing are an illusion brought on by hunger and dehydration, even as their skipper slips farther and farther into the utter blackness.

John Kennedy pries off his heavy shoes and lets them fall to the sea bottom, thinking that the reduced drag will allow him to swim more eas-ily. It doesn't. He drifts farther and farther out into the Pacific. No matter how hard he swims, the currents push him in the other direction. Finally, he stops fighting. Alone in the dark, his body now cold and his mind a jumble of conflicting thoughts, Kennedy bobs lifelessly. He is an enig-matic man. Despite his reputation for bedding as many girls as possible, he was raised in a Roman Catholic household. His faith has faltered in recent months, but it now serves him well. Even though his situation seems impossible, Kennedy has hope.

And he never lets go of his lamp.

■ ■ ■

Kennedy floats, as alone and powerless as a man can be, all night long. The skin of his fingers wrinkles, and his body grows even colder.

But it is not his time to die. Not yet. As the sun comes up, Kennedy is stunned to realize that the same currents once pulling him out to sea have now spun around and deposited him right back where he started.

He swims back safely to his men. After hours as a beacon in the darkness, the lamp finally extinguishes itself once and for all.

Days pass. Kennedy and his men survive by choking down live snails and licking moisture off leaves. They name their home Bird Island because of the abundance of guano coating the tree leaves. Sometimes they see aircraft dogfighting in the skies, but they never spot a rescue plane. Indeed, even as they struggle to survive, their PT brethren hold a memorial service in their honor.

After four days, Kennedy persuades George Ross of Highland Park, Illinois, to attempt a swim with him. This time they head for an island named Naru, where it is very possible they will run into Japanese soldiers. At this point in their ordeal, with the men's bodies racked by hunger and excruciating thirst, capture is becoming preferable to certain death.

The swim lasts an hour. At Naru, they come upon an abandoned enemy barge and see two Japanese men hurriedly paddling away in a canoe. Kennedy and Ross search the barge for supplies and find water and hardtack biscuits. They also discover a small canoe. After spending the day in hiding, Kennedy leaves Ross on Naru and paddles the one-man canoe out into the Ferguson Passage. No longer in possession of a lantern or other means of signaling a passing PT, JFK is now desperate, taking crazy gambles. And yet, despite long odds, he once again makes it through the night, paddling the canoe back to his men.

Finally, he receives a bit of good news. The men he mistook for Japanese soldiers were actually local islanders. They had spotted Kennedy and Ross, and then paddled to PT-109's crew to warn them about Japanese forces in the area.

Kennedy meets these islanders in person the next morning, when his canoe founders on the way back to Naru. These highly experienced men of the sea come out of nowhere to pluck him from the Pacific and paddle him safely to George Ross. Before the islanders depart, Kennedy carves a note into the shell of a fallen coconut: "NAURO ISL . . . COMMANDER . . . NATIVE KNOWS POS'IT . . . HE CAN PILOT . . . 11 ALIVE . . . NEED SMALL BOAT . . . KENNEDY."

With that cryptic message in their possession, the natives paddle away.

■ ■ ■

Night falls. Rain pours down. Kennedy and Ross sleep under a bush. Their arms and legs are swollen from bug bites and reef scratches. The islanders have shown them where yet another canoe is hidden on Naru, and Kennedy insists to Ross that they paddle back into the open sea one more time in search of a PT.

Only now the Pacific isn't placid. The rain turns torrential. The seas are six feet high. Kennedy gives the order to turn back, only to have the canoe capsize. The two men cling to their overturned boat, kicking as hard as they can to guide it toward land. Giant waves now pound against the reef. Kennedy is torn from the canoe. The sea's force holds him under and spins him around. Yet again he believes he is near death. But just when it seems all is lost, he comes up for air. He battles his way onto the reef. Ross is nearby, alive. As the rain pours down, they pick their way across the sharp coral and onto the beach, once again slicing open their feet and legs. This time there are no thoughts of barracuda, only survival. Too exhausted to care about being seen by the Japanese, they collapse onto the sand and sleep.

John Kennedy is out of solutions. He has done all he can to save his men. There is nothing more he can do.

As if in a mirage, Kennedy wakes up to see four natives standing over him. The sun is rising. Ross's limbs are horribly disfigured from his coral wounds, with one arm swollen to the size of a football. Kennedy's own body is beginning to suffer from infection.

"I have a letter for you, sir," one of the natives says in perfect English.

An incredulous Kennedy sits up and reads the note. The natives have taken his coconut to a New Zealand infantry detachment hidden nearby. The note is from the officer in charge. Kennedy, it says, should allow the islanders to paddle him to safety.

So it is that John F. Kennedy is placed in the bottom of a canoe, covered in palm fronds to hide him from Japanese aircraft, and paddled to a hidden location on New Georgia Island. When the canoe arrives at the water's edge, a young New Zealander steps from the jungle. Kennedy comes out from under his hiding place and climbs out of the canoe. "How do you do?" the New Zealander asks formally. "I'm Lieutenant Wincote." He pronounces his rank the British way: *LEFF*-tenant.

"Hello. I'm Kennedy." The two men shake hands. Wincote nods toward the jungle. "Come up to my tent and have a cup of tea."

Kennedy and his men are soon rescued by the U.S. Navy. And thus the saga of PT-109 comes to an end, even as the legend of PT-109 is born.

■ ■ ■

There is another incident that influences John Kennedy's journey to the Oval Office. Kennedy's older brother, Joe, is not as lucky about cheating death. The experimental Liberator bomber in which he is flying explodes over England on August 12, 1944. There is no body to bury and no memento of the tragedy to place on JFK's desk. But that explosion marked the moment when John F. Kennedy became a politician and began the journey into the powerful office in which he now sits.

■ ■ ■

Less than six months after the war ends, John Fitzgerald Kennedy is one of ten candidates running in the Democratic primary of Boston's Eleventh Congressional District. The veteran politicians and ward bosses of the deeply partisan city don't give him a chance of winning. But JFK studies each ward in the district, reveling in his role as the underdog. He recruits a well-connected fellow World War II veteran named Dave Powers to help run his campaign. Powers, a rising political star in his own right, is at first reluctant to help the skinny young man who introduces himself by saying, "My name is Jack Kennedy. I'm a candidate for Congress."

But then Powers watches in awe as Kennedy stands before a packed Legion hall on a cold Saturday night in January 1946 and gives a dazzling campaign speech. The occasion is a meeting of Gold Star Mothers, women who have lost sons in World War II. Kennedy speaks for only ten minutes, telling the assembled ladies why he wants to run for office. The audience cannot see that his hands shake anxiously. But they hear his well-chosen words as he reminds them of his own war record and explains why their sons' sacrifice was so meaningful, speaking in an honest, sincere voice about their bravery.

Then Kennedy pauses before softly referring to his fallen brother, Joe: "I think I know how all you mothers feel. You see, my mother is a Gold Star Mother, too."

Women surge forth as the speech concludes. Tears in their eyes, they reach out to touch this young man who reminds each of them of the sons they lost, telling him that he has their support. In that instant, Dave Powers is convinced. He goes to work for "Jack" Kennedy right then and there, forming the core of what will become known as Kennedy's "Irish Mafia." It is Dave Powers who seizes on PT-109 as a vital aspect of the campaign, mailing voters a reprint of a story about that August night in 1943 to show the selfless bravery of a wealthy young man for whom some might otherwise not be inclined to vote.

Thanks to Dave Powers's insistence on making the most of PT-109, John F. Kennedy is elected to Congress.

■ ■ ■

During his first months as president, the coconut on which Kennedy carved the rescue note is a reminder of the incident that started him on his path to the White House.

The coconut is also a daily reminder that JFK owes the presidency, in part, to the sharp political intuition of Dave Powers. The tall Boston native, five years JFK's senior, has been on the Kennedy payroll since that January night in 1946. As special assistant to the president, he is not a cabinet member, or even an official adviser—just a very close friend who always seems to anticipate the president's needs and whose company the always-loyal JFK enjoys immensely. Powers has been described as the president's "jester in residence," and it's true: his official capacity in the White House is largely social. Dave Powers is willing to do anything for John Kennedy.

But even Dave Powers, with his remarkable powers of intuition, cannot possibly know what "anything" means—nor can he predict that even as he witnessed John Kennedy's first-ever political speech, he will also witness his last.

2

~~

The president of the United States is naked, and on schedule. Almost every afternoon, at precisely 1:00 P.M., he slips into the indoor pool— always heated to a therapeutic ninety degrees—located between the White House and the West Wing. John Kennedy does this to soothe his aching back, a problem for him ever since he was a student at Harvard. His ordeal with the *Amagiri* exacerbated his back problems, and he has even endured surgery—to no avail. The pain is constant and so excruciating that Kennedy often uses crutches or a cane to get around, though rarely in public. He wears a corset, sleeps on an extra-firm mattress, and receives regular injections of the anesthetic procaine to ease his suffering. Aides know to look for a tightening of his jaw as a sign that the president's back is acting up. The half hour of breaststroke and the heat of the pool are part of Kennedy's therapy. His lack of a bathing suit for many of those swims stems from his notion of manliness. Real men do the breaststroke au naturel, and that's that.

The White House staff could never imagine the previous president, Dwight Eisenhower, swimming naked anywhere, anytime. The elderly general and his wife, Mamie, were as traditional as they come. Very little unexpected happened in the White House during the eight years the Eisenhowers lived there.

But now everything has changed. The Kennedys are much less formal than the Eisenhowers. Smoking is allowed in the staterooms. Receiving lines are being abolished, giving formal functions a more casual feel. The First Lady is having a stage set up in the East Room, to allow performances by some of America's most notable musicians, such as cellist and composer Pablo Casals and singer Grace Bumbry.

Still, the White House is a serious place. The president's daily schedule revolves around periods of intense work followed by restorative breaks. He rises each morning around seven and immediately begins reading the news of the day in bed, including dispatches from the *New York Times*, the *Washington Post*, and the *Wall Street Journal*. Kennedy is a speed-reader, capable of absorbing twelve hundred words every sixty seconds. He is done with the newspapers in just fifteen minutes, and then moves on to a pile of briefing books covering events going on around the world.

The president then takes breakfast in bed. It is a substantial meal: orange juice, bacon, toast slathered in marmalade, two soft-boiled eggs, and coffee with cream. By and large, he is not a huge eater. He meticulously keeps his weight at or below 175 pounds. But he is a creature of habit and eats the same breakfast almost every day of the week.

Shortly before 8:00 A.M., Kennedy slips into the tub for a brief soak. In the bath, as he will throughout the day, he has a habit of tapping his right hand constantly, as if the hand is an extension of his active thought process.

The president is in the Oval Office at nine o'clock sharp. He sits back in his chair and listens as his appointments secretary, Ken O'Donnell, maps out his schedule. Throughout the morning, as Kennedy takes calls and listens to advisers brief him on what is happening in the rest of the world, he is interrupted by his handpicked staff. In addition to court

President Kennedy and David Powers, his trusted aide and a member of the Kennedy White House's "Irish Mafia" in 1961. (Abbie Rowe, White House Photographs, John F. Kennedy Presidential Library and Museum, Boston)

jester Dave Powers and the quick-witted Kenny O'Donnell, son of the College of the Holy Cross's football coach, there are men such as the bespectacled special assistant and Harvard history professor Arthur Schlesinger; Ted Sorensen, the Nebraska-born special counselor and adviser; and Pierre Salinger, the former child prodigy pianist who serves as press secretary.

With the exception of the president's personal secretary, Evelyn Lincoln, the Kennedy White House is very much a fraternity, with every man deeply loyal to his charismatic leader. Conversation often lapses into the profane, as the president's naval background lends truth to the saying "swears like a sailor." "I didn't call businessmen sons of bitches," Kennedy once complained about being misquoted in the *New York Times*. "I called them pricks."

The tone is courtlier when women are around. The president, for instance, never refers to his secretary as anything other than Mrs. Lincoln. But even then, crudeness can be camouflaged. Once, in his wife's presence, Kennedy uses a version of the military's phonetic alphabet to lash out at a newspaper columnist, referring to him as a "Charlie-Uncle-Nan-Tare."

When the confused First Lady asks the president to explain, he deftly changes the subject.

■ ■ ■

Kennedy's half-hour midday swim is an effective tonic for his pain, but sometimes he also uses the swimming sessions to conduct business, inviting staff and even members of the press to put in laps alongside him. The catch? They have to be naked, too. Dave Powers, a regular swimming partner, is quite used to it. For some on the White House staff, however, the scene is almost surreal.

Enigmatically, the president's informal aquatic habits belie the fact that he is the polar opposite of his easygoing vice president. Lyndon Johnson is well-known for grabbing shoulders and slapping backs, but Kennedy keeps a physical distance between himself and other men. Unless he is campaigning, a chore he relishes, the president finds even the simple act of shaking hands to be a burden.

After swimming, Kennedy eats a quick lunch upstairs in the residence—perhaps a sandwich and possibly some soup. He then goes into his bedroom, changes into a nightshirt, and naps for exactly forty-five minutes. Other great figures in history such as Winston Churchill napped during the day. For Kennedy, it is a means of rejuvenation.

The First Lady wakes him up and stays with him to chat as he gets dressed. Then it's back to the Oval Office, most nights working as late as 8:00 P.M. His staff knows that after business hours, Kennedy often puts two feet up on his desk and casually tosses ideas back and forth with them. It is the president's favorite time of the day.

When everyone has cleared out, Kennedy makes his way back upstairs to the family's private quarters—often referred to as "the residence" or "the Mansion" by his staff—where he smokes an Upmann cigar, enjoys Ballantine scotch and water without ice, and prepares for his evening meal. Often, Jackie Kennedy puts together last-minute dinner parties, which the president tolerates.

Truth be told, JFK would rather be watching a movie. The White House theater can screen any film in the world, anytime the president wishes. His preferences are World War II flicks and Westerns.

Kennedy's fixation on movies rivals his other favorite recreational pursuit: sex.

The president's bad back does not discourage him from being romantically active, which is a good thing, because, as JFK once explained to a friend, he needed to have sex at least once a day or he would suffer awful headaches. He and Jackie keep separate bedrooms, connected by a common dressing room—which is not to say that John Kennedy limits his sexual relations to the First Lady. While happily married, he is far from monogamous.

■ ■ ■

The president's philandering aside, unquestionably the biggest change between the Kennedy and Eisenhower administrations is in the lady of the house. Jackie Kennedy, at thirty-one, is less than half the age of Mamie Eisenhower. The former First Lady was a grandmother while in the White House and a known penny-pincher who spent her downtime watching soap operas. By contrast, Jackie enjoys listening to bossa nova records and keeps fit by jumping on a trampoline and lifting weights. Like her husband, Jackie keeps her weight constant, a slim 120 pounds to compliment her 5-foot, 7-inch frame.

Her one true vice is her pack-a-day cigarette habit—either Salems or L&Ms—which she continues even throughout her pregnancies. As her husband does with his physical ailments, Jackie Kennedy keeps her

Jacqueline Bouvier Kennedy, pictured here at the 1961 inaugural ball, brought glamour to her role as First Lady. (Abbie Rowe, White House Photographs, John F. Kennedy Presidential Library and Museum, Boston)

smoking a secret—during the recent presidential campaign, an aide was charged with staying within arm's reach with a lighted cigarette so Jackie could sneak a puff anytime she wanted.

Jackie's parents divorced before she was twelve, and she was raised in wealth and splendor by her mother, Janet. She attended expensive girls' boarding schools and then Vassar College before spending her junior year in Paris. Upon her return to the United States, Jackie transferred to George Washington University, in D.C., where she got a diploma in 1951.

Throughout the First Lady's developmental years, she was taught to be extremely private and to hold thoughts deep within herself. She likes to maintain "a certain quality of mystery about her," a friend will later note. "People did not know what she was thinking or what she was doing behind the scenes—and she wanted to keep it that way."

The fact is that Jacqueline Bouvier Kennedy never fully reveals herself to anyone—not even to her husband, the president.

■ ■ ■

In far-off Minsk, Lee Harvey Oswald is having the opposite problem. The woman he loves just won't stop talking.

On March 17, at a dance for union workers, he meets a nineteen-year-old beauty who wears a red dress and white shoes and who styles her hair in what he believes to be "French fashion." Marina Prusakova is reluctant to smile because of her bad teeth, but the two dance that night, and he walks her home—along with several other potential suitors smitten by the talkative Marina.

But Lee Harvey is defiant, as always. He knows the other men will soon be distant memories.

And he is right. "We like each other right away," the defector writes in his journal.

After her mother's death two years before, Marina, who was born out of wedlock, was sent to live with her uncle Ilya, a colonel in the Soviet Ministry of Internal Affairs and a respected member of the local Communist Party. She is trained as a pharmacist, but quit her job sometime ago.

Oswald knows all this, and so much more about Marina, because between the nights of March 18 and 30, they spend a great deal of time together. "We walk," he writes. "I talk a little about myself, she talks a lot about herself."

Their relationship takes a sudden turn on March 30, when Oswald enters the Fourth Clinic Hospital for an adenoid operation. Marina visits him constantly, and by the time Lee Harvey is discharged, he "knows I must have her." On April 30 they are married. Marina almost immediately becomes pregnant.

Life is getting more and more complicated for Lee Harvey Oswald.

■ ■ ■

In the winter of 1961 the world outside the White House is turbulent. The cold war is raging. Americans are terrified of the Soviet Union and its arsenal of nuclear weapons. Ninety miles south of Florida, Fidel Castro has recently taken over Cuba, ushering in a regime thought to be friendly to the Soviets.

In America's Deep South, there is growing racial strife.

In the marketplace, there is a new contraceptive device known simply as "The Pill."

On the radio, Chubby Checker is exhorting young Americans to do the Twist, while Elvis Presley is asking women everywhere if they're lonesome tonight.

But inside the Kennedy White House, Jackie sees to it that none of these political and social upheavals intrude on creating the perfect environ- . ronment to raise a family. Her schedule revolves around her children. In a break from the traditional style of First Lady parenting, in which children are managed by the household staff, she is completely involved in the lives of three-year-old Caroline and baby John, taking them with her to meetings and on errands.

As she grows more comfortable in the White House, it will not be uncommon for Jackie to camouflage herself with a scarf and heavy coat and take the children to the circus or a park—discreetly followed by the Secret Service.

The sight of the First Lady playing with her children on the South Lawn will also soon become commonplace, causing one observer to note that Jackie is "so like a little girl who had never grown up." Indeed, she speaks with the same breathy, almost childlike voice of actress Marilyn Monroe.

The First Lady likes to think of herself as a traditional wife and dotes on her husband. But she also has a fiercely independent streak, breaking White House protocol by refusing to attend the myriad teas and social functions other First Ladies have endured. Jackie prefers to spend time with her children or concoct designs for a lavish renovation of the White

Jackie was a devoted mother to her children, Caroline and John F. Kennedy Jr., pictured here playing with his mother's necklace in the West Bedroom. (Cecil Stoughton, White House Photographs, John F. Kennedy Presidential Library and Museum, Boston)

House, an activity that does not interest her husband, who has little aesthetic sense when it comes to such matters. Jackie Kennedy refers to her new home as "the president's house" and takes her inspiration from Thomas Jefferson's White House, elaborately decorated by the former ambassador to France.

The current décor dates to the Truman administration. Many pieces of furniture are reproductions instead of actual period originals, giving America's most notable residence a cheap, derivative feel rather than an aura of grandeur. Jackie is assembling a team of top collectors to enhance the décor of the White House in every possible way.

She thinks she has years to finish.

At least four. Perhaps even eight.

She thinks.

3

APRIL 17, 1961
WASHINGTON, D.C./BAY OF PIGS, CUBA
9:40 A.M.

John F. Kennedy absentmindedly buttons his suit coat. He is seated aboard Marine One, his presidential Marine Corps helicopter, as it flares for a landing on the South Lawn of the White House. He has just spent a most unrelaxing weekend at Glen Ora, the family's four-hundred-acre rented country retreat in Virginia that the Secret Service has code-named Chateau.

The president is meticulous about his appearance and will change his clothes completely at least three more times today, on each occasion putting on yet another crisply starched shirt, a new tie, and a suit custom-tailored by Brooks Brothers. His suit coats are invariably charcoal or deep blue. But it is not vanity that drives John Kennedy's obsession with cloth-ing. Rather, it is a peculiar quirk of his personality that he is uncomfort-able if he wears a garment too long. He drives his longtime valet, George Thomas, crazy with his constant changes.

But right now Kennedy is not concentrating on his personal appearance, even though he does, as always, pat the top of his head to make sure every strand of hair is in place. Habits are hard to break.

Kennedy is preoccupied with Cuba. Roughly twelve hundred miles due south of Washington, D.C., a battlefield is taking shape. Kennedy has authorized a covert invasion of the island nation, sending fourteen hundred anti-Castro exiles to do a job that the U.S. military, by rule of international law, cannot do itself. The freedom fighters' goal is nothing less than the overthrow of the Cuban government. The plan has been in the works since long before Kennedy was elected. Both the Central Intelligence Agency and the Joint Chiefs of Staff have assured the president that the mission will succeed. But it is Kennedy who has given the go-ahead—and it is he who will take the blame if the mission fails.

Once the UH-34 helicopter touches down on the metal pads specially placed on the South Lawn as a landing spot, JFK emerges head-first out the door, stepping down onto the new spring grass. The president looks calm and unflappable, but his stomach is churning, literally. The stress of the weekend, with its last-minute planning of the risky attack, has brought on severe diarrhea and a debilitating urinary tract infection. His doctor has prescribed injections of penicillin and a diet of liquefied food to make his afflictions more bearable. Yet he feels miserable. But as awful as things seem right now, the president knows that his Monday is about to get much worse.

The president walks purposefully through the serenity of the White House Rose Garden, even as the Cuban exiles comprising Brigade 2506 are in grave danger, pinned down on a remote stretch of sand in Cuba.

This inlet will go down in infamy as the Bay of Pigs.

John F. Kennedy steps through the Rose Garden entrance into the Oval Office, with its gray carpet and off-white walls. During the winter, when there are no leaves on the trees, it is possible to gaze out toward the National Mall from the tall windows behind Kennedy's desk. At the far end, hidden from JFK's view by the Old Executive Office Building, rises the Lincoln Memorial. But Kennedy doesn't sit down, nor does he glance out in the direction of Mr. Lincoln.

He is much too anxious about the events in Cuba to have a seat.

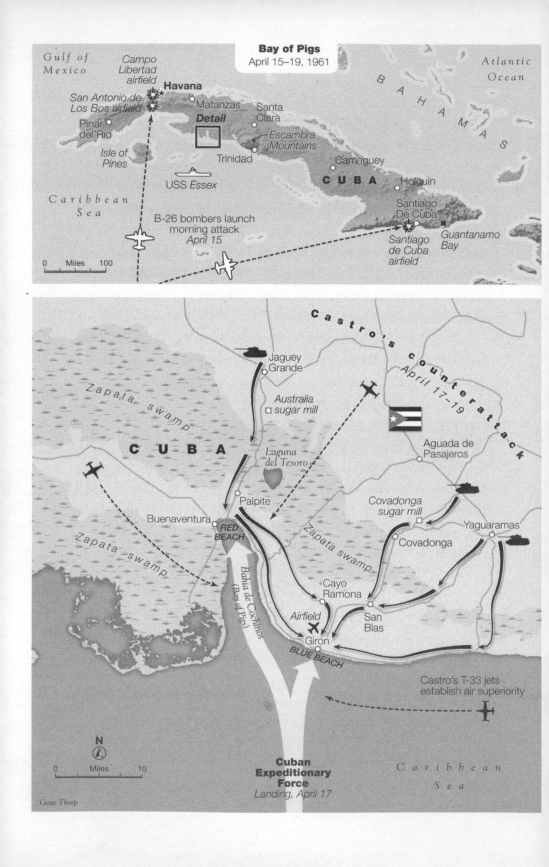

Bay of Pigs
April 15–19, 1961

Gulf of Mexico

Campo Libertad airfield

Havana

San Antonio de Los Bos airfield

Pinar del Rio

Matanzas

Santa Clara

Detail

Escambra Mountains

Trinidad

Isle of Pines

USS *Essex*

Caribbean Sea

Camaguey

C U B A

Holguin

Santiago De Cuba

Santiago de Cuba airfield

Guantanamo Bay

Atlantic Ocean

B A H A M A S

B-26 bombers launch morning attack April 15

0   Miles   100

Castro's counterattack April 17–19

Jaguey Grande

Zapata swamp

Australia sugar mill

C U B A

Laguna del Tesoro

Palpite

Buenaventura

RED BEACH

Zapata swamp

Zapata swamp

Aguada de Pasajeros

Covadonga sugar mill

Covadonga

Yaguaramas

San Blas

Cayo Ramona

Bahía de Cochinos (Bay of Pigs)

Airfield

Giron

BLUE BEACH

Castro's T-33 jets establish air superiority

N

0   Miles   10

Gene Thorp

Cuban Expeditionary Force
Landing, April 17

Caribbean Sea

■ ■ ■

It has not been a good week for America. On April 12 the Soviets stunned the world by launching the first man into space, proving to one and all that they have rockets capable of carrying nuclear warheads all the way to the United States. The cold war that has raged between the two nations for more than a decade is now clearly tipped in the Soviets' favor. Many in Washington believe that overthrowing the pro-Soviet Castro will go a long way toward restoring equilibrium to the cold war.

Kennedy knew he had the backing of the American people when he authorized the invasion. Fear about the global spread of communism is rampant in the United States. Anything he does to stop it will be applauded. And while invading another country is an enormous diplomatic risk, the president enjoys a 78 percent approval rating after his first months on the job, political capital with which to gamble. Newspapers and magazines are gushing about the young president, calling Kennedy "omniscient" and "omnipotent."

But no man is all-knowing, and even the president of the United States is not all-powerful. Kennedy is about to make the sort of sworn enemies that come with a colossal blunder. By the time the Bay of Pigs is over he will count among these enemies not only Castro but also one of the highest-ranking officials of the U.S. government: the wily CIA chief, Allen Dulles.

■ ■ ■

Kenny O'Donnell greets Kennedy in the Oval Office and quickly briefs him on the day's schedule. The president then strides out through another of the Oval Office's four doors. His path takes him past the desk of his loyal personal secretary, Evelyn Lincoln, and into the Cabinet Room, where Secretary of State Dean Rusk awaits.

A brilliant man, Rusk attended Oxford as a Rhodes scholar and served as a chief of war plans as an army officer in the China-Burma-India Theater during World War II, organizing covert missions very much like the Bay of Pigs. The Georgia native sat in on the many planning meetings leading up to the weekend's invasion. Yet he was not Kennedy's first choice to head the State Department, and just three months into his new job, the new secretary of state remains tentative with his boss, wary of speaking his mind. At a time when Kennedy desperately needs solid advice, Rusk is unwilling to share his professional misgivings about the Bay of Pigs, including his belief "that this thin brigade of Cuban exiles has a snowball's chance in hell of success."

Rusk's reluctance to advise him in an open and honest fashion is the least of the president's troubles at this point. Nobody, it seems, will level with Kennedy. As JFK awaits word from the battlefront, he craves the company of someone who will tell him the unvarnished truth.

Sensing a crisis, the president picks up a phone and dials.

■ ■ ■

Cuba.

Americans of means once made this steamy, rum-soaked paradise their favorite tropical playground. The country's sandy white beaches are sensual and the casinos legendary. Ernest Hemingway wrote of Cuba's many charms, then unwound with his favorite rum libation, the daiquiri. Behind the scenes, America's organized crime bosses such as Meyer Lansky and Lucky Luciano were as comfortable in the Cuban capital, Havana, as they were in New York City. And for decades, U.S. corporations took advantage of Cuba's climate and thoroughly corrupt government to set up vast sugarcane plantations, oil fields, and cattle ranches.

In fact, ever since that epic moment in 1898 when Teddy Roosevelt and his Rough Riders charged up San Juan Hill to liberate Cuba from Spain, the Cuban-U.S. relationship was mostly peaceful, free of tension, and, in a word, easy.

Until 1959.

Corruption reached an all-time high under the American-friendly regime of General Fulgencio Batista, sparking rebellion among Cubans. After four years of fighting, Fidel Castro, the thirty-two-year-old bastard child of a wealthy Cuban farmer, led his guerrilla army into Havana and toppled Batista. (The general died of a heart attack in exile in Portugal, just two days before Castro's team of assassins could complete its mission.) The United States responded to Batista's overthrow by officially recognizing the new government.

■ ■ ■

Castro is a man of many secrets. In perhaps his most egregious episode, eleven days after overthrowing Batista's government in 1959, seventy-five political prisoners were marched in the dead of night toward an open field outside the city of Santiago, hands tied behind their backs. There was no path, and those who slowed down or stumbled felt the sharp jab of a soldier's bayonet in their ribs. Suddenly, a row of army trucks turned on their headlights, revealing a trench six feet deep and fifty yards long. Bulldozers were parked alongside the trench, blades lowered and ready to plow the fresh mounds of dirt back into the massive hole.

The executions were supposed to be a secret, but the prisoners' wives and girlfriends found out and kept vigil, following the procession from a distance and gasping with horror as those headlights illuminated what would soon be a mass grave. As the women's sobs and wails punctured the still night air, Castro's soldiers lined their husbands and sons and boyfriends shoulder to shoulder along the edge of the ditch, all the while taunting the women with jeers and catcalls. The women wept and prayed right up until that inevitable moment when the machine guns opened fire and their loved ones toppled into the abyss.

Thus marked the beginning of Fidel Castro's reign of terror. Soon after, a Cuban judge was shot through the head for pardoning military pilots who had flown against Castro's forces during his guerrilla campaign. Castro then ordered the pilots convicted of genocide. When the new judge sentenced them to hard labor instead of death, he, too, was shot dead. The Cuban leader, in his own words, is "violent, given to tantrums, devious, manipulative, and defiant of all authority."

The Cuban people soon realized that they were paying a high price for supporting the rise of Castro. But overseas, Castro's popular facade as a revolutionary hero took hold. One British newspaper wrote that "Mr. Castro's bearded, youthful figure has become a symbol of Latin

America's rejection of brutality and lying. Every sign is that he will reject personal rule and violence." In April 1959, Castro spoke at the Harvard University Law School in Cambridge, Massachusetts. Even though he had used his knowledge of the law to suspend Cuba's writ of habeas corpus, and even though the January 12 massacre was reported in the *New York Times*, Castro's Harvard speech was interrupted time after time by enthusiastic cheering and applause.

On that same trip to America, the Cuban leader met with Vice President Richard Nixon, who was immediately impressed by Castro. In fact, Nixon wrote in a four-page secret memo to Eisenhower that "the one fact we can be sure of, is that he has those indefinable qualities which makes him a leader of men."

John F. Kennedy, then a U.S. senator still months away from beginning his campaign for the presidency, knew that Batista was a ruthless despot who had murdered more than twenty thousand of his own people. Kennedy saw nothing wrong with Castro's rise to power. And, like Hemingway, he was also fond of a daiquiri from time to time.

In 1959, Kennedy and Castro were on the verge of becoming two of the twentieth century's greatest rivals. Both were charismatic, idealistic young men beloved by their fanatical followers. Both enjoyed a good cigar and had had long political winning streaks that resulted in each man ruling his nation. But each had a setback during his rise to power— Castro was imprisoned in the early years of his revolution; Kennedy's painful back condition and a potentially deadly adrenal gland condition known as Addison's disease each nearly killed him. Perhaps the most striking similarity between the two men is that Kennedy and Castro were the sort of highly competitive alpha males who never accept losing, no matter what the circumstances, no matter how high the cost.

■ ■ ■

In Cuba the costs of revolution are very high. With blood running in the streets of Havana, it was only a matter of time before America comprehended the truth. In February 1960, thirteen months after Castro seized power, a CIA briefing to the National Security Council warned of the Soviet Union's "active support" for Castro, while also lamenting the disorganization of anti-Castro forces. The Eisenhower administration quietly began making plans to overthrow Castro's regime, authorizing the CIA to begin paramilitary training of Cuban exiles at a secret base in Guatemala.

Castro became a hot-button issue of the 1960 presidential campaign. Kennedy vigorously attacked the Eisenhower administration, using the situation in Cuba to illustrate its weakness against communism. "In 1952 the Republicans ran on a program of rolling back the Iron Curtain in Eastern Europe," Kennedy warned the nation. "Today the Iron Curtain is 90 miles off the coast of the United States."

The question of a Cuban invasion became not a matter of if, but when. In a speech on December 31, 1960, Castro warned America that any landing force would suffer far greater losses than on D-Day. "If they want to invade us and destroy the resistance they will not succeed . . . because as long as a single man or woman with honor remains[,] there will be resistance," he railed. A few days later, on January 3, 1961, Castro inflamed the cold war fears of every American by announcing that "Cuba has the right to encourage revolution in Latin America."

As John Kennedy prepared to take office, roughly one in every nineteen Cubans was a political prisoner. America had severed diplomatic relations with Havana. On January 10, the *New York Times* ran a front-page story entitled "U.S. Helps Train Anti-Castro Forces at Guatemalan Air-Ground Base," revealing that commandos were being trained in guerrilla warfare for a planned attack against Cuba. The *Times* article got the attention of Castro, who responded by ordering the placement of land mines at potential invasion zones.

Inside the Washington Beltway, the CIA and its longtime director, Allen Dulles, have become obsessed with killing Fidel Castro. It will one day be estimated that they concocted more than six hundred plans to assassinate him, including such unorthodox methods as a Mafia-style hit and exploding cigars. On March 11, a year after Dwight Eisenhower authorized the training of rebel forces, President Kennedy was formally presented with CIA plans for a landing. The invasion would take place in daylight, and the location would be a beach code-named Trinidad.

The operation presented Kennedy with a major dilemma. On the one hand, he had run for president on a platform of change, promising the nation a new start after the cold war policies of Dwight Eisenhower. On the other hand, he had fanatically ridiculed Eisenhower about Castro and knew he would look soft on communism if he did nothing to deter the brutal dictator. On April 7 the *New York Times* ran another front-page story, this one saying that the Cuban rebels were breaking camp and preparing to launch their invasion, prompting Kennedy to remark privately that Castro didn't need spies in the United States—all he had to do was read the paper.

On April 12 the Communist Party in Guatemala reported to Moscow that the anti-Castro American-sponsored guerrillas would launch their invasion within a matter of days. The Soviets, however, were unsure of the intelligence and didn't pass along the news to Castro. That very same day, President Kennedy attempted to disavow any American involvement in an invasion, explaining, "There will not be, under any conditions, any intervention in Cuba by United States forces." Kennedy carefully left out any mention of U.S. financing, training, and planning of a rebel-led assault.

The young American president was attempting a deft diplomatic maneuver, hoping to confront a very real threat by not allowing U.S. military personnel actually to take part. His remarks stretched the truth, but the subtext couldn't have been clearer: the invasion had become personal. It was no longer about the United States versus Cuba, but about John F. Kennedy versus Fidel Castro, two extremely competitive men battling for ideological control over the Western Hemisphere. In the days to come, each would take the actions of the other as a personal affront. And each man would remain determined to win at all costs.

In Moscow, another brutal dictator, Nikita Khrushchev, who murdered his way up the ladder of Soviet Union politics, was confused: "Why should an elephant be afraid of a mouse?" he wondered. Castro's ongoing defiance of the United States was keeping his popularity in Cuba very high. Khrushchev understood that even if the Cuban invasion succeeded, the Cuban people would be hard-pressed to accept an American puppet as their new leader. An ensuing guerrilla war against the United States by Castro's supporters might benefit the Soviet Union by allowing it to establish a military presence in the Western Hemisphere to aid the Cuban dictator.

The bottom line for Khrushchev, of course, had little to do with Castro or Cuba. His goal was world domination. Anything that distracted or in any way diminished the United States was good for the Soviet Union.

■ ■ ■

In the days leading up to the scheduled invasion, President Kennedy soured on the CIA's plan. The Trinidad beach was too much like the Normandy landing zones. The president wanted the invasion to seem as if it had been generated solely by Cuban exiles, thereby masking American involvement. Kennedy wanted an out-of-the-way location where men and supplies could come ashore quietly, then slip into the countryside unnoticed.

The CIA response was to offer a new location, known as Bahia de Cochinos—loosely translated as the "Bay of Pigs." The landing would take place at night. Unlike the broad beachheads of Trinidad or even Normandy, miles of impenetrable swamp bordered the Bay of Pigs, and few roads led in or out.

Yet, while the United States has a history of successful large-scale amphibious invasions, very few of them have taken place in darkness. There are only two ways the mission can succeed. First, the invasion force will have to get off the beach immediately and take control of the access roads. Second, rebel planes need to take control of the skies, wipe out Castro's air force, and then gun down Castro's troops and tanks as they race toward the Bay of Pigs. Without overwhelming airpower, the mission will fail.

Kennedy is a man fond of spy novels—James Bond is a personal favorite—and enchanted by the cloak-and-dagger world of undercover agents. CIA director Alan Dulles, an urbane and wealthy gentleman in his late sixties, epitomizes that aura of secrecy and covert intrigue. He assured Kennedy that the plan would succeed.

The president initially believed him. On April 14, just two days after giving a press conference in which he promised there would be no intervention by U.S. forces in Cuba, Kennedy gave Operation Zapata, as the Bay of Pigs invasion was known, the official go-ahead.

April 14 was a Friday. After launching the invasion, there was nothing for the president to do but wait. So he flew to Glen Ora to be with Jackie and the kids, where he endured a gut-wrenching weekend waiting for news from Cuba. When word finally came, almost none of it was good.

It started on Saturday morning, when eight B-26 bombers piloted by Cuban freedom fighters attacked three Cuban air bases. The original plan called for sixteen planes, but Kennedy had gotten cold feet and ordered the number cut in half.

As a result, the bombings were ineffectual, barely damaging the Cuban air force at all. But Fidel Castro was furious. He immediately turned up the heat on the Kennedy administration by launching public accusations of U.S. involvement in the attack.

Things only got worse after that. A diversionary landing on Saturday was supposed to put roughly 160 anti-Castro Cuban freedom fighters ashore near Guantanamo Bay, but was canceled due to the breakdown of a crucial boat. In a separate incident, Cuban forces arrested a small band of freedom fighters who were already on the island with a large cache of arms.

By Saturday afternoon, the Cuban ambassador to the United Nations was addressing the General Assembly, denouncing the United States for its attack—in response to which Adlai Stevenson, the U.S. ambassador to the UN, repeated JFK's promise that no American forces would ever wage war in Cuba.

As all this was taking place, John Kennedy hid in the country. Each event so far had been a prelude to the real invasion. But the pressure has already gotten to Kennedy. He canceled a second wave of bombings, even though he knew full well the move might doom the invasion.

In the dead of night, just after Sunday turned to Monday, the landing force of 1,400 Cuban exiles from Brigade 2506 powered toward the Bay of Pigs aboard a small fleet of freighters and landing vessels. Their hopes were high—their dream was to regain control of their homeland.

Very few of the invaders were actually soldiers. They were men from all across the social strata who had been trained by American World War II and Korea veterans—and those hardened U.S. vets were impressed by what they saw.

But when they landed, the brave freedom fighters had no idea that the president had called off a second wave of air strikes. Now the men of Brigade 2506 would have to secure the beachheads on their own—an almost impossible task.

On Monday morning, even as those Cuban freedom fighters encountered the first wave of Castro's defenders, the president boarded Marine One and flew back to Washington, hoping that the freedom fighters might find a way to do the impossible.

■ ■ ■

Other than John Kennedy, only two men are allowed to enter the Oval Office through the Rose Garden door: Vice President Lyndon Johnson and Attorney General Robert Kennedy. That privilege, along with their mutual disdain, is all the two men have in common.

The six-foot, four-inch Texan is a self-made man and career politician, a former high school teacher whose towering physique belies a fragile and sometimes insecure persona. The fifty-one-year-old LBJ, as he is known, was perhaps the most successful and powerful Senate majority leader in U.S. history, adept at building partnerships and fortifying his party faithful to pass important legislation.

Bobby, at a shade over five foot nine, speaks with the same clipped Boston accent as his brother. He is a physical fitness buff who was born into privilege and has never held elective office. LBJ knows this and revels in the fact that as leader of the Senate, he is a cut above the relatively inexperienced Kennedy political machine.

Their feud dates to the autumn of 1959, when Bobby Kennedy went

President Kennedy and his brother Attorney General Robert F. Kennedy had a
contentious relationship with Vice President Lyndon B. Johnson. (Abbie Rowe,
White House Photographs, John F. Kennedy Presidential Library and Museum,
Boston)

to visit Johnson at his expansive Texas ranch. His brother had sent him to
Texas to gauge whether Johnson would run against Kennedy for the
Democratic nomination in 1960.

It was LBJ's habit to take important guests deer hunting on his vast
property, and Bobby's visit was no different. At first, Bobby and LBJ got
along extremely well—that is, until Bobby shot at a deer. The rifle's
recoil knocked him flat and opened a cut above one eye. Johnson, reaching down to help Bobby to his feet, couldn't resist taking a swipe: "Son,"
he told Bobby, "you've got to learn to shoot a gun like a man."

No one speaks to Bobby Kennedy that way. Of such small moments
are great feuds made.

As the election of 1960 drew nearer, it was Bobby who fought hardest against Lyndon Johnson as the choice for vice president. And it was also Bobby who personally visited Johnson's hotel suite during the Democratic convention in Los Angeles to offer him the job—though not before trying to talk him out of accepting.

Now the Bay of Pigs will mark the moment when their careers officially veer in two radically different directions. Bobby's stature will quickly rise, with his brother soon referring to him as the "second most powerful man in the world."

Johnson, who privately refers to Bobby as "that snot-nosed little son of a bitch," is already regretting leaving the Senate. LBJ is a man in decline. President Kennedy doesn't trust him and barely tolerates him. The president is so dismissive of Johnson that he even wonders to Jackie, "Can you imagine what would happen to the country if Lyndon were president?"

Being vice president, noted John Nance Garner, Franklin Delano Roosevelt's first VP, is like being "a pitcher of warm spit." John Adams once described being in the position as "I am nothing." Lyndon Johnson knows precisely what his predecessors meant. He no longer has a constituency, no longer has political leverage, and no longer has a whit of authority.

For instance, the vice president does not have a plane of his own. When his duties require him to travel, Johnson must ask one of Kennedy's aides for permission to use a presidential plane. Though he is technically second in command of the nation, Johnson's request carries no more weight than that of a cabinet member. Sometimes his request is denied. When that happens, the vice president of the United States might even be forced to fly commercial.

The greatest insult, however, isn't that Johnson has lost his political pull in Washington, it's that he has lost almost all his clout in his home state of Texas. Despite Johnson's crucial role in delivering Texas to Kennedy on Election Day, Senator Ralph Yarborough is now moving in to take control of Texas politics, and Secretary of the Navy John Connally is making plans to run for governor. One, or both, of them will soon control political power in the Lone Star State. Johnson is becoming expendable. If Kennedy chooses another running mate when he seeks a second term in office, LBJ will be out of politics entirely.

For now, however, Johnson possesses that rare privilege of entering the Oval Office through the Rose Garden door. But when Kennedy picks up the phone to call for help on the morning of April 17, he does not call Lyndon Johnson.

It is Bobby Kennedy who answers the phone. He is in Virginia, giving a speech. "I don't think it's going as well as it could," the president tells his younger brother. "Come back here."

John Kennedy has purposely focused his brother on domestic policy issues, preferring to let others advise him on international matters. Despite their frequent phone conversations, the president sees his younger brother as a guy who's benefited from nepotism, for it was Joseph Kennedy who insisted that JFK hire Bobby as attorney general. But now, in a moment of great insecurity, John Kennedy understands his father's wisdom. Even though Bobby hasn't had a CIA briefing on the Cuban operation in three months, he is the one man the president believes he can count on.

Meanwhile, Lyndon Johnson drifts farther and farther from the center of political power.

■ ■ ■

John Kennedy stands in the Oval Office, helpless to stop what he has started. The president could have called off the invasion right up to the moment on Sunday night when the highly trained men and teenage boys of Brigade 2506 clambered down from their transport ships and transferred to the boats that would carry them to shore.

But reversing course would have taken extraordinary courage. Kennedy would have lost face with Allen Dulles, the CIA, his close advisers, and the Joint Chiefs of Staff.

Yet that is the sort of unpopular decision he had been elected to make. And now Kennedy's unwillingness to make those tough choices is threatening to devastate his administration.

He has come a long way since his days as the young commander of PT-109. But he is still learning, as Abraham Lincoln also learned, that the decision to use force should not be determined by men whose careers depend upon its use.

But it was not the CIA or the Joint Chiefs who ordered the invasion; it was John Kennedy.

Bobby has sped back from Virginia and now steps into the Oval Office to find his older brother in a pensive mood. "I'd rather be called an aggressor than a bum," JFK laments. The news from the landing beaches is not good: the freedom fighters have failed to secure key roads and other strategic points. There is no way off the beach for the men of Brigade 2506. Cuban forces have pinned them down. The invasion is stalled.

A distraught JFK openly shares his fears with Bobby. The president knows when speaking with his brother that he is safe from security leaks or attempts to undermine his authority. But even now, with Bobby at his side, John Kennedy feels the crushing loneliness of being the president of the United States. He has made this mess in Cuba, and he alone must find a way to turn a potential fiasco into a rousing victory.

■ ■ ■

But it's not to be.

By Tuesday, April 18, Castro himself is on the beach in a T-34 tank, fighting off the invaders. Tens of thousands of Cuban militia have taken up positions to contain the rebel advance. The Cubans now control the three main roads leading in and out of Bahia de Cochinos. Most important of all, thanks to Kennedy's cancellation of air cover, the Cuban air force and its T-33 jets easily control the skies.

At noon on April 18, National Security Adviser McGeorge Bundy meekly reports to the president that the "Cuban armed forces are stronger, the popular response is weaker, and our tactical position is feebler than we had hoped. Tanks have done in one beachhead, and the position is precarious at the others."

That evening, at a White House meeting shortly after midnight, Kennedy is dressed in white tie as he listens to yet another report on the failure of the invasion. Earlier that night he was called away from a White House reception for Congress—formal duties call even in the midst of the crisis.

The Cabinet Room is decorated with a map of the Caribbean, on which tiny magnetic ships have been placed to show the location of the various vessels on station to support the invasion. Among them are the aircraft carrier *Essex* and her protective escort vessels.

"I don't want the United States involved in this," snaps an incredulous JFK as he surveys the map.

Admiral Arleigh Burke, head of the U.S. Navy, takes a deep breath and speaks the truth: "Hell, Mr. President, we *are* involved."

In a last-ditch attempt to salvage the invasion, the president reluctantly authorizes one hour of air cover from 0630 to 0730 by six unmarked jets from the *Essex*. The jets are to rendezvous with B-26 bombers piloted by Cuban freedom fighters and keep the Cuban aircraft at bay. However, the U.S. Navy pilots are not to attack ground targets or actively seek out air-to-air combat—yet another sign that JFK has lost his nerve.

After the midnight meeting, the president steps through that Oval Office door into the Rose Garden, the weight of the free world and the fate of more than a thousand men on his shoulders. He is alone for an hour pacing in the wet grass.

On the morning of April 19, more bad news: incredibly, the CIA and the Pentagon didn't account for the time zone difference between Cuba and the freedom fighters' air base in Nicaragua. Jets from carrier *Essex* and the B-26 bombers from Central America arrive at the rendezvous one hour apart. The two groups of aircraft never meet up. As a result, several B-26s and their pilots are shot down by the Cuban air force. Pierre Salinger, the president's press secretary, discovers Kennedy alone in the White House residence weeping after hearing the news.

Jackie has never seen her husband so upset. She has seen JFK cry only twice before and is startled when he puts his head in his hands and sobs. Bobby asks the First Lady to stay close, because the president needs comfort. On this day, Kennedy doesn't even worry about his usually meticulous personal appearance, greeting one senator for a meeting in the Oval Office with his hair a mess and his tie twisted at an odd angle.

Bobby Kennedy rushes to his brother's defense when Lyndon Johnson complains that he's been kept out of the loop. Bobby paces the floor of the Cabinet Room, glaring now and again at the Caribbean map and those magnetic ships. "We've got to do something, we've got to do something," he says again and again. When the CIA and military leaders don't reply, he wheels around and sharply says, "All you bright fellows have gotten the president into this, and if you don't do something now, my brother will be regarded as a paper tiger by the Russians."

Meanwhile, the president passes the rest of the day wallowing in grief, making no attempt to hide his depression from the White House staff. "How could I have been so stupid?" he mutters to himself, often interrupting a completely different conversation to repeat those words. "How could I have been so stupid?"

■ ■ ■

By 5:30 P.M. on the night of April 19, Cuban forces have taken complete control of the Bay of Pigs. The invasion is over.

In addition to the dead and captured on the ground, Castro's forces have sunk almost a dozen invasion vessels, including those carrying food and ammunition, and shot down nine B-26 bombers.

The defeat is a major humiliation for the United States. Kennedy is forced to give a press conference and take full blame. "There's an old saying that victory has a hundred fathers and defeat is an orphan. What matters," he says, is that "I am the responsible officer of the government."

One day JFK will look back and speculate that the Bay of Pigs blunder could have given the U.S. military reason to interfere with the civilian American government on the grounds that the president was unsuited for office.

Six months later, however, it is CIA director Allen Dulles who is fired. The CIA chief is extremely bitter. The slight is one that the old spymaster and his agency will not soon forget.

■ ■ ■

A week after the Bay of Pigs debacle, Kennedy calls his advisers, including Bobby, into the Cabinet Room. Bobby's attendance at a foreign policy meeting is unusual, and at first the president's brother holds his tongue.

The president leans back in his chair and softly taps a pencil against his teeth as Undersecretary of State Chester Bowles reads a lengthy statement that absolves the State Department from any blame concerning the Bay of Pigs.

JFK can see that Bobby is seething. The two brothers find Bowles whiny and self-righteous.

The president knows from a lifetime of observing his little brother in action that an explosion is coming soon. He has also authorized Bobby to speak for him. JFK waits, keeping his expression blank, listening, tapping that pencil against his teeth.

Finally Bobby Kennedy takes the floor. He brutally tears into Chester Bowles with words designed to humiliate.

"That's the most meaningless, worthless thing I've ever heard. You people are so anxious to protect your own asses that you're afraid to do anything. All you want to do is dump the whole thing on the president. We'd be better off if you just quit and left the foreign policy to someone else," Bobby growls, his voice growing louder. The president watches, his face impassive, that pencil making just the slightest clicking noise on his perfect white teeth.

"I became suddenly aware," Kennedy adviser Richard Goodwin will later write, "that Bobby's harsh polemic reflected the president's concealed emotions, privately communicated in some earlier, intimate conversation. I knew, even then, that there was an inner hardness, often volatile anger beneath the outwardly amiable, thoughtful, carefully controlled demeanor of John Kennedy."

If Lyndon Johnson is the vice president, it will one day be written, then Bobby Kennedy is soon to become the assistant president—but only after the Bay of Pigs bonds the brothers and transforms the way JFK does business in the White House. From now on, when President Kennedy wants a contentious point made to his cabinet or advisers, he will rely on Bobby, who will then speak for the president and endure any subsequent criticism or argument so as not to weaken his big brother.

■ ■ ■

Amazingly, Kennedy's approval ratings rise to 83 percent after the invasion, proving to the president that the American people firmly stand behind his actions against Castro. Behind the scenes, U.S. plots to overthrow the Cuban leader continue to be hatched, and Castro becomes openly defiant of Kennedy, further cementing the widespread belief that each man wants the other dead.

Meanwhile, even as Kennedy's approval ratings temporarily make him one of the most popular presidents of the twentieth century, he knows that something must be done to restore America's prestige among the international community. In an interview with James Reston of the *New York Times*, Kennedy sets aside the Cuban situation. Instead, he candidly admits that "we have a problem making our power credible and Vietnam looks like the place."

Vietnam.

Small, and until now almost completely overlooked by America, the Asian nation is in the throes of its own Communist uprising. Now President Kennedy deems it vital to American security. In May 1961, JFK tasks Vice President Lyndon Johnson with a fact-finding trip to Vietnam, sending him farther away from the Oval Office than ever before.

The reasons have as much to do with national security as the president's awareness of the toll that being powerless is taking on the vice president. "I cannot stand Johnson's damn long face," JFK confides to one senator. "He just comes in, sits at cabinet meetings with his face all screwed up. Never says anything. He looks so sad."

When Kennedy's good friend Senator George Smathers of Florida suggests Johnson go on an around-the-world trip, JFK is delighted, calling it "a damn good idea."

Just to reinforce the journey's importance, the vice president is allowed the use of a presidential airplane.

■ ■ ■

More than 110 men would not have died if JFK had canceled the Bay of Pigs invasion. And more than 1,200 freedom fighters would not have been captured and sentenced to Castro's brutal prisons. The Bay of Pigs not only exposed flaws in Kennedy's international policy, but it also eroded the power the voters had given him—even if this was unbeknownst to them at the time. Kennedy was indecisive at a time when he should have been resolute. He allowed himself to be misled. It is impossible to ascertain why. But there is no question that in the first major test of his administration, Kennedy's leadership failed.

The harrowing days of April 1961 taught the Kennedy brothers an indelible lesson: they are on their own. Their advisers are not worth shoe polish. In order to restore America's power position, the Kennedy brothers will have to find a way to defeat their enemies, both abroad and, especially, in Washington, D.C.

■ ■ ■

Meanwhile, in the Soviet Union, the U.S. State Department has decided to return Lee Harvey Oswald's American passport and allow him to return home. But while Oswald is quite anxious to leave the Soviet Union, he is no longer the unattached nomad who defected nearly two years earlier. He delays his departure until a time when Marina and their unborn child can travel with him.

He also delays telling Marina that they are going anywhere.

Finally, Oswald breaks the news. "My wife is slightly startled"—he writes in his journal on June 1, after finally telling Marina that they are leaving the Soviet Union, most likely forever—"but then encourages me to do what I wish to do."

Marina is on the verge of leaving behind everything she knows for a life of uncertainty with a man she barely knows. But she accepts this hard reality because she has already learned one great truism about Lee Harvey Oswald: he always does what he wants to do, no matter how many obstacles are thrown in his path.

Always.

4

❦

The First Lady glides alone down a hallway, walking straight toward the six-foot-high television camera bearing the logo of the CBS eye. Her outfit and lipstick are a striking red, accenting her full lips and auburn bouffant hairdo. The camera will broadcast only in black and white, so this detail is lost on the forty-six million Americans tuning in to NBC and CBS to watch her televised tour of the White House. This is Jackie's moment in the national spotlight, a chance to show off the ongoing effort to restore her beloved "Maison Blanche."

Jackie pretends that the camera is not there. This is the way she goes through life as well, feigning ignorance and keeping a discreet distance from all but a few trusted confidants. Despite her practical detachment, Jackie is anything but unaware of her circumstance, having written and edited the show's script herself, filling the document's margins with small reminders about a piece of furniture's history and the names of wealthy donors. She knows not only the renovation status of each of the

White House's fifty-four rooms and sixteen baths but also the complete history of the 170-year-old building itself.

And yet, as America will learn over the course of the broadcast, the First Lady does not come across as a pompous know-it-all. In fact, she doesn't even like to be called "the First Lady"; she thinks it sounds like the name of a racehorse. This ability to laugh at herself gives Jackie that precious gift of appearing vulnerable and shy, rather than aloof, even as she speaks with an upper-crust accent. Many men find her sexy, and many women see her as an approachable icon. Throughout the first year of her husband's presidency, her perceived accessibility has endeared Jackie Kennedy to America and the world.

President Kennedy made light of this when they visited Paris in June 1961, on a state visit to meet French president Charles de Gaulle. The Bay of Pigs had taken place just six weeks earlier, and JFK's image had been vastly diminished in the estimation of many European leaders. But not so Jackie's image. When Air Force One touched down at Orly Airport, she was hailed as the very picture of glamour, poise, and beauty. The president couldn't help but notice the popping flashbulbs that followed in her wake. Speaking before a host of dignitaries at the Palais de Chaillot, JFK opened his remarks with somber tones as he delivered an apt description of his status in the eyes of Paris and the world. "I do not think it altogether inappropriate for me to introduce myself to this audience," he said with a straight face. "I am the man who accompanied Jacqueline Kennedy to Paris—and I have enjoyed it."

■ ■ ■

After her walk past the CBS camera, the First Lady starts her television special by narrating a brief history of the White House. Viewers hear her demure voice as images of drawings and photographs fill the screen. There is drama in her words, underscoring her emotional attachment to the building. She speaks in approving tones about Theodore Roosevelt's addition of the West Wing, which moved the offices of the president and his staff from the cramped second-floor environs of the White House residence into a far more spacious and businesslike environment.

There is an air of tragedy in her voice as she describes how the White House had to be gutted in 1948. President Truman's study floor had begun vibrating as if on the verge of collapse. An inspection revealed that the entire building was about to implode because it had not been renovated or reinforced for decades. "The whole inside was scooped out. Only the exterior walls remained," Jackie says breathily as photographs of giant bulldozers tearing out the historic original floors and ceilings flash on the screen. "It would have been easier and less expensive to demolish the whole building. But the White House is so great a symbol to Americans that the exterior walls were retained."

The First Lady finishes her monologue with a reminder that she has immersed herself in the details of all renovations, past and present: "Piece by piece, the interior of the president's house was put back together. The exterior views were exactly those which Americans had seen throughout the century, except for the balcony on the South Portico—which President Truman added."

The scripted words are a coy barb. Truman was roundly denounced in 1947 for adding the balcony, which was seen as a desecration of the White House's exterior architecture. President Kennedy was initially nervous about Jackie's restoration, fearing that she would come under the same sharp criticism as Truman. But rather than defer to her husband, as she does so often, the First Lady refused to back down. This "won't be like the Truman Balcony," she insisted, assuring her husband that her efforts would be viewed positively. Her focus would be the interior, finally finishing the work those bulldozers began in 1948. Her goal is nothing less than to transform the White House from the very large home of a bureaucrat into a presidential palace.

Mamie Eisenhower was once fond of referring to the White House and its objects as her personal property—"my house" and "my carpets." She also had a passion for the color pink. Jackie, who doesn't get along with her predecessor, has gotten rid of all of Mamie's cheap furniture and carpeting and painted over the pink.

As Americans are about to see for themselves, the White House now belongs to Jacqueline Bouvier Kennedy.

The First Lady once again steps before the camera to take viewers on a walk around her new home, now followed by the show's host, Charles Collingwood of CBS. Jackie's personal touches are everywhere, from the new draperies, whose designs she sketched herself; to the new guidebook she authorized to raise funds for the restoration (selling 350,000 copies in just six months). She has done away with oddities such as the water fountains that made the White House look more like an office building than a national treasure.

The First Lady has scoured storage rooms and the National Gallery, turning up assorted treasures such as paintings by Cézanne, Teddy Roosevelt's drinking mugs, and James Monroe's gold French flatware. President Kennedy's new desk was another of Jackie's finds. The *Resolute* desk, as it is known, was carved from the timbers of an ill-fated British vessel and was a gift from Queen Victoria to President Rutherford B. Hayes in 1880. Jackie found it languishing in the White House broadcast room, buried beneath a pile of electronics. She promptly had it relocated to the Oval Office.

No one other than longtime household staff knows the White House and its secrets quite as well as Jackie. But despite her vast knowledge, there is also a great deal she does not *want* to know.

Foremost on that list are the names of the women her husband is sleeping with. And they are many. There is Judith Campbell, the mistress who serves as Kennedy's clandestine connection to Chicago Mafia kingpin Sam Giancana—and who complains that JFK is less tender as a lover since becoming president. And twenty-seven-year-old divorcée Helen Chavchavadze, whom JFK has been seeing since before the inauguration. There are the girls brought in by Dave Powers. The president's mistresses even include some of Jackie's friends and personal staff. Jackie makes it a habit to leave for the couple's Glen Ora estate in Virginia most Thursdays for a weekend of horseback riding. She does not return until Monday. The president has full run of the White House while she is away. So the list of his consorts grows by the day.

Jackie Kennedy is not stupid. She has known about JFK's affairs since he was in the Senate. Her feelings are deeply hurt, but she sets the president's indiscretions aside for the sake of appearances, for the prestige of being First Lady, and most of all because she loves her husband—and believes that he loves her.

The First Lady has a fascination with the European aristocracy and knows that it is common, perhaps even natural, for powerful men in Europe to have affairs. Her beloved father, John "Black Jack" Bouvier, strayed often. And her father-in-law, Joseph Kennedy, is notorious for his dalliances. The First Lady has no reason to believe that the president of the United States, the most powerful man in the world, will be any different. Besides, it's a family tradition. "All Kennedy men are like that," she once commented to Joan, the wife of JFK's youngest brother, Teddy. "You can't let it get to you. You can't take it personally."

Once, while passing through Evelyn Lincoln's office with a French reporter, Jackie spied Lincoln's assistant, Priscilla Wear, sitting to one side of the small room. Switching from English to French, Jackie informed the reporter that "this is the girl who supposedly is sleeping with my husband."

However, despite outward acceptance, deep inside Jackie takes it very personally. From time to time, her friends notice the quiet sadness about her marriage. Even the Secret Service agents, who genuinely like and respect her, can see that the First Lady is suffering.

Even in the midst of her pain, however, the First Lady is practical. She makes a point to keep Kenny O'Donnell aware of the precise time she plans to leave for and return from any trip outside the White House, just to make sure she doesn't stumble upon the president in flagrante delicto with a consort.

The First Lady has thought of taking a lover. She often dines alone with Secretary of Defense Robert McNamara. They flirt with each other and read poetry together. And when Jackie is in New York she visits the apartment of Adlai Stevenson, America's ambassador to the United Nations. They always kiss when they say hello and enjoy trips to the ballet and opera together.

She is intrigued by these men and knows that there are rumors she has had a fling with actor William Holden, but it is her husband whose love she craves. Until recently their lovemaking was hardly spectacular.

There was little attempt at foreplay—indeed, for all his sexual adventures, the president made love to Jackie as if it were a duty. She often wondered why he felt the need to sleep with other women and began to question whether *she* was the problem. Despite the adoration of millions of men around the world, there had to be some reason that her own husband seemed oblivious to her sexual charms.

Then, in the spring of 1961, when Jackie twisted her ankle playing touch football at Hickory Hill, Bobby's Virginia home, Bobby asked his neighbor, Dr. Frank Finnerty, to treat the injury. Finnerty was a thirty-seven-year-old cardiologist who taught medicine at Georgetown University. He was also extremely handsome and likeable. Jackie found him to be a good listener. A week later, her ankle healed, she asked Finnerty if she could call him from time to time, just to talk. A surprised Finnerty was more than happy to agree.

Sex was definitely on Jackie's mind when she made the proposition, but not sex with Dr. Finnerty. Over the course of several conversations, she told Finnerty the names of the women her husband was involved with and admitted how bad JFK's affairs made her feel about herself. The Kennedy marriage was designed, in Jackie's words, as "a relationship between a man and a woman where a man would be the leader and a woman be his wife and look up to him as a man." That construct extended to the bedroom, where his pleasure was paramount. She wondered why the president made love so quickly, without any concern for her pleasure. It was all about him, and she felt left out. "He just goes too fast and falls asleep," she complained.

Dr. Finnerty came up with a solution. He scripted a discussion that Jackie might have with the president, suggesting ways that their love-making might be more mutual. Finnerty coached her to speak matter-of-factly and use precise descriptions of what she wanted and of how she might also be able to enhance the president's enjoyment.

Thus fortified, Jackie nervously broached the subject to JFK over dinner one night. As the president listened in amazement, his usually shy and sexually inhibited wife told him precisely what she wanted from him in bed. Jackie lied when he asked how she had suddenly become so knowledgeable, claiming that she had gotten the answers from a priest, a gynecologist, and several very descriptive books.

The president was impressed. He "never thought she would go to that much trouble to enjoy sex," Finnerty would later recall.

Jackie reported back to the doctor that the sex with JFK had improved, and whatever anxieties she had had about her own performance were gone for good.

Not that the president has stopped sleeping around. But at least Jackie now knows that he is getting satisfaction in the marital bed.

■ ■ ■

"Thank you, Mr. President," concludes reporter Charles Collingwood. "And thank you, Mrs. Kennedy, for showing us this wonderful house in which you live, and all of the wonderful things you're bringing to it."

John Kennedy has joined his wife on camera for the last few minutes of the broadcast special, explaining the importance of Jackie's ongoing efforts and what the White House means as a symbol of America. The First Lady says nothing as she smiles warmly and gazes into the camera. Jackie looks utterly unflappable as the special comes to an end, not a hair out of place, the strands of pearls around her neck perfectly aligned.

But looks are deceiving. The White House tour was actually recorded a month ago, and the hour-long broadcast took seven hours to film. A nervous Jackie chain-smoked her L&Ms whenever the cameras weren't rolling and wound down afterward by combing out her bouffant so that her hair hung straight down.

She also downed one very large scotch.

■ ■ ■

Jackie's White House tour is one of the most watched shows in the history of television. In fact, it earns the First Lady a special Emmy Award. America is now completely smitten. Jacqueline Kennedy is a superstar.

Meanwhile, the White House restoration continues. Far down on the list of items to be addressed are those gray Oval Office curtains, which will not be replaced until late in November 1963.

5

〜

March 24, 1962
Palm Springs, California
7:00 P.M.

John F. Kennedy is tired but alert. He is in the resort city of Palm Springs, standing on the patio of the Spanish-style home of show business legend Bing Crosby. But Crosby is not present this evening, having turned his comfortable house over to JFK and his entourage for the weekend. Kennedy watches as the party unfolds around the crowded pool on this warm spring evening. Sounds of laughter and splashing fill the night air. Beyond the pool, the president sees boulder-strewn mountains rising above the one-acre property, forming a stunning desert backdrop.

Yesterday, Kennedy gave a rousing speech to eighty-five thousand people at the University of California, Berkeley. He spoke of democracy and freedom, key themes throughout the cold war. He then flew south on Air Force One to Vandenberg Air Force Base, where he watched his first-ever missile launch. The slim white Atlas rocket blasted off without incident, proving that the United States was catching up in the space race, which was going strong, with the Soviet Union having just this week reached an agreement to share outer space research with America's cold war adversaries.

Palm Springs, and Crosby's secluded home, is the perfect weekend hideaway after the hectic West Coast trip. There was a brief bit of official business earlier in the day, when the president met with Dwight Eisenhower to discuss foreign policy. But now JFK can finally unwind with a cigar and a daiquiri or two.

But the president is not completely relaxed. He knows he has offended good friend and longtime supporter Frank Sinatra by canceling his plans to spend the weekend at Sinatra's house and staying at the home of Crosby, a Republican, of all things—but the president will deal with that symbolism later. Tonight he just wants to have fun.

A lot of fun.

It's Saturday, which normally means that Jackie and the children are spending the weekend at the Glen Ora estate. But the First Lady, as the whole world knows from the many media accounts, is halfway around the globe on an official visit to India and Pakistan. The success of her television special confirmed what her husband has known for years: Jacqueline Bouvier Kennedy is John Fitzgerald Kennedy's number one political asset. He's already making plans to leverage her popularity for his 1964 reelection campaign.

And while the president would be a fool to damage their marriage (and his career) by a brazen act of public infidelity, there are moments when this normally pragmatic man is helplessly self-destructive.

Such as now.

Among the guests at Bing Crosby's estate is the most glamorous and perhaps the most troubled woman in Hollywood. JFK has cultivated a relationship with her for almost two years and is quite certain that tonight Marilyn Monroe is finally his for the taking.

The president of the United States takes another pull on his cigar and steps into the bedroom. His wife is eight thousand miles away. He

The First Lady on a boat cruise on Lake Pichola in Rajasthan during her official visit to India and Pakistan in 1962. (Cecil Stoughton, White House Photographs, John F. Kennedy Presidential Library and Museum, Boston)

can do anything he wants tonight. Anything. And there's absolutely no chance his wife will walk in on him.

■ ■ ■

"My wife had her first and last ride on an elephant!" JFK spontaneously informed the packed stadium at the University of California the day before. The crowd roared and laughed in approval.

That's how JFK talks to America about his Jackie: as if they're eavesdropping on a private conversation. People crave even the smallest intimate nugget of information about their marriage. The president's keen political instincts tell him, though he never admits it aloud, that the Kennedys aren't just the most glamorous couple in America—they're the most glamorous couple in the entire world. The cool heat of their relationship is an inspiration to lovers everywhere.

The Kennedy children would often play in the Oval Office while the president attended to his official duties. (Cecil Stoughton, White House Photographs, John F. Kennedy Presidential Library and Museum, Boston)

And it's true: the Kennedys *do* love each other. JFK is a doting father and husband who cherishes his family. He lets Caroline and John play in the Oval Office as he works, and the presidential bathtub is often filled with floating rubber ducks and pink pigs, because he knows they amuse baby John. He spends a few minutes in Jackie's bedroom each morning before walking down to the office and likes it when his wife does the same for him each afternoon—waking him up from his nap, the two of them catching up on the news of the day as he gets dressed.

The president's only complaint about his wife is that Jackie has a profound indifference to fiscal discipline. She spends more money on clothes than the U.S. government pays him to be president. (JFK's net worth is more than $10 million. He dedicates his $100,000 presidential salary to charities such as the Boy Scouts and the United Negro College Fund.)

Yet there is an enormous contradiction in the Kennedys' otherwise charmed marriage. The president's voracious sexual appetite is the elephant that the president rides around on each and every day while pretending that it doesn't exist.

There's no way the First Lady can keep up. She's raising a family, restoring the White House, and juggling a busy social calendar. Jackie would have to be superhuman to meet the president's physical needs. Plus, he wouldn't be satisfied with just one woman. The sheer volume of call girls, socialites, starlets, and stewardesses escorted into the White House whenever Jackie and the kids are away is beyond the realm of most men's moral or physical capacities. It's gotten to the point where the Secret Service no longer even checks the names and nationalities of all the women Dave Powers procures for the president.

More than one federal agent believes the situation is dangerous. The number of women who have access to the president is, of course, a security breach that could bring down the presidency, whether through blackmail or even, say, covert assassination via hypodermic injection. It is a topic of discussion among the Secret Service. But its job is to protect the president, not lecture him. The agents turn a blind eye to his behavior, and some even provide cover for him. Being a member of the White House detail means being married to the job, and the fifty to eighty hours of overtime every month can increase a Secret Service agent's paycheck by more than $1,000 a year. An agent would be a fool to give that up for the sake of a morality lesson.

The White House press corps also looks the other way. The president's private life is none of their business, or that of the public's. White House reporters know that the president cherishes loyalty and will cut them off from full access if he doesn't get it. Not a word about suspected infidelities is printed or broadcast. In fact, the Washington bureau chief for *Newsweek*, Ben Bradlee, a very close friend of the president's, will forever claim to know nothing about JFK's philandering.

Meanwhile, the president is having sex with Bradlee's sister-in-law.

Sometimes the objects of Kennedy's flirtations actually work in the White House, as in the case of Jackie's secretary, Pamela Turnure, and

Evelyn Lincoln's assistant, Priscilla Wear. This makes the president's courting easier from a logistical and security standpoint, but brings about its own unique dangers.

For instance, the president is quite fond of the occasional afternoon swim with the two twentysomething secretaries Priscilla Wear and Jill Cowen—nicknamed Fiddle and Faddle by the Secret Service. A Secret Service agent is always positioned outside the door to make sure no one enters.

But one day the First Lady appeared at the pool door, eager to go for a swim. This had never before happened. The panic-stricken agent barred the door and tried to explain to Jackie that she was not allowed to use the pool of the very White House she was so lovingly restoring.

Inside, JFK heard the commotion, quickly pulled on his robe, and fled the pool just before he could be caught. Agents would later recall that his large wet footprints and the smaller prints of his female swim partners left a very clear trail, which Jackie did not see, having left in a huff.

■ ■ ■

Even as one part of the president's brain strategizes clever ways to deal with Fidel Castro, Nikita Khrushchev, and Charles de Gaulle, another part strategizes ways to have as much sex as he wants without Jackie walking in on him. And as Kennedy gets more and more comfortable in the White House, his affairs get more and more outrageous.

"We got to the point where we'd say, 'What else is new?'" one member of the Kennedy Secret Service detail later remembered. "There were women everywhere. Very often, depending on what shift you were on, you'd either see them going up, or you'd see them coming out in the morning. People were vacuuming and the ushers were around. There were several of them that were regular visitors. Not when Jackie was there, however."

When Kennedy goes more than a few days without extramarital sex, he becomes a different man—so much so that the Secret Service breathes a sigh of relief whenever Jackie takes the kids away for the weekend. "When she was there, it was no fun," a longtime agent would later admit.

"He just had headaches. You'd really see him droop because he wasn't getting laid. He was like a rooster getting hit with a water hose."

Sex is John Kennedy's Achilles' heel. Why in the world does he do this to Jackie? And what is he doing to the nation in the process?

■ ■ ■

Just a few short weeks after being named attorney general, Bobby Kennedy received a special file from J. Edgar Hoover, the pug-nosed and Machiavellian head of the Federal Bureau of Investigation. In the file was evidence about the president's extramarital affairs. It turns out that while the newspapers were looking the other way, the FBI had been tracking JFK's liaisons since the late 1940s, because he was seeing a woman thought to be a spy for Nazi Germany. The file is Hoover's idea of job security. He wants everybody to know the FBI will never be diminished—and that there's nothing illicit going on in America that he doesn't know about. For reasons of national security, not even the president of the United States is above the scrutiny of the FBI.

In early 1962, as President Kennedy's visit to Palm Springs is being planned, a Justice Department investigation into organized crime reveals that singer Frank Sinatra is deeply involved with the Mafia. This is trouble for the Kennedys—Americans know that Sinatra not only supports the president but is also a close personal friend. And if that isn't enough to compromise the attorney general and the president of the United States, their sister Patricia's husband, movie actor Peter Lawford, is a member of Sinatra's famous Rat Pack.

Making the matter more delicate is a brand-new file from Hoover delivered to Bobby just a few weeks before the Palm Springs trip. This one indicates that the president of the United States is having sex with a consort of Sam Giancana, not only one of the most notorious mobsters in the country, but also at the top of the list of Mafia kingpins whom Bobby Kennedy is trying to bring down. The woman's name is Judith Campbell, and Hoover is describing her as a major security risk. Unbeknownst to Patricia Kennedy Lawford, her husband owes that affiliation to her family heritage. Sinatra has long wanted to be closer to the throne of power. Once he realized that the Kennedys were on the verge of becoming the most powerful family in America, he allowed Lawford into his inner circle. In addition, it was Patricia Kennedy Lawford who bankrolled the script for *Oceans 11*, assuming her husband would costar with Sinatra. But Dean Martin was given the role instead. Sinatra treats Peter Lawford like a hanger-on, suspecting that Patricia Kennedy Lawford, like most people outside the Hollywood bubble, will do almost anything to bask in the reflected glow of movie stars' fame.

And Sinatra is correct. Despite numerous snubs, the Lawfords remain keen to be part of the Rat Pack "vibe."

Thus, the woman who extended Sinatra's invitation for JFK to stay in his Palm Springs home on his visit to the city is none other than Patricia Kennedy Lawford.

After reading Hoover's Sinatra file, Bobby Kennedy tells the president to stay somewhere else in Palm Springs. Bobby doesn't care that this slight might sever a long-standing political relationship with Sinatra, who not only campaigned extensively on behalf of Kennedy in 1960, but also worked overtime to coordinate the inaugural gala.

The truth is that Bobby has no choice. Sinatra has had repeated contact with ten of the biggest names in organized crime. The FBI reports detail not only the times and dates when the singer is phoning Mafia heads from home, but also reveal that the mobsters are dialing his private number. "The nature of Sinatra's work may, on occasion, bring him into contact with underworld figures," reads the report. "But this does not account for his friendship and/or financial involvement with people such as Joe and Rocco Fischetti, cousins of Al Capone, Paul Emilio D'Amato, John Formosa and Sam Giancana—all of whom are on the list of racketeers."

The FBI has been keeping files on Sinatra since the late 1940s, chronicling his associations with other famous gangsters such as Lucky Luciano and Mickey Cohen. As early as February 1947 there were reports that he had vacationed in Havana with Luciano and his bodyguards, and that the trio were seen together at "the race track, the gambling casino, and at private parties." What made these sightings so extraordinary was

President Kennedy was once close friends with Frank Sinatra, shown here in California. (AFP/Getty Images)

that Luciano had recently been paroled from prison and deported to Sicily. Such a high-profile appearance in Havana was his way of thumbing his nose at U.S. law enforcement.

The list of alleged associations goes on and on. Bobby's true surprise about Sinatra, however, is not that the singer is connected with the Mafia. Rather, it's that the FBI has evidence linking the Kennedy White House with organized crime through the singer. In fact, Hoover has years of files documenting the close relationship between Sinatra, the Kennedys, and high-profile members of the Mafia such as Giancana—who wears a sapphire pinkie ring given to him by none other than Frank Sinatra. The most damning bits of the report state that Giancana frequently visits Sinatra's Palm Springs estate. Agents also found a number of calls from Giancana's good friend Judith Campbell to Evelyn Lincoln, the president's secretary, suggesting a clear link between the Kennedy White House and organized crime.

Frank Sinatra and John Kennedy have shared many laughs, many drinks, and, as the FBI suggests, a woman or two. In a separate investigation in February 1960, the FBI observed JFK at the Sands Hotel in Las Vegas with the Rat Pack and noted that "show girls from all over town were running in and out of the Senator's suite." Sinatra and the Rat Pack sang the national anthem to open the 1960 Democratic National Convention in Los Angeles. Sinatra has visited the Kennedys' family estate at Hyannis Port and once startled guests by performing an impromptu concert at the living room piano. Sinatra even reworded his 1959 hit song "High Hopes" to make it an anthem for the Kennedy campaign.

There are also rumors that the Kennedys used the Mafia to help influence voters during the 1960 election.

The file is just a warning: Hoover is letting Bobby know that the connection between the Kennedys and organized crime is on the verge of becoming widespread public knowledge. And only Hoover can stop that.

Despite their significant history, JFK listens to Bobby and cuts Sinatra off in an instant. They're done. The singer has become a snare that could potentially entangle Kennedy and bring him down—and no friendship is worth the presidency. *Ruthless* might be a word commonly associated with Bobby, but now and again the president can be just as cold-blooded.

■ ■ ■

Bobby phones Peter Lawford to break the news that the president will not be staying with Sinatra. Lawford owes his career to Sinatra. He fears the man and is reluctant to make the call to Sinatra canceling the presidential weekend.

So JFK himself gets on the phone to Lawford. "As President, I just can't stay at Sinatra's and sleep in the same bed that Sam Giancana or some other hood slept in," he tells his brother-in-law. Kennedy then demands two favors. The first is to find him someplace else to rendezvous with Monroe during his weekend in Palm Springs. The second is to buck up and break the news to Frank.

Peter Lawford has no choice but to make the calls. Chris Dumphy, a Florida Republican, connects Lawford with Bing Crosby, solving Lawford's first problem. The president's womanizing is an open secret. Crosby, who is out of town, suspects what might go on at his house, but he doesn't care. He's worked in Hollywood long enough to know that infidelity is as common as sunrise.

Delivering the news to Sinatra is not so simple.

The forty-six-year-old singer has been anticipating this visit for months. He has purchased extra land next to his property and built cottages for the Secret Service. He has installed special state-of-the-art phone lines. A gold plaque has been hung in the bedroom the president will use, forever commemorating the night when "John F. Kennedy Slept Here." Pictures of JFK are hung all over the main house. A flagpole is erected so that the presidential standard can fly over the compound. And most important, Sinatra has built a special new cement landing pad for the president's helicopter. Sinatra is giddy about the visit. So giddy, in fact, that it doesn't even bother him that the president will be rendezvousing with Sinatra's former girlfriend, Marilyn Monroe.

The truth is, the Kennedys are somewhat embarrassed that Sinatra believes his home will become the western White House. It's not that the Kennedy clan doesn't like Sinatra—although Jackie can't stand him—but they prefer to keep the flamboyant singer at arm's length.

Finally, Lawford breaks the news by phone. Sinatra listens, but only for as long as it takes to realize that he is being cast out of the president's circle of friends. The singer slams down the receiver and hurls the phone to the floor. "Do you want to know where he's staying?" Sinatra screams to his valet. "Bing Crosby's house. That's where. And he's a Republican!"

Sinatra will never forget this slight. He calls Bobby Kennedy every name in the book, then phones Lawford back and cuts him off from *his* inner circle. He races around his house and tears Kennedy photos from the walls, then finds a sledgehammer and storms outside to single-handedly destroy the concrete helipad.

■ ■ ■

John Kennedy stands just outside a back door watching the crowd drifting in and out of Bing Crosby's home. Secret Service agents hover at the edges of the lawn and in the shadows of the palm trees and shrubbery ringing the grounds. Marilyn Monroe is already by the president's side. There is an intimacy in their movements that leaves no doubt they will be sleeping together tonight.

Monroe has been drinking. A lot. Or so it appears.

The thirty-five-year-old movie star is not a stupid woman, although she often plays that role both on- and offscreen. "I thought you were dumb," her character in *Gentlemen Prefer Blondes* is told. "I can be smart when it's important," she replies, "but most men don't like it."

It is a line that Norma Jean Baker herself suggested. After spending much of her youth in foster homes, she began modeling in her teens and landed a movie contract in 1946, changing her name to Marilyn Monroe. Born a brunette, she dyed her hair and began cultivating the "dumb blonde" persona that became her calling card. Her career path led her to a number of high-profile performances in movies such as *How to Marry a Millionaire*, *The Seven Year Itch*, and *Some Like It Hot*. She has been married and divorced three times, and has developed a reputation for abusing alcohol and prescription drugs. Substance abuse is slowly destroying her career. But she is still voluptuous, vivacious, and clever enough in her lucid moments that her true intelligence reveals itself.

Kennedy first met Monroe at a dinner party in the 1950s. Their relationship ramped up on July 15, 1960, the night he accepted the Democratic nomination for president. The two flirted that night, much to the dismay of Kennedy's staff, who were immediately concerned the pair would be caught having an affair during the campaign. Patricia Kennedy Lawford went so far as to pull Marilyn aside and warn her not to have sex with her brother.

But that was almost two years ago—and ironically, it was Patricia who invited Marilyn and JFK to a dinner party at her New York home in late February 1962. Marilyn marched in late, as was her custom. She'd been drinking sherry. Her dress was a small beads-and-sequins affair. "It was the tightest goddam dress I ever saw on a woman," the legendary show business manager Milt Ebbins would later remember of Monroe's pre-party preparations—specifically of pulling the dress on over Monroe's head: "We couldn't get it past her hips. Of course, typical of Marilyn, she wasn't wearing any underwear either. So there I was, on my knees in front of her . . . pulling down this dress with all my might, trying to get it [down] past her big ass."

Ebbins was eventually successful with the dress, and JFK immediately gravitated to Monroe's side as she sashayed into the party. A photographer attempted to take their picture, but the president quickly turned his back so they wouldn't be photographed together. For good measure, the Secret Service demanded the film.

Before the night was over, JFK had casually invited Marilyn to meet him in Palm Springs on March 24. To close the deal, he confided that "Jackie won't be there."

■ ■ ■

Now Marilyn Monroe wears a loose robe as the party swirls at the Crosby estate. She is "calm and relaxed," in the opinion of one partygoer.

The president is entranced by her wit and intellect and would be thrilled to add such a famous sex symbol to his list of conquests. He also finds her nurturing. After Kennedy complains of his chronic back pain, Monroe phones her friend Ralph Roberts, an actor and masseur knowledgeable about back issues. When she puts Kennedy on the phone, Roberts doesn't know it's the president he's talking to, but he can't help but think that the man on the other end sounds just like John Fitzgerald Kennedy. Roberts offers a quick diagnosis and hangs up after a few minutes, thinking to himself that Marilyn is once again up to no good.

In some ways, she can't help herself. Monroe has been married to two very famous and powerful men—baseball player Joe DiMaggio and playwright Arthur Miller—but JFK eclipses them by far. "Marilyn Monroe is a soldier," she later tells her therapist, speaking in the third person. "Her commander-in-chief is the greatest and most powerful man in the world. The first duty of a soldier is to obey the commander-in-chief. He says do that, you do it." The attorney general has caught her attention, as well. "It's like the Navy—the president is the captain and Bobby is his executive officer," she will tell her therapist. "Bobby would do anything for his country, and so would I. I will never embarrass him. As long as I have memory, I have John Fitzgerald Kennedy."

Yet despite her passion and beauty, Marilyn Monroe is damaged goods. Her three marriages aren't socially acceptable in the Kennedys' Catholic world, nor is her affair with Frank Sinatra. JFK knows that she broke up Arthur Miller's previous marriage so that she could marry the playwright. More ominously, the president suspects that Monroe has visions of moving into the White House sometime soon. He has even made a point of telling her that she's "not First Lady material."

No, Marilyn is not going to replace Jackie, no matter what the movie star might believe during the two nights she spends with the president in Palm Springs. Marilyn gives JFK a chrome Ronson Adonis cigarette lighter as a gift to remind him of their special time together, although the president certainly needs no reminder of his time with the world's leading sex symbol.

■ ■ ■

News of the Kennedy-Monroe liaison would be about as explosive as it gets. The question lingering in the minds of Kennedy's Secret Service detail and the president's close-knit Irish Mafia cronies is why the president continues to take such risks. Some believe it's a carryover from the old days of the Kennedy heritage in Ireland, where the leader of a clan commonly had free rein to sleep with women outside of marriage. Until his recent stroke, the president's father, Joseph Kennedy, behaved in just such a manner.

In addition, some believe that John Kennedy's personal tragedies—the death of his brother and of his infant child, and his own brushes with death—have given him a fatalistic attitude. All the sex is his carpe diem way of living life to the utmost.

And then there is the issue of his chronic physical pain. John Kennedy's appearance may be robust, but he suffers from a nervous stomach, back pain, and Addison's disease. His physical activity is limited to walking, sailing, and the occasional nine holes of golf. He can barely ride a horse. And the Kennedy family's legendary games of touch football don't include him as much as they used to.

Sex is the president's physical release of choice. He's an adrenaline junkie, and his psyche requires illicit excitement. As he told a family friend, "The chase is more fun than the kill."

■ ■ ■

"Happy Birthday, Mr. President."

Two months after their weekend in Palm Springs, Marilyn Monroe stands before a dazzled crowd in New York's Madison Square Garden, singing the traditional birthday song in the most salacious manner possible. Her skintight dress leaves little to the imagination, both front and back, even as her breathless words inspire a thousand questions. Marilyn, still stung by JFK's blunt assessment that she is not First Lady material, is desperately trying to rekindle the Palm Springs nights of romance.

"Happy Birthday to you," she purrs into the microphone.

The date is May 19, 1962, ten days before JFK's actual birthday. Jackie, once again, is not in attendance, but she knows all about Marilyn. She's not so much hurt as disgusted, correctly sensing that the president is taking advantage of an emotionally troubled woman who is easy prey for such a powerful man.

The president never comes in contact with the seemingly tipsy Marilyn as he climbs to the lectern at Madison Square Garden. But he does favor her with a lupine gaze that one journalist will later remember as "quite a sight to behold, and if I ever saw an appreciation of feminine beauty in the eyes of a man, it was in John F. Kennedy's at that moment."

Marilyn Monroe has become so obsessed with JFK that she calls the

"Happy Birthday, Mr. President." Marilyn Monroe serenaded JFK at his birthday gala in 1961. (Getty Images)

White House constantly, but her singing performance falls on deaf ears. The president has moved on, putting as much distance between himself and Marilyn as he did between himself and Frank Sinatra.

Like Sinatra, Marilyn is a snare that could easily entangle Kennedy and bring down his presidency. This is where the pragmatist in JFK returns, overriding his libido. He is willing to take great personal risks to satisfy his sexual needs, but he does not gamble when it comes to remaining in power. Better to have Monroe and Sinatra and the Mafia as enemies whom he can view from a wary distance, rather than as friends who could drag him down.

At the lectern before the party faithful in New York City, the president adopts the chaste mien of an altar boy. "I can now retire from politics after having 'Happy Birthday' sung to me in such a sweet and wholesome way," the president speaks into the microphone, his wry delivery suggesting that he is above such sexual shenanigans.

But the president hasn't given up on extramarital affairs. He is just beginning a new long-term relationship with a nineteen-year-old virgin whom he deflowers on Jackie's bed.

■ ■ ■

The presidency is a daunting and lonely job. Moments like the Madison Square Garden party offer a welcome respite from the pressure. JFK basks in the birthday appreciation, which comes in the midst of a campaign rally that raises more than $1 million for the Democratic Party.

The president has no way of knowing that he will celebrate this special day just one more time.

■ ■ ■

In the faraway Soviet city of Minsk, Lee Harvey Oswald has finally cleared the tangle of red tape that has prevented him from returning home.

The plan now is for him, Marina, and five-week-old June Lee to take the train to the American embassy in Moscow to pick up their travel documents.

On May 18, Oswald is discharged from his job at the Gorizont (Horizon) Electronics Factory. Few are sad to see him go. The plant director thinks Oswald is careless and oversensitive and lacks initiative. Even Marina thinks her new husband is lazy and knows he resents taking orders.

The Oswalds arrive in Moscow on May 24, 1962, the same day that navy test pilot Scott Carpenter becomes the second American astronaut to orbit the earth. President Kennedy is quick to commend Carpenter for his courage and skill, even as he grapples with Congress over the issue of affordable nationwide health care.

On June 1 the Oswalds board a train from Moscow to Holland. Lee Harvey carries a promissory note from the U.S. embassy for $435.71 to help start his life anew in America. On June 2, as Secretary of the Navy John Connally wins a runoff to become the Democratic nominee for

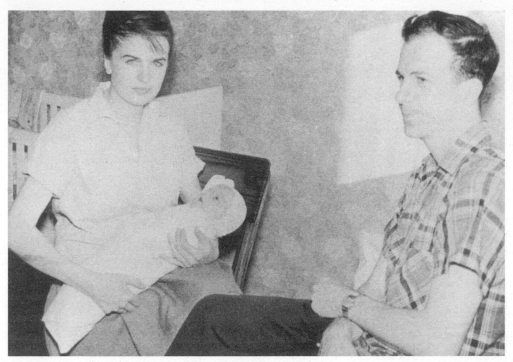

Marina and Lee Harvey Oswald with their daughter, June Lee, in 1962. (Getty Images)

governor of Texas, the Oswalds' train crosses the Soviet border at Brest. Two days later they board the SS *Maasdam*, bound for America, where they stay belowdecks most of the journey. Oswald is ashamed of Marina's cheap dresses and doesn't want her to be seen in public. He passes the time in their small cabin writing rants about his growing disillusionment with governmental power.

The *Maasdam* docks in Hoboken, New Jersey—Frank Sinatra's hometown—on June 13, 1962. The Oswalds pass through customs without incident and take a small room at New York City's Times Square Hotel. The plan is to stay there until they can afford to fly to Texas, where Oswald's brother Robert lives. There, Oswald can finally settle down and find work.

The next morning, in far-off Vietnam, South Vietnamese soldiers are flown aboard U.S. helicopters to combat a Communist stronghold, a move that forces President Kennedy to backpedal publicly on the issue of direct U.S. involvement in Southeast Asia, a war that he believes is vital to stanching the worldwide spread of communism.

Meanwhile, thanks to a loan from his brother, Lee Harvey Oswald and his family fly to Dallas. The city simmers with a rage that mirrors Oswald's ongoing personal unhappiness in many ways. The Deep South swung in President Kennedy's favor during the election, but there are pockets of militant anger about Kennedy being the first Roman Catholic president, his desire to bring about racial equality, and what some perceive as his Communist tendencies.

This is the environment into which the Oswald family arrives. They land at a Dallas area airport called Love Field, where the president and First Lady will touch down aboard Air Force One in seventeen short months.

Oswald is unhappy that his return to the United States has not attracted widespread media attention—or any media attention, for that matter. But even as he fumes that the press is nowhere in sight, he has no idea that he is being secretly watched—by a very powerful concern.

6

August 23, 1962
Washington, D.C./Beirut, Lebanon
Midday

The president is impotent.

Or so thinks Nikita Khrushchev, leader of the Soviet Union. Not physically, of course, but in the bruising global arena of realpolitik.

Khrushchev has watched Kennedy closely since the Bay of Pigs, searching for signs of the same weakness and indecisiveness that defined the U.S. president's handling of that crisis. The sixty-eight-year-old Khrushchev, who came to power after a brutal political battle to replace Joseph Stalin, well knows how to evaluate an opponent's strengths and weaknesses. He does not see a worthy adversary in Kennedy. September will mark Khrushchev's tenth anniversary in power. He plans on marking the occasion with a celebration of Soviet dominance in the world. If he can humiliate an American president in the process, so much the better.

The Russians, as the Soviets are often called, are flaunting their control of outer space by sending not one but two spaceships into orbit at the same time. The cosmonauts piloting each craft then further parade

Soviet mastery of missile technology by speaking to each other through a device known as a radio telephone.

In addition, Khrushchev and his Politburo are thumbing their noses at an international nuclear test ban by exploding two 40-megaton nuclear weapons over the Arctic, one week apart.

They are also building an eighty-seven-mile-long wall through the heart of Berlin, Germany. The wall separates the Soviet-controlled sector from the rest of the city, which is controlled by the Western Allies. The barrier is not meant to keep people out, but to imprison the citizens of Communist East Germany, preventing them from fleeing to the freedom of West Germany. The results are horrific. On August 23, 1962, East German border guards shoot a nineteen-year-old railway policeman who is trying to sprint to the West through a hole in the still-unfinished wall. They watch as the young man struggles to crawl the final few yards to freedom, then do nothing to help him as he collapses and dies.

The same thing happened a week earlier, when another young German was shot while trying to escape East Germany. Again, border guards watched for an hour as the man slowly bled to death. No one was allowed to go to his rescue. Riots broke out in West Berlin to protest the Soviet behavior, but it continues without apology.

Through it all, President Kennedy has refrained from making public threats or even critiquing the Soviet atrocities. Still, the American people overwhelmingly support JFK. He is the most popular president in modern American history, with an average approval rating of 70.1 percent— almost six points higher than Eisenhower's and a whopping 25 points higher than Harry Truman's. But the public will not forgive another misstep like the Bay of Pigs, so JFK tiptoes carefully through the high-stakes arena of foreign policy.

■ ■ ■

Lyndon Johnson does not tiptoe when it comes to foreign relations. The vice president—whose Secret Service code name is Volunteer—now stands up in the front seat of a convertible in Beirut, Lebanon. This

"Paris of the Middle East" loves him. He waves to the huge crowds lining the road as he is driven to the Phoenicia Hotel.

No matter where in the world he travels, the vice president wades into crowds, handing out ballpoint pens and cigarette lighters with the initials LBJ stamped on them. Then he launches into a pep talk. Whether it's a leper in Dakar or a shirtless beggar in Karachi, the vice president is keen to shake his hand and tell him that the American dream is not a myth—that there is hope, even in the midst of poverty.

And best of all, LBJ believes this. Johnson was raised in poverty himself. He knows firsthand the ravages of neglect and substandard living conditions. In many ways, the vice president has a far deeper emotional connection with the unwashed crowds along the side of the road than with the wealthy diplomats who host him.

Johnson is larger than life, a towering dynamo with basset hound bags under his eyes and sweat rings soaking his shirt. Back in Washington, he mopes around, bemoaning his lack of power. But when he travels abroad, Johnson is a rock star. His foreign antics are becoming legendary, particularly his impulsive habit of halting motorcades so he can jump out of his personal convertible limousine and into crowds to press the flesh.

Beirut is no different. This is the first layover on a nineteen-day trip that will also see stops in Iran, Greece, Turkey, Cyprus, and Italy. Lebanon was just supposed to be a refueling stop for his 707, but when Johnson learns that he is the highest-ranking American official ever to visit the Land of Cedars, he can't help himself. The refueling stop suddenly becomes an official visit, and the vice president is soon whisked from the airport and into the heart of Beirut.

As his motorcade slows down, Johnson spots a crowd of children at a roadside melon stand. He orders his driver to halt. Whipping off his sunglasses to make eye contact, Johnson bounds over to the startled kids and tells them about the power of the American dream. Some of the children look confused. A teenager wearing a "Champion Spark Plugs" cap is told that the United States stands behind the "liberty and integrity" of Lebanon.

Johnson's voice is booming, and he waves his arms as he speaks. Secret Service agents hasten to surround him, once again annoyed at the vice president's ignorance about security. Then, in a flash, Johnson is back in the front seat of his car, standing tall, waving to the crowds with both hands as he continues into the heart of Beirut.

Lyndon Johnson is a persnickety traveler. In addition to his limousine, he travels with cases of Cutty Sark scotch and a special shower nozzle whose needlelike jets of water he prefers. He demands a seven-foot-long mattress in each hotel room, to accommodate his large frame—not that he sleeps much: long after his staff has gone to sleep, LBJ is still at work, making phone calls back to Washington and reading diplomatic cables.

Originally, Johnson fought JFK over being used as a roving ambassador, but now he has come to love this aspect of his job. In Washington his craving for authority has many in the White House referring to him as Seward, a reference to Abraham Lincoln's power-hungry secretary of state. But on the road, Johnson truly does have power. He speaks for the president, but just as often veers off message to speak his own mind, which are moments he relishes.

But the Kennedys, John and Bobby, are annoyed with Johnson, especially when he speaks irresponsibly. On one trip to Asia, he praises South Vietnam's president, Ngo Dinh Diem, a man who tortured and killed an estimated fifty thousand suspected Communists. Incredibly, Johnson pronounces Diem to be the "Winston Churchill of Asia," a pronouncement that leads some to question the vice president's very sanity.

In Thailand, LBJ conducts a 3:00 A.M. press conference in his pajamas. On that same trip, he is warned that patting people on the head is considered an offense in Thai culture—whereupon he immediately bounds onto a local bus and rubs his very large hands on the heads of its passengers.

Johnson does one better in Saigon: while holding a press conference in his steamy hotel room, he suddenly strips naked, towels the sweat from his body, and puts on a fresh suit—all while answering questions from the media.

But there's no need for disrobing in Beirut. The Phoenicia Hotel is just two blocks from the blue Mediterranean. The August heat is tempered by a cool sea breeze. This will be one of the longest trips Johnson has ever undertaken, but the vice president is reveling in every minute, because for each one of these nineteen days away from the United States, he will be the most powerful and respected man in the room.

■ ■ ■

At the same time, at home, Bobby Kennedy is engaged in a completely different power struggle, one best epitomized by an incident that happened seven years ago.

Mississippi, 1955. A fourteen-year-old African American boy named Emmett Louis "Bobo" Till is visiting relatives in the Mississippi Delta town of Money. Till is from Chicago and has come to the Deep South to see for himself where his mother grew up. He had polio as a small child, which caused him to develop a stuttering problem. But though just five foot, four inches, Emmett now looks mature enough that he often passes for an adult. A close look at his smooth face, however, reveals that he is still very much a child.

Emmett's mother has warned him that there is a big difference between Chicago and Mississippi, and she isn't talking about the weather. Just a week before Emmett's trip south, a black man was shot dead in front of a courthouse not far from Money. His killers will soon be acquitted.

Emmett tells his mother he understands the southern racial climate and promises to be careful. This will turn out to be a false promise.

The teenager arrives at the small two-bedroom home of his sixty-four-year-old great-uncle Moses Wright on August 21, 1955. Three days later, on a Wednesday, he and some of his teenage relatives drift over to Bryant's Grocery and Meat Market, a small mom-and-pop operation that caters mostly to local sharecroppers. It is 7:30 at night. The twenty-four-year-old owner, Roy Bryant, a former soldier, is away in Texas, hauling shrimp from New Orleans to San Antonio. His twenty-one-year-old wife, Carolyn, a petite woman with black hair and dark eyes, is running the store.

Emmett is among eight young blacks who pull up to the store in a 1946 Ford. All are between thirteen and nineteen years old. They meet up with another group of black teens that is already playing checkers at tables on the store's front porch. Emmett, hundreds of miles from home and trying his best to fit in, shows the group a picture of a white girl in his wallet and then brags that she was a sexual conquest.

The crowd, which now numbers almost twenty teenage boys and girls, can't believe their ears. Such an intermingling of the races is unheard of in Mississippi. Public restrooms, drinking fountains, and restaurants there are segregated. A black man would never even dream of shaking hands with a white man, unless the white man extended his hand first. Blacks lower their gaze when talking to whites, always showing them respect, referring to them as "Mister" or "Missus" or "Miss," and never by their first name. So Emmett Till's claim that he not only spoke with a white girl but also took her clothes off and lay with her is met with monumental disbelief.

So they tell Emmett to prove it. They dare him to go inside the grocery and talk to Carolyn Bryant. Sensing danger, Emmett tries to back out. But that spurs the group on, and they begin taunting him for being chicken. Emmett surrenders. He pulls open the screen door and steps into the store. He walks over to the candy case, where he asks for two cents' worth of bubble gum. When Carolyn hands him the gum, Emmett places his hand over hers and asks the married mother of two young boys for a date.

Back home in Chicago, a man touching a woman's hand might not be considered a big deal. But in the Deep South, skin-on-skin contact between blacks and whites is forbidden. When money is exchanged in stores, a black person will place it on the counter rather than into the white person's hand. Similarly, when the change is returned, it is also placed on the counter. And Emmett didn't just touch a married white woman, he asked her for a date.

Carolyn pulls away, astonished. Emmett reaches for her again, this time around her waist. "You needn't be afraid of me, baby," he assures her. "I been with white girls before."

Angrily, she pushes him away. Emmett finally leaves the store. But he is soon followed by the furious woman, who is racing to her car to get her husband's handgun. It's getting late, and she now fears for her safety.

But Emmett Till means her no harm. He is in the habit of substituting whistling for words when his stutter sets in, as he does now, whistling at Bryant. Carolyn Bryant is shocked again. And so are the black teenagers watching the scene unfold. They "knew the whistle would cause trouble," the official FBI report will read. "And they left in haste, taking Till with them."

When Roy Bryant returns home and hears what happened, he wastes no time in conducting his own personal criminal investigation. On August 28, at 2:30 A.M., he bangs on the door at the home of Emmett's great-uncle, Moses Wright. Roy is accompanied by his friend, J. W. "Big" Milam.

Big Milam is twelve years older than Roy Bryant. He is a hulking, extroverted Mississippian who quit school after the ninth grade and fought the Germans in World War II. Each man carries a Colt .45 handgun—a revolver for Bryant and an automatic for Milam. The men force Moses to take them to "the nigger who did the talking."

A frightened Moses leads the two men into a small back bedroom, where Emmett and three cousins share a bed. Big Milam shines a flashlight in the boy's face. "You the nigger who did the talking?"

"Yeah," comes the response.

"Don't say yeah to me. I'll blow your head off. Get your clothes on."

Moses and his wife beg for the two men to reconsider, even offering them money to let the whole thing slide, but Roy and Big won't listen. They march Emmett out to Big's pickup truck and drive off into the night.

Their plan is to take Emmett to a cliff along the Tallahatchie River, where they will pistol-whip the youth and scare him by pretending that they're going to throw him over the side. But in the dark, Big can't find the spot. After three hours of driving, Big drives the pickup to his own house, where he has a two-room toolshed in his backyard. They bring Emmett inside and pistol-whip him, each man smashing his face hard with his gun. But instead of backing down, Emmett is defiant. "You bastards. I'm not afraid of you. I'm as good as you are," he tells them, his face badly bruised but not bleeding.

This sets Big Milam into a rage. "I'm no bully," Milam will explain to *Look* magazine. "I never hurt a nigger in my life. I like niggers—in their place—I know how to work 'em. But I just decided it was time a few people got put on notice. As long as I live and can do anything about it, niggers are gonna stay in their place."

But apparently, Emmett doesn't know his place, because he continues to tell his captors that he is their equal, and even brags about having sex with white women. This belief in the equality of blacks and whites, something that Emmett finds relatively common in integrated Chicago, infuriates Milam and Bryant. "I stood there in that shed and listened to that nigger throw that poison at me," Milam will remember. "And I just made up my mind. 'Chicago boy,' I said, 'I'm tired of 'em sending your kind down here to stir up trouble. Goddam you, I'm going to make an example of you—just so everybody can know how me and my folks stand.'"

Big and Roy are no longer interested in just scaring Emmett. Now they want to murder him.

Big remembers that a nearby cotton company has just changed the fan on one of their gins. The replaced part is perfect for what Big now has in mind. The fan is enormous—three feet across and weighing seventy-five pounds. They drive to the Progressive Ginning Company, steal the discarded fan, and continue on to a hidden spot along the Tallahatchie where Big likes to hunt squirrels. They force Emmett to carry the fan to the river's edge, then they force him to strip.

"You still as good as I am?" Big asks.

"Yeah." Even standing naked before men two decades older than he, Emmett Till finds a way to be courageous. Blood streams down his face, and his cheekbones are broken. One of his eyes has been gouged out.

"You still 'had' white women?"

"Yeah."

Big raises his .45 and shoots Emmett point-blank in the head. The bullet makes a small hole as it enters near the right ear and kills the fourteen-year-old in an instant. Big and Roy then run a strand of barb-wire around Emmett's neck and attach it to the fan. They roll his body, anchored by the giant hunk of metal, into the river, and then drive home to wash out the blood that's pooling in the back of the pickup.

Despite the heavy fan tied around his neck, Emmett's body drifts with the current. Three days later, fishermen find his bloated corpse bobbing in the water some eight miles downstream. His head is almost flattened from the pistol blows.

When Emmett's body is returned to Chicago, his mother insists on an open casket at the funeral, so that the whole world can see the crime perpetrated against her son. Pictures of Emmett Till's battered and flattened head are published in magazines nationwide. Tens of thousands attend the viewing, and public outrage about the murder spreads across the country.

But not in Mississippi. Though police later arrest Roy Bryant and Big Milam, both men are acquitted of the crime by a jury of their peers (whites) three months later. Taking advantage of the judicial concept of double jeopardy, which does not allow an individual to be tried twice for the same crime, the two men later boast to a *Look* magazine writer about the day they murdered Emmett Till.

■ ■ ■

Until 1962 JFK was not eager to lead the fight for civil rights, knowing that taking a pro-black position could hurt him within the Democratic Party. In fact, the president's record on race issues was middling at best when he was in the Senate. Since the landmark 1954 *Brown v. Board of Education* ruling by the Supreme Court, which ordered that schools be integrated, tension between whites and blacks in the South has reached an all-time high, and events such as the murder of Emmett Till are no longer an exception. "Human blood may stain southern soil in many places because of this decision," an editorial in a Mississippi newspaper correctly prophesied shortly after the ruling.

But beginning with his May 1961 Law Day address at the University of Georgia Law School, Bobby Kennedy made it plain he would use his Justice Department as a bully pulpit to enforce civil rights throughout America, particularly in the Deep South. He is taking up an exhausting, never-ending battle, one that originated on the day the first African slaves were brought to America in 1619. The Kennedy brothers do so with the knowledge that this intense fight will gain them a whole new group of very dangerous enemies.

Bobby Kennedy was instrumental in helping civil rights activists known as Freedom Riders travel by bus into the South to fight segregation in 1961. The Greyhound Company, fearing its buses might be vandalized, had initially denied the northern activists passage. Kennedy pressured Greyhound, and the company relented.

But RFK could not stop what happened next. As soon as the activists tried to get off some of the buses, they were beaten with pipes and clubs by angry mobs. Local law enforcement did little to stop the brutality.

Despite—or perhaps even because of—the violence, the civil rights movement continues to gain momentum, and Robert Kennedy is now paying close attention to one of its most prominent leaders, a thirty-three-year-old charismatic Baptist minister named Dr. Martin Luther King Jr.

Reverend King is as intense and enigmatic as President Kennedy. He is a man of deep religious values who also sleeps with women outside his marriage. His speaking tone and rhetoric are bold and impassioned, but he advocates the same nonviolence to achieve his methods as Gandhi used in India. King also appears to be a Communist sympathizer. This puts Bobby in the unlikely position of having to monitor King to determine whether the reverend is indeed a Communist, while at the same time ensuring that King is protected from harm and guaranteed free speech as he pushes the cause of civil rights. One assassination attempt has already been made on King, when a deranged black woman stabbed him in the chest in 1958, and there are constant fears that the reverend will one day be lynched during his travels through the Deep South.

Truth be told, the civil rights movement is an enormous headache for Bobby Kennedy. His main enforcement arm, the FBI, has little con-

FBI director J. Edgar Hoover kept dossiers on many civil rights leaders and even had a file on the president. (Abbie Rowe, White House Photographs, John F. Kennedy Presidential Library and Museum, Boston)

cern for civil rights, or even for making inroads into Bobby's other major legal concern, organized crime. Instead, J. Edgar Hoover is entirely focused on stopping the spread of communism. He is all too happy to play the part of Pontius Pilate, washing his hands of racial bloodshed. In fact, in 1962 the FBI has only a handful of black agents in the field.

Hoover, however, does take an interest in Reverend King—but only because of the widespread belief within the FBI that the civil rights movement is part of a larger Communist plot against America. One of the bureau's division leaders, William C. Sullivan, will characterize King as "the most dangerous Negro of the future in this nation from the standpoint of communism, the Negro, and national security."

■ ■ ■

The truth—and Bobby Kennedy knows this—is that in large parts of the South, black Americans have little protection from prejudice and violence.

Although the Kennedy tradition is to put politics above social concerns, the two brothers raised in affluent northern liberalism have become increasingly interested in righting the wrongs of racial injustice.

J. Edgar Hoover believes this preoccupation is folly and that Reverend King's comments will one day be forgotten. For Hoover, civil rights are just a passing trend. So he will continue with the political game he's played since he joined the Justice Department during World War I. He will endure Bobby Kennedy's overeager style, just as he will continue to chronicle, yet keep silent on, the president's indiscretions. First and foremost, he will keep his job.

But that doesn't mean the FBI chief has to like the Kennedy boys— and he doesn't.

Bobby knows that one of JFK's first official acts after being reelected in 1964 will be to fire J. Edgar Hoover. So he soldiers on, investigating civil rights violations without the FBI director's support. It's tough going. Something as simple as getting a judge approved by the Senate for an open spot in a federal court is stymied when the senator in charge of the subcommittee orders that the proceedings be halted indefinitely. Not surprisingly, the judge up for approval, Thurgood Marshall, is black. And also not surprisingly, the senator who halted the proceedings is white.

But Robert Kennedy is the U.S. attorney general, sworn to uphold the nation's laws. And as long as young men such as Emmett Till are being lynched for the color of their skin, Bobby has no choice but to wage this war.

■ ■ ■

It is brutally hot in Fort Worth, Texas, on August 16, 1962. FBI special agents John Fain and Arnold J. Brown, warriors in J. Edgar Hoover's war against communism, have been waiting all day to see Lee Harvey Oswald. They sit in an unmarked car, just down the street from Oswald's newly rented duplex apartment on Mercedes Street, right around the corner from the Montgomery Ward department store.

Special Agent Fain is just two months away from finishing his twenty years with the bureau. He's going to retire to Houston. There, he'll live off his pension while working for his brother, an orthopedic surgeon. This will mark yet another major career change for the veteran agent. Fain is a complicated man in his mid-fifties who taught school, ran for public office, and passed the Texas state bar before joining the bureau in 1942. The Oswald case is nothing new to him. Back when Oswald first defected to the Soviet Union, it was Fain who was assigned a minor investigation of Oswald's mother because she had mailed twenty-five dollars to her son in the Soviet Union. When it comes to rooting out Communists, no stone is too small to be left unturned by Hoover's FBI.

It is also John Fain who spoke face-to-face with Oswald just eight weeks earlier, on June 26, 1962. Oswald's case has been designated as an "internal security" investigation, based on the belief that his defection might make him a threat to national security. Fain's job is to find out whether the Russians have trained and equipped Oswald to perform a job against the United States. It is protocol with all internal security investigations to have two agents present, so that all statements can be corroborated.

Something about the first interview, which lasted two hours, doesn't sit well with Fain. He doesn't like Oswald's attitude, thinking him "haughty, arrogant . . . and insolent." And his answers to most questions seemed incomplete. Fain has in-depth knowledge of Oswald's struggle to return to America and knows that the Russians originally would not allow Marina and the baby to leave with him. But Oswald refused to leave without his wife, and the Soviet authorities finally relented. The one question that Oswald has never answered in a completely truthful manner is whether the Russians demanded anything in return for letting him come to America.

John Fain needs that question answered. He's a very thorough man and takes it upon himself to interview Lee Harvey Oswald one more time.

At 5:30 P.M. the two agents see Oswald sauntering down the street, on his way home from his new job as a welder at the Leslie Machine Shop. Oswald lied on his job application, stating that his Marine Corps discharge was honorable when it was not. Oswald was kicked out of the

Corps for a series of minor infractions. He also neglected to tell his employer about his time in the Soviet Union. And while he's been on the job only a month, Oswald is already sick of the menial labor. He wants to quit and find better work in Dallas.

Fain drives up alongside the walking Oswald. "Hi, Lee. How are you?" he says out the car window. "Would you mind talking with us for just a few minutes?"

"Won't you come in the house," Oswald answers politely, remembering Fain from the last interview. Special Agent Brown is a new face. A different agent accompanied Fain back in June.

"Well, we will just talk here," Fain responds. "We will be alone to ourselves and be informal, and just fine."

Brown gets out to let Oswald into the backseat. Fain stays up front behind the wheel, but Brown slides in next to Oswald. Fain twists around to explain that they didn't contact Oswald at work, not wanting to embarrass him with his new employer. And they don't want to speak with him inside, for fear of rattling Marina. Thus the car.

The three men talk for a little over an hour. The car windows are open just enough to take the edge off the stifling humidity. But the men still perspire—particularly the G-men, in their coats and ties. Oswald has already put in a hard day of blue-collar labor, and the smell of his body odor wafts through the car. Despite the discomfort, Oswald is friendlier than before, less defensive. He explains that he's been in touch with the Soviet embassy, but only because it is required for Soviet citizens such as Marina to inform the embassy of their location on a regular basis. When pressed on whether this involved discussions with Soviet intelligence officials, Oswald is coy, wondering aloud why anyone would want to discuss spying with a guy like him. "He didn't feel like he was of any importance to them," Fain will later testify. "He said that he would cooperate with us and report to us any information that would come to his attention."

But Fain still is not satisfied. He presses Oswald again and again as to why he went to the Soviet Union in the first place. To the agent, it doesn't make sense. U.S. Marines are known for their motto, Semper

Fidelis, "Always Faithful." Why would one of them willingly renounce America and take up residence in a nation that poses the greatest threat to the United States?

It is the one question Oswald doesn't answer. He dances around it, talking about "his own personal reasons" and that "it was something that I did."

At 6:45, Oswald is released from the car and goes inside his home. His time with the agents was actually a respite from tension in his household. He and Marina have been fighting, sometimes quite violently, for more than six months. The strife has become worse since they came to America. It used to be that Oswald was the only person Marina could talk to in America, because she doesn't speak English. But now she's made new friends within Dallas's small local Russian expat community. Among these is a man named George de Mohrenschildt, who not only may have CIA connections, but also knew Jackie Kennedy when she was a child. De Mohrenschildt was a close friend of Jackie's aunt Edith Bouvier Beale. Marina's new friends find her husband rude and take her side in their marital battles.

And the battles are many. Oswald likes to be "the Commander" in their marriage, dictating the details of their life and refusing to let Marina learn English, for fear he'll lose control over her. She is embarrassed by her bad teeth and wants corrective dental work, but he puts it off. He often plays out his need for power by hitting his wife in anger.

But Marina is no shrinking violet. She screams at him for not making enough money and complains that he is indifferent to her. Their sexual relations are so infrequent that she accuses him of not being a man. She nags him constantly, and when he compares himself with the great men in the historical biographies he enjoys reading, she sarcastically derides him. Marina even writes to a former boyfriend in the Soviet Union, telling him she made a terrible mistake marrying Oswald. Unfortunately for her, the letter is returned for not having enough postage. Oswald opens and reads it, then beats her. Oddly, Marina condones Oswald's violence. Even that little bit of passion, however misguided, is better than the cold side of his character that she finds so frustrating.

The marital friction, coupled with his surprise FBI interrogation, would normally be enough to send Oswald into one of his trademark rants—the kind where he rails on and on about suppressive governments. But tonight his new copy of the *Worker*, the newsletter of the American Socialist Workers Party, awaits him. Oswald settles in to read.

It is Special Agent Arnold J. Brown, not John Fain, who prepares the final report concerning the conversation in the car. The papers are submitted on August 30, 1962. But it is Fain, the twenty-year veteran, who will decide if there is any reason to believe that Lee Harvey Oswald is a secret agent for the Soviet Union, planted within the United States to do the nation harm.

Content with the answers Oswald has given them, and looking forward to retirement, Special Agent John Fain requests that the Lee Harvey Oswald internal security investigation now be considered closed. After all, Oswald doesn't own a gun or otherwise appear to be a threat.

And so the case is closed.

But Lee Harvey Oswald and the FBI will soon meet again.

7

October 16, 1962
The White House
8:45 a.m.

The president of the United States is rolling around on the bedroom floor with his children. Jack LaLanne is on the television telling JFK, Caroline, and John to touch their toes. Kennedy wears just a T-shirt and underpants. The carpeting and a nearby easy chair are cream-colored, providing perfect accents to the blue-patterned covers on the president's four-poster canopy bed.

The TV volume is "absolutely full blast" in Jackie's words, as JFK and his son and daughter tumble around—loud enough that Jackie comes in from her bedroom to see what's going on. She loves her husband's lack of self-consciousness and how at ease he is in all situations. But as she can plainly see, morning with the kids is when John Kennedy is at his most relaxed. He dotes on his children, letting Jackie be the disciplinarian, and takes unbridled pleasure in being close to them. She worries about their rambunctious behavior. The president thinks it a blessing. His one great lament is that his bad back prevents him from tossing young John into the air and catching him, a game the president's son loves. Instead, JFK depends upon members of his staff and even visiting dignitaries to do the throwing for him.

As president, JFK no longer needs to campaign or spend hours in his Senate office. He works at home. What was once a solitary morning ritual has become a family affair. He has drawn closer to his children than ever before and relishes each and every moment they spend together. They start each morning in his bedroom, even as he bathes, shaves, stretches, and eats.

The president has just finished his bath and will soon get dressed. The kids will stick around and watch cartoons. Jackie might return to her bedroom, or she might come sit with him as he wraps his back brace into place before slipping on the tailored shirt that longtime valet George Thomas has laid out for him. Then will come the president's shoes, the left one with a quarter-inch medical lift. Then, a quick glance into the bedroom mirror above the dresser to double-check his appearance. The mirror's frame is a clutter of postcards, family photographs, and other minutiae, such as the Sunday Mass schedules for St. Stephen's and St. Matthew's cathedrals. He attends Mass and takes the sacrament regularly, although Kennedy bridles when photographers shoot pictures of him leaving confession. A time of atonement should also be a time of humiliation and privacy.

Sometimes during the day, John and Caroline walk into the Oval Office and play on the floor or even beneath the presidential desk. Jackie fiercely protects the children from the public eye. But the president takes a larger view, realizing that America is enthralled by such a young First Family and clamors for every morsel of news about their daily life. Caroline and John have become celebrities in their own right, although they don't know it. Photographers, writers, news magazines, and daily newspapers chronicling their young lives are just a fact of daily life.

John, almost two years old, likes to stop at Evelyn Lincoln's typewriter on his way in to the Oval Office and pretend to type a letter. Caroline, who is nearly six years old, likes to bring one or all of the family's three dogs when she pays a visit to her father. In fact, the Kennedy children have turned the White House into a veritable menagerie, with dogs, hamsters, a cat, parakeets, and even a pony named Macaroni. JFK is allergic to dog hair, but he never lets on.

Sometimes the president returns the favor by paying a surprise visit to Caroline and her classmates at their small private school on the third floor of the White House. The school is unique, set up by Jackie Kennedy to protect her children and those of her sister-in-law Ethel Kennedy. The First Lady has brought in two teachers to give the children the best possible education.

At nights the president is a great storyteller, making up tales about the fictitious giant in "Bobo the Lobo" and the sock-eating creatures of the deep in "The White Shark and the Black Shark."

The drop-in visits, forays to the schoolroom, and bedtime stories are unscheduled, but rolling around on the floor is a cherished morning routine. Kennedy, like every president since John Adams became the White House's first resident in 1800, has learned that life inside the White House is complicated. Mornings are the only time the president can be carefree, unrehearsed, and, best of all, *unwatched* by a curious public.

But on this Tuesday morning in October, a knock on the president's bedroom door intrudes on his private time with the children. That knock will change everything.

■ ■ ■

National Security Adviser McGeorge Bundy steps through the door. The razor-sharp creases of his suit pants and his polished shoes give the slim, bespectacled scholar an outward look of complete organization, which conflicts with his internal feelings of utter disarray.

Bundy is about to deliver very bad news. He learned of it last night but has intentionally waited until now to tell the president. John Kennedy was in New York to deliver a speech and didn't return to the White House until very late. The national security adviser wanted to make sure Kennedy received a full night of sleep before Bundy stepped into the presidential bedroom and broke the news. Bundy knows that from now until the moment this problem is solved, the president will be lucky to get any rest. For what McGeorge Bundy is about to tell JFK could change the course of history.

"Mr. President," the forty-three-year-old Bundy calmly informs Kennedy, "there is now hard photographic evidence, which you will see later, that the Russians have offensive missiles in Cuba."

U-2 spy planes flying over Cuba have confirmed that six Soviet medium-range ballistic missile sites and twenty-one IL-28 medium-range bombers are now just ninety miles from the United States. Each of the airplanes is capable of launching nuclear weapons from thousands of feet up in the air. Each of the medium-range ballistic missiles (MRBMs) can fly as far as Montana.

The detonated nuclear warheads could kill eighty million Americans within a matter of minutes. Millions more would die later from the radioactive fallout.

The president has dealt with crisis after crisis since taking office twenty-one months ago. But nothing—not the Bay of Pigs, not civil rights, not the Berlin Wall—can even remotely compare to this.

■ ■ ■

The Bay of Pigs, in its own mismanaged way, has shaped John Kennedy's presidency. Now, listening to National Security Adviser Bundy, JFK is not nervous, as he was in April 1961. He is not overwhelmed. Instead, he behaves like the president of the United States, a man who long ago stopped defining himself by party affiliation.

Kennedy knows that he needs to tread carefully. The Bay of Pigs will forever be a fresh wound. A second misstep in Cuba could be devastating—not only to his presidency, but also to his own children. The thought of losing Caroline and John to an atomic bomb terrifies Kennedy, for his children are always on his mind when he deals with the Soviets and the issue of nuclear war. The president is lobbying for an international nuclear test ban and characterizes himself as "President of generations unborn—and not just American generations."

Once, on a visit to a New Mexico nuclear testing ground, Kennedy was astounded at the enormity of the crater left by a recent underground test explosion. Even more troublesome was the opinion of two physicists, who explained, with broad smiles on their faces, that they were designing a more powerful bomb that would leave a much smaller crater.

"How can they be so damned cheerful about a thing like that?" the president groused to a writer afterward. This was highly uncharacteristic. Kennedy's typical behavior is outwardly friendly and inwardly guarded. He usually gives away nothing. So this sharing of his feelings is glaring evidence of his anxiety. "They keep telling me that if they could run more tests they could come up with a cleaner bomb. If you're going to kill a hundred million people, what difference does it make whether it's clean or dirty?"

■ ■ ■

JFK orders McGeorge Bundy to immediately schedule a top secret meeting of the national security staff. He then phones Bobby, telling him that "we have some big trouble. I want you over here." The president decides not to deviate from his normal schedule, not wanting the news about Cuba to get out quite yet. One reason is that he doesn't want to panic the American public. He knows very little about the situation and doesn't have a plan for moving forward. Leaking word prematurely, at a time when he doesn't have answers to the many questions the press will ask, will make him appear weak and indecisive.

Another reason for keeping this "second Cuba" quiet has to do with JFK's political best interests. The president long ago assured the American public that he would not allow the Soviets to install offensive weapons in Cuba. Khrushchev is calling Kennedy's bluff at a time when midterm congressional elections are just a few weeks away. The president has no way of knowing whether the Soviets ever plan to use the missiles, but their mere presence shows that Khrushchev continues his quest to secure the upper hand in the U.S.-Soviet relationship.

This must not happen. As with all midterms, the votes being cast across the nation will be a referendum on Kennedy's policies and administration. His party holds a majority in the House and Senate, making it

President Kennedy, with brothers Robert and Teddy. (Cecil Stoughton, White House Photographs, John F. Kennedy Presidential Library and Museum, Boston)

easier for JFK to promote his presidential agenda. Losing those majorities will complicate his job—and could perhaps cost him the election in 1964.

There is another, even more personal, reason JFK wants his policies viewed in a popular light: his youngest brother, Teddy, is running for the Senate in Massachusetts. Something as catastrophic as a mishandling of this new Cuba situation could destroy any hopes of Teddy winning.

JFK is proud of his thirty-year-old brother's bid for office but has given it a wide berth during the campaign. The president's official statement on the matter was a terse "His brother prefers that this matter be decided by the people of Massachusetts and that the president should not become involved." JFK bristles at the widespread media coverage of Teddy's run, including a sarcastic *New York Times* column about the youngest Kennedy brother's relative inexperience and other newspaper articles warning of a Kennedy dynasty.

None of this really bothers the president, personally. But he knows that if Teddy loses in the Kennedys' home state, it will be a reflection on JFK's political strength—or lack thereof.

The final, and by far the most important, reason the president doesn't want word leaking out about the missiles in Cuba is that he does not want the Russian leadership to know that he is onto their secret. In that way, he believes, he can gain some control over the unsettling turn of events.

Because on the morning of October 16, as Kennedy leaves his bedroom and strolls down to the Oval Office to start his day, one fact is very clear: if the Soviets launch those missiles, the midterm elections, Teddy's bid for office, and even the opinion of the American people won't matter anymore. Because there may no longer be a Washington, D.C.—and there may no longer be much left of the United States of America.

Whatever happens next has nothing to do with being a Democrat or a Republican, and everything to do with what's best for the American people. If anything shows how much JFK has grown since taking the Oath of Office, it is this resolve, at this moment.

■ ■ ■

At 10:00 A.M. the president emerges from a brief meeting in the Oval Office with Mercury astronaut Wally Schirra, who spent nine hours in outer space two weeks earlier. JFK walks next door into Kenny O'Donnell's office. The appointments secretary has previously voiced an opinion that America's voters don't care about Cuba anymore. "You still think the fuss about Cuba is unimportant?" Kennedy asks innocently.

"Absolutely. The voters don't give a damn about Cuba."

The president calmly shares with O'Donnell the news McGeorge Bundy delivered just an hour ago.

"I don't believe it."

"You better believe it," Kennedy tells him before marching back to the Oval Office.

Two hours later, JFK steps away from his desk yet again. He joins Caroline in the nearby Cabinet Room, then shoos her back to the residence as he convenes the top secret meeting about the Soviet missiles. He takes a seat at the center of the table, not the head. Bobby sits across from him, as does LBJ. Eleven other men are in attendance, all hand-picked for their expertise and loyalty to the president.

Photos taken by U-2 spy planes show that the Soviet missiles are still being prepared for launch, but for the time being, they probably lack the nuclear warheads that would make them lethal. The talk shifts to military options. After listening to the various opinions, the president provides his own list. The first is a limited air strike. The second is a broader air strike, on a broader number of targets. The third is a naval blockade of Cuban waters, preventing the Soviet ships carrying nuclear warheads from reaching the missiles.

Bobby, who has listened quietly throughout the seventy-minute meeting, finally speaks up, suggesting that a full-scale invasion of Cuba might be necessary. It is the only way to prevent Russian missiles from ever being placed on Cuban soil.

Even as military force seems like the only solution, JFK is still troubled by the question of motive. Why is Nikita Khrushchev trying to provoke the Americans into war?

The president doesn't know the answer. But two things are apparent: those missiles must be removed and, far more important, those nuclear warheads cannot be allowed to reach Cuba.

Ever.

■ ■ ■

It is Saturday afternoon, October 20. John Fitzgerald Kennedy is spending the weekend in downtown Chicago, rallying the Democratic Party faithful at a fund-raiser.

Two days ago he met privately with Soviet foreign minister Andrei Gromyko. It was Gromyko who requested the meeting, not knowing that the Americans had discovered that the Soviets had placed offensive missiles in Cuba. The topics of discussion were the goings-on in Berlin and

Soviet leader Khrushchev's pending visit to America. Kennedy skillfully guided the subject toward the topic of nuclear weapons. Gromyko then lied to the president's face, stating most adamantly that "the Soviet Union would never become involved in the furnishing of offensive weapons to Cuba."

For this reason, Kennedy now refers to Gromyko as "that lying bastard."

The mood in Chicago is a radical departure from the tension in Washington. When Air Force One lands at O'Hare Airport, the president is greeted by an army of bagpipers and local politicians, and an estimated half million people line the Northwest Expressway to witness the president's motorcade. After JFK's speech at a $100-a-plate fund-raising dinner on Friday night, a fireworks show lights up the sky over Lake Michigan. As if by magic, the display features the president's face in profile.

But the public adulation is a stark contrast to the private inner hell John Kennedy is living right now. He hasn't even told his wife what is going on in Cuba. What will become known as the Cuban missile crisis is now four days old, and his ExComm team—short for Executive Committee of the National Security Council—is close to formulating an aggressive strategy to avert a nuclear attack. One hundred and eighty naval ships are being sent to the Caribbean. The army's First Armored Division is being relocated from Texas to Georgia. The air force's Tactical Air Command has transferred more than five hundred fighter jets and tankers to Florida and is hustling to find enough munitions to supply them.

The legendary Strategic Air Command has squadrons of B-47 and B-52 bombers ready to launch, the pilots sequestered in secure "Alert" facilities. Most of these long-range bomber bases are in the northern portion of the United States—Maine, New Hampshire, and northern Michigan. The primary reason for this is simple: it's the shortest route to the Soviet Union, which has long been thought to be the primary target once war comes. The pilots and navigators are familiar with those coordinates and have practiced them for years. The straight shot down to Havana is brand-new territory.

The president calls the First Lady from his Chicago suite. Jackie and the children are at the Glen Ora estate in Virginia.

"I'm coming back to Washington this afternoon. Why don't you come back there?" he asks her. Jackie senses "something funny" in JFK's voice.

"Why don't you come down *here*?" she answers playfully. Jackie and the children have just arrived. The autumn weather is warm enough that Jackie is lying in the sun when she takes her husband's call.

But something about that tone in JFK's voice alerts Jackie. He knows how important those weekends in Virginia are to her and how much she treasures unwinding from the pressures of the White House. He's never before asked her to cut a weekend short.

"Why?" the First Lady asks again. She will later remember the alarm she felt, realizing that "whenever you're married to someone and they ask something—yeah, that's the whole point of being married—you must sense some trouble in their voice and mustn't ask why."

But she asks anyway.

"Well, never mind," JFK answers, not telling her his reasons. "Why don't you just come back to Washington?"

Then, suddenly, the president changes his mind. At a time like this, he wants nothing more than to relieve his burden and be with his family. So the president finally tells Jackie about the possibility of a nuclear war.

"Please don't send me away to Camp David. Please don't send me anywhere," Jackie answers. She now pleads with her husband, disregarding her safety. Jackie knows that in event of an attack, the family will be evacuated to the Maryland presidential retreat, which will take her and the children away from JFK—perhaps forever. "Even if there's no room in the bomb shelter in the White House. Please, then I just want to be on the lawn when it happens. I just want to be with you, and I want to die with you, and the children do too."

The president assures his wife he will not send her away. Then, instructing Pierre Salinger to explain to the press that he has a cold, JFK flies back to Washington, D.C. The *New York Times* will report that a "slight upper respiratory infection" is the reason the president is cutting short the three-day trip; the paper is unaware that the president is flying back to Washington in an effort to prevent global thermonuclear war.

Jackie and the children are waiting when he arrives.

■ ■ ■

There is no day and there is no night in the Kennedy White House as the Cuban confrontation escalates. The president is in such pain from his back that he gets around on crutches, further adding to the tension. He sleeps just one or two hours at a time, then rises and talks on the phone for hours in the Oval Office, before returning to bed for another short nap. Jackie sleeps with him now, whether night or day. Sometimes they sleep in his small bed; at others, in her bedroom, in the two double beds, which have been pushed together to form one large king. They often talk late at night about the crisis. Once, Jackie wakes up to see Mac Bundy standing at the foot of their bed to wake her husband, whereupon JFK rises instantly and disappears for several more hours of top secret phone calls.

Jackie will later remember these days and nights as the time she felt closest to her husband. She walks by the president's office all the time, cheering him up by bringing the children for surprise visits. She arranges for dinner from a favorite Miami seafood restaurant to be flown to Washington. The president and First Lady often slip into the Rose Garden for a quiet walk, where he confides in her about the escalating tension.

When the president returns to his work, he is not alone—nor is Jackie. While Bobby Kennedy works closely with his brother, his wife, Ethel, and their three children are frequently at the White House. It is Ethel who gives White House nanny Maud Shaw a pamphlet on how to prepare children for nuclear war—a pamphlet that Jackie snatches away moments later. "Don't you know that panic is catching? And that children are susceptible?" the First Lady scolds Shaw.

This is not the demure Jackie the public sees, but a fiercely protective mother and wife taking charge of her household.

For two days, the president and his small White House entourage debate the top secret threat to the United States. Photos taken by U-2 spy planes show that the Soviets are working around the clock to complete the missile sites, meaning that warheads could be launched toward the United States within a matter of days. No one "bitches it up," in JFK's words, by leaking this information to the press, even though it's clear that some journalists already know. Not even the Congress is told.

On the night of Monday, October 22, the scene changes. President John Fitzgerald Kennedy appears on national television to inform America about the potentially lethal missiles in Cuba—and what he plans to do about them. The end of the world is no time to keep the American people uninformed.

■ ■ ■

"Good evening, my fellow citizens," John Fitzgerald Kennedy greets the nation from his study at the White House. There are deep grooves under his greenish-gray eyes, giving him a haggard look instead of the vibrant, youthful countenance the nation is used to seeing.

JFK's face is puffy from his chronic hypothyroidism. He wears a crisp blue suit, blue tie, and starched white shirt, though the television audience can see him only in black and white. It is 7:00 P.M. in Washington, D.C.

This broadcast from the White House is quite the opposite of Jackie's lighthearted tour of just ten months earlier. John Fitzgerald Kennedy must make the most powerful speech of his life. He does not smile. His face is stern. There is menace in his eyes. He is not optimistic, nor even hopeful. His words come out angrily, with a vehemence that shocks some viewers. Kennedy speaks the words of a man who has been bent until he will bend no more. And now he's fighting back.

"Within the past week, unmistakable evidence has established the fact that a series of offensive missile sites is now in preparation on that imprisoned island. The purpose of these bases can be none other than to provide a nuclear strike capability against the Western Hemisphere."

Here the president pauses, letting the words sink in. He then recounts Soviet foreign minister Andrei Gromyko's visit to his office the previous

Thursday, quotes Gromyko on the subject of missiles in Cuba—and then calls Gromyko a liar, for all the world to hear.

"The 1930s taught us a clear lesson: Aggressive conduct, if allowed to grow unchecked and unchallenged, ultimately leads to war. This nation is opposed to war. We are also true to our word. Our unswerving objective, therefore, must be to prevent the use of these missiles against this or any other country and to secure their withdrawal or elimination from the Western Hemisphere."

The president's cadence is quicker now, as he grows angrier and angrier. The word *Cuba* comes out as *Cuber.*

After his speech is done, the president will enjoy a quiet dinner upstairs with Jackie, Ethel, Bobby, and a handful of invited guests. Watching the speech, the president's dinner guests—among them designer Oleg Cassini and Jackie's sister, Lee Radziwill—are stunned to learn that their dinner will not be the typical easygoing White House gathering. Even though they will sip French wine in the newly redecorated Oval Room, on the second floor, and JFK, with his usual understated style, will play the part of the congenial host, the tension at the dinner table will be something they will remember for the rest of their lives.

■ ■ ■

Thirteen hundred miles away, in Dallas, Texas, Lee Harvey Oswald is listening to Kennedy's speech. Unlike the majority of his peers, Oswald believes that the Soviets have every right to be in Cuba. From his perspective, the Russians must protect Castro's people against terrorist behavior by the United States. Oswald is firmly convinced that President Kennedy is putting the world on the brink of nuclear war by taking such an aggressive stance against the Soviets. To him, JFK is the villain.

Oswald finalized his move from Forth Worth to Dallas earlier in the month and rented a P.O. box, number 2915, at the post office on the corner of Bryan and North Ervay Street. A few weeks before that, Oswald found a job at the firm of Jaggars-Chiles-Stovall, as a photographic trainee. Amazingly, the firm has a contract with the U.S. Army Map

Service that involves highly classified photographs taken by the U-2 spy planes flying over Cuba. It is Marina Oswald's Russian friend George de Mohrenschildt who arranged for Oswald to be hired there. If the FBI, in all its zeal to stop the spread of communism, is concerned that a former Soviet defector has access to such top secret U-2 data at the peak of cold war tension, it's not proving it by paying attention to his case.

■ ■ ■

On television, the president is about to throw down the gauntlet. "Acting, therefore, in the defense of our own security and of the entire Western Hemisphere, and under the authority entrusted me by the Constitution as endorsed by the resolution of Congress, I have directed that the following initial steps be taken immediately."

Then, after months of being diplomatic and appearing weak in Soviet eyes, the president shows his true mettle. JFK promises to "quarantine" Cuba, using the might of the U.S. Navy to prevent any Soviet vessel from entering Cuban waters. He declares that he is prepared to use military might in the form of an invasion, if necessary. He states unequivocally that any missile launched by the Cubans or Soviets will be considered an act of war and that the United States will reciprocate with missiles of its own. The president then places the blame squarely on his nemesis. The entire speech has been building to this moment. "And finally, I call upon Chairman Khrushchev to halt and eliminate this clandestine, reckless and provocative threat to world peace and stable relations between our two nations. I call upon him further to abandon this course of world domination and to join in an historic effort to end the perilous arms race and transform the history of man."

The power of the president's speech, and the terrible news that he now delivers to the public, will make this moment stand forever in the minds of everyone who is watching. Kennedy once noted that "the only two dates that most people remember where they were was Pearl Harbor and the death of President Roosevelt."

His Cuban missile crisis speech now joins that list.

For as long as they live, men and women will be able to recount where they were and what they were doing when they got this terrible news. They will describe the people standing nearby and how their reactions compared. They will talk about the headlines the next day and how their world was transformed by the traumatic news. They will suddenly appreciate each sunrise, each sunset, each mirthful peal of a child's laughter.

Tragically, another event in JFK's short life will also soon join that list of unforgettable moments. Its shock and horror will eclipse this news of Cuba and missiles and Soviet lies. John Kennedy will never know it happened.

That event is exactly thirteen months from today. But for now, the Cuban missile crisis is drama enough.

John Kennedy, being his charismatic self, is incapable of concluding a speech without a stirring moment to galvanize his listeners. Whether with his Gold Star Mothers speech in a Boston American Legion hall during his first run for Congress, or with his inaugural address in 1961, or now on national television, JFK knows how to grab his listeners by the heart—or by "the nuts," as he so often likes to say—and rally their emotional support.

"Our goal is not the victory of might, but the vindication of right. Not peace at the expense of freedom, but both peace and freedom—here in this hemisphere and, we hope, around the world. God willing, that goal will be achieved."

The White House set fades to black.

■ ■ ■

American forces around the world immediately prepare for war. All navy and marine personnel are about to have their duty tours extended indefinitely. American warships and submarines are forming a defensive perimeter around Cuba, preparing to stop and search the twenty-five Soviet ships currently sailing toward that defiant island.

At Torrejón Air Base in Spain, the men of the 509th B-47 bomber wing hear the president's words over loudspeakers in their rooms, part of a global alert going out to all U.S. military. Captain Alan Dugard, a young bomber pilot, is packing for a week's leave in Germany. When the air force's defense readiness condition (Defcon) is upgraded to Defcon 2—only Defcon 1, which means that nuclear war is imminent, is higher—Captain Dugard instantly realizes that there will be no vacation.

U.S. Air Force bombers are already in the air around the clock. The crews will circle over European and American skies in a racetrack pattern, awaiting the "go" code to break from their flight plan and strike at the heart of the Soviet Union. Their contrails are a visible reminder of what is at stake.

The nonstop air brigade means just one thing: the United States is ready to retaliate and destroy the USSR.

■ ■ ■

Five thousand miles away, in Moscow, a furious Nikita Khrushchev composes his response to JFK's televised message.

The Soviet leader is the dashing JFK's polar opposite in appearance and aplomb. He is just five foot three, weighs almost two hundred pounds, and is as bald as a circus clown. Khrushchev has an enormous mole under his right eye, a wide gap between his front teeth, and a very unstatesmanlike habit of mugging for the camera. When he stepped off the plane on his 1959 visit to the United States, a woman in the crowd took one look at him and exclaimed, "What a funny little man."

But there is nothing funny about Nikita Khrushchev. He believes in diplomacy by "balance of fear." His decision to place missiles in Cuba is calculated and ruthless. "I came to the conclusion that if we did everything secretly, and the Americans found out about it only after the missiles were in place and ready to be launched, they would have to stop and think before making the risky decision to wipe out our missiles by military force," Khrushchev will later write.

However, now, as he begins his response to Kennedy's speech, the Soviet dictator turns crafty and chooses his words carefully. "You, Mr. President, are not declaring a quarantine," Khrushchev dictates to a secretary, "but rather are setting forth an ultimatum and threatening that if we do not give in to your demands you will use force. Consider what you are saying!

"The Soviet government considers that the violation of the freedom to use international waters and international air space is an act of aggression which pushes mankind toward the abyss of a world nuclear missile war," Khrushchev lectures JFK. "Naturally, we will not simply be bystanders with regard to piratical acts by American ships on the high seas. We will then be forced on our part to take the measures we consider necessary and adequate in order to protect our rights. We have everything necessary to do so."

It was Khrushchev alone who devised the plan to place missiles in Cuba. He presented his idea to the Soviet government's Central Committee, and then to Fidel Castro just three months earlier. He believed the missiles could be hidden from the United States and, even if they were discovered, that Kennedy would refuse to act.

Khrushchev also claims the decision was a goodwill gesture to the Cuban people, in case of another Bay of Pigs–style invasion by the United States. Having participated in World War II, the Soviet leader knows that the logistics of launching a war in another hemisphere are just about impossible. So he wants his arsenal closer to America, and Cuba provides that opportunity. The weapons he has persuaded Castro to take are Soviet-made, manned by Soviet soldiers and technicians, tipped with Soviet nuclear warheads—and brought to Cuba aboard Soviet ships.

Having been a former political commissar in the Red Army, Khrushchev understands the power of words. He tells the world that the Soviet Union has "a moral and legal justification" for placing missiles in Cuba. Soviet ships have every right to enter Cuban waters and unload any cargo they like and that the American naval quarantine—a fancy way of saying "blockade," which is an act of war—is reprehensible. Khrushchev feels persecuted by the Americans. He is outraged that the Soviet Union has suffered two world wars on its soil, while the United States has suffered very little homeland devastation. Khrushchev also knows quite well that the atomic bomb dropped on Hiroshima had an explosive force

Soviet premier Nikita Khrushchev collaborated with Cuban prime minister Fidel Castro to challenge President Kennedy in the Western Hemisphere, far from the seat of Soviet power. (Associated Press)

equivalent to 20,000 tons of TNT. That makes the Soviet dictator smile: his nuclear warheads are equivalent to *1 million* tons.

Nikita Khrushchev is no stranger to mass death. He served at the Battle of Stalingrad during World War II, where more than a million men died—including many of the German soldiers Khrushchev personally interrogated. But those killings pale next to the sadistic methods a younger Khrushchev employed to climb the Communist Party ladder in the early 1930s.

When Joseph Stalin, the serial killer who ran the Soviet Union for thirty years, ordered a "Great Purge" of his enemies in 1934, Nikita Khrushchev was an eager participant in this plan. Millions of suspected disloyal Communists were executed or relocated to Siberian prisons. Khrushchev personally ordered thousands of murders and authorized the killing of some of his own friends and colleagues. He gave a speech in 1936 stating that the executions were the only way to rid the Soviet

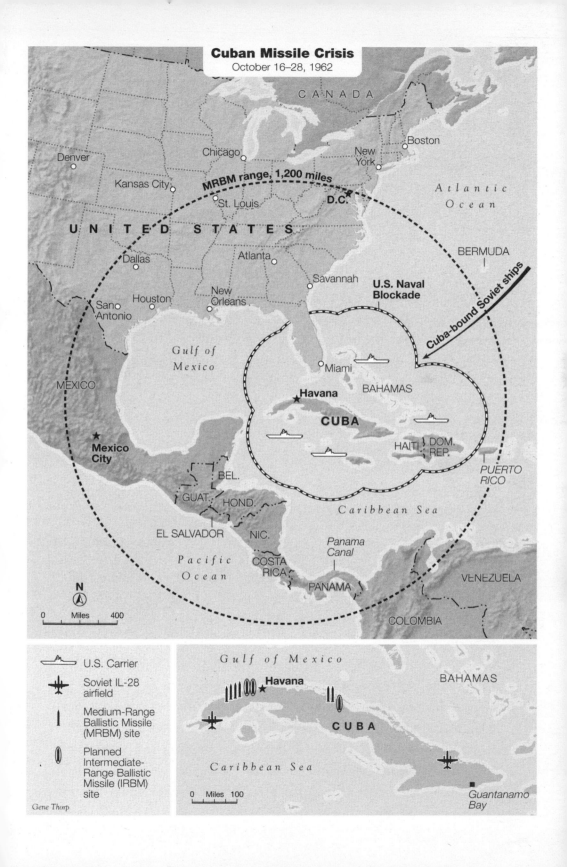

Cuban Missile Crisis
October 16–28, 1962

CANADA

Denver

Chicago

Boston

New York

Kansas City

MRBM range, 1,200 miles

St. Louis

D.C.

Atlantic Ocean

UNITED STATES

BERMUDA

Dallas

Atlanta

Savannah

U.S. Naval Blockade

Cuba-bound Soviet ships

Sano Antonio

Houston

New Orleans

Miami

Gulf of Mexico

MEXICO

Havana

BAHAMAS

CUBA

Mexico City

HAITI

DOM. REP.

PUERTO RICO

BEL.

GUAT.

HOND.

Caribbean Sea

EL SALVADOR

NIC.

Panama Canal

Pacific Ocean

COSTA RICA

PANAMA

VENEZUELA

COLOMBIA

N

0   Miles   400

Legend

U.S. Carrier

Soviet IL-28 airfield

Medium-Range Ballistic Missile (MRBM) site

Planned Intermediate-Range Ballistic Missile (IRBM) site

Gene Thorp

Gulf of Mexico

Havana

BAHAMAS

CUBA

Caribbean Sea

Guantanamo Bay

0   Miles   100

Union of the dissidents striving to undermine its grand success. The following year, Stalin appointed Khrushchev as head of the Communist Party in Ukraine. By the time World War II ended his tenure there in 1939, Khrushchev had overseen the arrest and murder of almost every member of the local party leadership. Hundreds of Ukrainians were murdered. Few politicians survived.

Now Nikita Khrushchev's relentless quest for power has put the world on the brink of nuclear war.

But there's a problem: Khrushchev is surprised to learn that his adversary, John Kennedy, is deadly serious about defending his country at all costs. But Khrushchev tells associates he will not back down. He is a firm believer in the old Russian adage, "Once you're in a fight, don't spare yourself. Give it everything you've got."

John Kennedy was ignorant of that adage eighteen months ago, during the Bay of Pigs invasion. Now Nikita Khrushchev is gambling that the president of the United States will make the same mistake once again.

On the evening of October 24, Khrushchev orders that his letter be transmitted to Kennedy. In it the Communist leader states calmly and unequivocally that the president's proposed naval blockade is "a pirate act." Soviet ships are being instructed to ignore it.

■ ■ ■

President Kennedy receives Premier Khrushchev's letter just before 11:00 P.M. on October 24. He responds less than three hours later, coolly stating that the blockade is necessary and placing all blame for the crisis on Khrushchev and the Soviets.

It's becoming clear that Kennedy will *never* back down. The U.S. Navy soon boards a freighter bound for Cuba. Appropriately, the destroyer USS *Joseph Kennedy Jr.*, named for the president's late brother, is the ship tasked with enforcing the risky quarantine.

"Did you send it?" Jackie asked her husband, referring to the ship, when she learned of this coincidence.

"No," the president replied. "Isn't that strange?"

■ ■ ■

While the Soviet leadership waits for JFK to crack, he instead goes on the offensive. The president spends Friday, October 26, planning the invasion of Cuba. No detail is too small. He requests a list of all Cuban doctors in Miami, just in case there will be a need to airlift them into Cuba. He orders that a U.S. naval vessel loaded with sensitive radar be moved farther off the coast of the island nation, to make it less vulnerable to attack. Kennedy knows where each invasion ship will assemble, and even scrutinizes the wording of the leaflets that will be dropped to the Cuban people. All the while, the president frets that "when military hostilities first begin, those missiles will be fired at us."

JFK is privately telling aides that it's now a showdown between him and Khrushchev, "two men sitting on opposite sides of the world," deciding "the end of civilization."

It's a staring contest. The loser blinks first.

But John Kennedy has seen Nikita Khrushchev blink before. In the early days of Kennedy's presidency, shortly after the Bay of Pigs incident, the two men held a summit meeting in Vienna. Khrushchev tried to bully his younger adversary on the subject of West Berlin, hoping to take control of the entire city because more and more citizens of Soviet-controlled East Berlin were risking their lives in the name of freedom by escaping into the adjacent territory controlled by the United States and her World War II allies. Kennedy refused to back down, and a chastened Khrushchev began construction of the Berlin Wall to save face.

But time is on Khrushchev's side on this occasion. Construction of the missile launch facilities in Cuba is nearly complete.

So, while the rest of the world prepares for imminent doom, Nikita Khrushchev spends the early evening of October 26 at the Bolshoi Ballet. "Our people and the foreigners will see this, and it will have a calming effect," he exhorts his comrades in the Soviet leadership. "If Khrushchev and the other leaders are going to the theatre at a time like this, then it must be possible to sleep peacefully."

But Nikita Khrushchev is the most anxious man in Moscow, and there's no way he can rest now. At least a dozen Soviet ships have either been intercepted by U.S. warships or turned back of their own accord. The lightly armed Russian vessels are no match for the American firepower.

After the ballet, Khrushchev spends all night in the Kremlin—just in case something violent transpires. The Soviet leader is uncharacteristically pensive. Something is on his mind. Shortly after midnight, he sits down and dictates a new message to President Kennedy.

■ ■ ■

It is 6:00 P.M. in Washington and 2:00 A.M. in Moscow when the message is delivered. JFK has spent the day fine-tuning the upcoming invasion of Cuba. He is bone tired, running on a hidden reserve of energy. His aching body is in a state of chaos. The president has long suffered from a condition known as autoimmune polyendocrine syndrome type 2 (APS-2), which has caused not only his hypothyroidism (insufficient thyroid hormone) but also his Addison's disease, which must be closely monitored at all times. Addison's causes his body to fail to produce the necessary hormones, such as cortisol, that regulate blood pressure, cardiovascular function, and blood sugar. Left unchecked, Addison's causes exhaustion, weight loss, weakness, and even death. In 1946, before the disease was diagnosed, Kennedy collapsed at a parade and turned so blue and yellow that he was thought to be suffering from a heart attack.

That must not happen now.

So JFK is receiving injections of hydrocortisone and testosterone to battle his Addison's. He is taking antispasmodic drugs to ward off his chronic colitis and diarrhea. And the president is suffering from another painful urinary tract infection, which requires antibiotics. All of this is in addition to relentless excruciating back pain. A less driven man would have taken to bed long ago, but John Kennedy refuses to let his constant pain and suffering interfere with his performing his duties.

Jackie has chosen not to worry about Jack's fatigue, having seen him drive himself hard through many a campaign, attending a fund-raising dinner until late in the night and then waking up before dawn to stand outside some factory or steel mill to shake hands with the workers arriving for their shift. But this is different, and she doesn't know how much longer he can go on. She sees the awkward way he eases himself into his favorite rocking chair for meetings to lessen the pain in his back.

More ominously, Jackie knows about the time his Addison's almost killed him, fifteen years earlier. She also remembers that, in 1954, a metal plate was inserted into her husband's spine (to counter a degenerative condition) and a postoperative infection put him in a coma. Once again, John Kennedy was administered the last rites of the Roman Catholic Church. And once again he battled back.

That makes three times—PT-109, Addison's, and the back surgery—in which JFK defeated death. Jackie Kennedy knows that her man, the president of the United States, is extremely tough. He will persevere. He always has.

But it's actually the men of ExComm who have the First Lady concerned. Jackie has pressed her ear to the door and eavesdropped on their meetings. She has heard the strain. She believes these men are working to "the peak of human endurance" to save the world.

McGeorge Bundy, too, is quite sure that the ExComm men are all about to crack. They've been awake night and day for almost two weeks. These staid men have become emotional because of their extreme exhaustion and have cultivated opinions and petty jealousies that will define their relationships for years to come. One of the most powerful voices among them is that of air force general Curtis E. LeMay, who sees nothing wrong with blowing Cuba off the map.

■ ■ ■

Then Khrushchev's message arrives. The letter's wording is personal, an appeal from one leader to another to do the right thing. The Soviet leader insists that he is not trying to incite nuclear war: "Only lunatics or suicides, who themselves want to perish and to destroy the whole world before they die, could do this," he writes. The Soviet ruler rambles on, questioning Kennedy's motivations.

Khrushchev concludes his letter by negotiating with Kennedy in a

somewhat confusing fashion. The paragraph that draws the most attention states: If you have not lost your self-control, and sensibly conceive
what this might lead to, then, Mr. President, we and you ought not to pull
on the ends of the rope in which you have tied the knot of war, because
the more the two of us pull, the tighter the knot will be tied. And a
moment may come when that knot will be tied so tight that even he who
tied it will not have the strength to untie it, and then it will be necessary
to cut that knot."

The ExComm crew does not believe that Khrushchev's message is
the sign of an outright capitulation. But they all agree it's a start.

For the first time in more than a week, John F. Kennedy feels hopeful. Yet he does not lift the blockade. There are still nearly a dozen Soviet
vessels steering directly toward the quarantine line—and these ships
show no signs of turning around.

The tension increases the next afternoon, when word reaches JFK
that Cuban surface-to-air missiles have shot down an American U-2 spy
plane. The pilot, Major Rudolf Anderson Jr., has been killed.

In retaliation, the Joint Chiefs of Staff demand that the president
launch U.S. bombers in a massive air strike on Cuba within forty-eight
hours, to be followed by an outright invasion.

Worst of all, spy plane photographs now confirm that some of the
Soviet missile installations are complete. There are twenty-four medium-
range ballistic missile launchpads, and forty-two MRBMs. Once the
warheads are attached, the MRBMs can be launched. Each has a range
of 1,020 miles—far enough to reach Washington. Soviet diplomats in
their Washington, D.C., embassy are so convinced war is imminent that
they have begun burning sensitive documents.

The crisis isn't over. The prospect of nuclear war has never been
greater. The United States is so close to invading Cuba that one bad joke
in the nonstop series of ExComm meetings is that Bobby Kennedy will
soon be mayor of Havana.

White House appointments secretary Kenny O'Donnell sums up the
mood best, describing the ExComm meeting on Saturday evening,

October 27, as "the most depressing hour that any of us spent in the White House during the president's time there."

President Kennedy secretly sends Bobby to meet with Soviet officials in Washington, promising not to invade Cuba if the missiles are removed, and also to meet a Khrushchev demand that he withdraw U.S. missiles from Turkey that are currently in range of the Soviet Union. The Turks won't like it, and the missiles are technically under control of the North Atlantic Treaty Organization (NATO), but the president is willing to make this one concession if it will stave off war.

It is a war that could be just hours away.

■ ■ ■

Then Khrushchev blinks.

The Communist leader is so sure that Kennedy is bluffing that he has not mobilized the Soviet army to full alert. Yet Khrushchev's intelligence reports now show that the United States is very serious about invading Cuba. And if that happens, the Russians will be forced to fire nuclear missiles. Failure to do so would make Khrushchev and the Soviet Union an international laughingstock. Far worse, the world will think that John Kennedy is more powerful than Nikita Khrushchev.

There is no way the Soviet leadership or the Soviet people will stand for that humiliation. Khrushchev will be toppled from power.

Despite this possibility, the Soviet leader becomes less bellicose. The "funny little man" is introspective when it comes to the subject of war. He lost his first wife to typhus during World War I. Khrushchev may be remembering his beloved Yefrosinia when he says of war "it has rolled through cities and villages, everywhere sowing death and destruction." The Russian dictator sees that the American president is willing to conduct a nuclear war if pushed to the limit. Yes, the United States will be gone forever. But so will the Soviet Union.

On Sunday morning, at 9:00 A.M., Radio Moscow tells the people of the Soviet Union that Chairman Khrushchev has saved the world from annihilation. The words are also aimed directly at JFK when the commentator states that the Soviets choose to "dismantle the arms which you described as offensive, and to crate and return them to Soviet Russia."

After thirteen long days, the Cuban missile crisis is over.

■ ■ ■

In Dallas, Lee Harvey Oswald has been following the action closely. His reaction is to show solidarity with the Russians and Cubans by joining the Socialist Workers Party.

Oswald is alone in the new two-story brick apartment he has rented on Elsbeth Street and is eager for Marina to join him. She and baby June are living with friends in Fort Worth, and he is lonesome for her company despite their violent history. Yet when Marina finally arrives in Dallas, on November 3, their domestic battles resume. She calls their squalid new dwelling a "pigsty." They scream at each other for two solid days. Oswald swears that he's going to "beat the hell out of her," and then goes one step further by threatening to hit her so hard and so long that he'll kill her.

Marina has had enough. She leaves him again, moving in with some of her Russian friends. So complete is their split that she doesn't even give Oswald her new address. The members of the Russian community in Dallas, who never liked Oswald, refuse to assist him in his search for his wife.

Outcast, misunderstood, and alone, Lee Harvey Oswald, who considers himself a great man, destined to accomplish great things, festers in a quiet rage.

He has now become desperate.

■ ■ ■

On November 6, 1962, Teddy Kennedy is one of the first beneficiaries of the outcome of the defused crisis, sweeping into office as the newly elected U.S. senator from Massachusetts. There will now be three Kennedys in Washington. And while the Cuban missile crisis has seen JFK's approval rating soar to 79 percent, not everyone is happy about the growing Kennedy influence. The Joint Chiefs of Staff are irate that JFK did not, and now *will not,* invade Cuba. Fidel Castro feels sold out by the Soviets and is already seeing his influence in Latin America plummet because he has been exposed as a Russian puppet. Seething, he blames Kennedy.

With good reason. The Cuban missile crisis does not mark the end of efforts to get rid of Castro. And while the president has promised Khrushchev that he will not meddle in Cuban affairs, this does not mean that the CIA's Operation Mongoose has come to an end. The brainchild of JFK, Mongoose involved inserting teams of Cuban exiles into Cuba to foment rebellion against Castro. Initially, the Mafia was also secretly enlisted, with the primary aim of killing Castro. The president never used the word *assassinate* to describe the operation's ultimate mission, but the Mafia is not a military organization, and their well-documented involvement took Mongoose beyond a popular overthrow by the exiles and into the realm of carefully plotted political murder.

■ ■ ■

The bond between Jack and Bobby Kennedy became tighter than ever during the Cuban missile crisis, even as Lyndon Johnson once again stumbled. The vice president made the crucial mistake of being disloyal to President Kennedy, initially aligning himself with the hawkish generals who advocated a full-blown invasion. Bobby, meanwhile, took the opposite point of view. He thought an attack on Cuba would remind the world of Pearl Harbor—an opinion mirroring that of JFK.

Now, with the crisis successfully defused, John Fitzgerald Kennedy is elated. He sees a comparison between the successful outcome of the Cuban missile crisis and Abraham Lincoln's stable leadership that brought about the end of the Civil War. "Maybe this is the night I should go to the theater," JFK jokes to Bobby, remembering that Lincoln attended a play as the war ended—only to be assassinated.

It is a bold joke, a playful poke at a fellow president's murder, almost tempting fate. And it is out of character for John Kennedy, a man with echoes of Lincoln everywhere in his life: from sleeping in the Lincoln Bedroom on the night of his inauguration, to having a secretary surnamed

Lincoln, to being driven in a bubble-top convertible Lincoln Continental limousine. But after the nail-biting tension of the recent crisis, John Kennedy feels he is allowed a touch of black humor. Even such a morbid joke feels lighthearted after the darkness that has enveloped his life these last thirteen days and nights.

The president and the attorney general laugh.

"If you go" to the theater, Bobby answers, "I want to go with you."

Little do they know how macabre those words actually are.

PART II

The Curtain Descends

8

~

Jackie Kennedy's bare, tanned shoulders accentuate the pink color of her strapless Oleg Cassini gown. She wears dangling diamond earrings designed by legendary jeweler Harry Winston. Long white gloves come up past her elbows. She makes small talk with a man she adores, André Malraux, the sixty-one-year-old writer who serves as the French minister of culture. The First Lady's eyes sparkle after a restful family Christmas vacation in Palm Beach, Florida.

On this night, the First Lady is truly a vision.

And, unbeknownst to all but one of the thousand people filling the West Sculpture Hall of the National Gallery of Art, she is also pregnant.

The president stands less than three feet away, paying no attention whatsoever to his wife. He gazes at a dark-haired beauty half his age named Lisa Gherardini. She is blessed with lips that are full and red, contrasting seductively with her smooth olive skin. Her smile is coy. The plunging neckline of her dress hints at an ample bosom. She bears the faintest of resemblances to the First Lady.

There are television cameras, newspaper reporters, and those thousand guests. The president's every move is being scrutinized, but he is unafraid as his gaze lingers on this tantalizing young woman. He is the president of the United States, a man who has just rescued the world from global thermonuclear war. Everything is going his way. Surely John Kennedy can be allowed the minor indiscretion of appreciating this lovely twentysomething.

Playing to those who might be watching closely, JFK smiles at young Lisa. But he is a changed man since the Cuban missile crisis, and far more enchanted by Jackie than by other women—at least for the time being. That near-catastrophic experience reminded him how deeply he loves his wife and children.

The new Congress begins tomorrow, and the president's State of the Union address is less than a week away. Kennedy will push for "a substantial reduction and revision in federal income taxes" as the "one step, above all, essential" to make America more competitive in the world economy. But that tax cut will be controversial, a hard sell with the new Democratic Congress. Tonight the burdens of being president of the United States are far more pressing than spending time with Lisa Gherardini.

The president moves on.

▪ ▪ ▪

But Jackie stays, turning away from Malraux to gaze at the same bewitching young woman. Lisa Gherardini is not actually here in person, but in a painting hanging on the gallery wall. She is also known as *La Gioconda*, or the *Mona Lisa*, a wife and mother of five children who sat for this portrait in the early sixteenth century.

Jackie revels in the *Mona Lisa*'s presence with a feeling of profound success, for it was her persistent dream to bring the world's most famous painting to the National Gallery of Art, in Washington. About a year ago she made a discreet request to Malraux, who then arranged the loan— much to the outrage of Parisians, many of whom consider America a cultural wasteland.

But this is hardly the first time the *Mona Lisa* has traveled. Napoléon once hung her on his bedroom wall, gazing upon her each morning. In 1911 the painting was stolen from the Louvre and not returned to the Paris museum for two years. She was moved several times during World War II, to prevent her from falling into Nazi hands. And now Jackie has brought Leonardo da Vinci's masterpiece to America, where "Mona Mania" is about to break out. Millions of Americans are lining up to view the painting before its return to France in March—and all because of Jackie Kennedy.

John Walker, director of the National Gallery, was against the loan, fearful that his career would be ruined if he failed to protect the *Mona Lisa* from theft or the damage that might accompany moving a fragile 460-year-old painting across an ocean in the dead of winter. In fact, on October 17, just as JFK and his staff were first grappling with the realities of Soviet missiles in Cuba, Walker called the First Lady and gently told her that bringing the painting to America was a horrible idea. The mere thought of it filled him with dread.

Then, like the rest of America, Walker was soon distracted by the barrage of radio and television reports documenting the Cuban missile crisis. He was deeply touched by Jackie's maternal nature and the fact that she had insisted on remaining at the White House to be with her husband. Walker realized that the First Lady was a woman of substance, not just a wealthy young lady with a passion for French culture.

So he changed his mind. Long before the Cuban missile crisis was over, he began arranging the *Mona Lisa's* trip to America.

Walker's task was made much easier when JFK ordered the world's most elite bodyguards to watch over the precious work of art—none other than the men who would willingly take a bullet to protect the president himself: the Secret Service.

■ ■ ■

The president's Secret Service code name is Lancer. The First Lady's is Lace. Caroline and John are Lyric and Lark, respectively. Almost everything and everyone in the First Family's lives has a code name: LBJ is

Volunteer, the presidential Lincoln is SS-100-X, Dean Rusk is Freedom, and the White House itself is Castle. Things that exist temporarily have code names, such as Charcoal, the name given to the president's residence when he is not in the White House. Most subsets of names and places begin with the same first letter: *L* for the first family, *W* for the White House staff, *D* for Secret Service agents, and so on.

The Secret Service protection given President Kennedy is constant, and contrasts sharply with the protection given Abraham Lincoln a hundred years ago. Back then, the Secret Service did not exist. The agency was not founded until three months after Lincoln's assassination. Even then, its primary role was to prevent currency fraud, not to protect the president.

In Lincoln's day, private citizens could walk into the White House whenever they wished. Vandalism was rampant as overenthusiastic visitors stole pieces of the president's home to keep as souvenirs. The Department of the Interior responded by hiring a select group of officers from Washington's Metropolitan Police to protect the great building. But as death threats against Abraham Lincoln mounted in the waning days of the Civil War, these police officers shifted their protective focus to the president. Two officers remained at his side from 8:00 A.M. to 4:00 P.M. Another stayed with Lincoln until midnight, and a fourth man covered the graveyard shift. Each officer carried a .38-caliber pistol.

President Lincoln was never completely safe, though, as his assassination proved. On the night Lincoln was shot in the head, John Parker, the officer who was supposed to be protecting him, was instead drinking beer in a nearby tavern. And even though the president of the United States was shot to death after Parker left his post, the officer was never convicted of dereliction of duty—and, incredibly, was even allowed to remain on the police force.

Before Lincoln's assassination, there were many (including Lincoln himself) who believed that Americans were not the kind of people who killed their political leaders. One pistol shot by John Wilkes Booth blatantly disproved that theory. Still, some people continued to believe the myth of presidential safety. Lincoln's death was thought to be an anomaly— even when a second president, James Garfield, was assassinated sixteen years later. Compulsory protection of the *vice* president didn't begin until 1962, reinforcing the notion that the vice presidency is a thankless job.

■ ■ ■

John Kennedy's bodyguards sport the telltale bulge of .38 revolvers beneath their suit coats. But every other aspect of their protection is furtive. The Secret Service's motto is "Worthy of trust and confidence," and the agents reinforce that message through their poise and professionalism. They are athletic men, many of them possessing college degrees and military backgrounds. Drinking beer on duty is out of the question. There are eight agents on each of the three eight-hour shifts, and every agent is trained to handle a variety of deadly weapons. The Secret Service headquarters in the White House is a small windowless office at the north entrance to the West Wing, where an armory of riot guns and Thompson submachine guns provides additional firepower. There are several layers of security between JFK and a potential assassin, beginning at the White House Gates and continuing right up to the black-and-white-tiled hallway outside the Oval Office, where an agent remains on duty whenever the president is working. Should Kennedy need to summon that agent at a moment's notice, the president can push a special emergency button beneath his desk.

The easiest place to attack the president is outside the White House. The Secret Service need only look to recent events in France for proof. President Charles de Gaulle is virtually untouchable inside the Élysée Palace, where he lives and works. But on August 22, 1962, terrorists opened fire on his motorcade in the French suburb of Petit Clamart. One hundred and fifty-seven shots were fired. Fourteen bullets struck the car, puncturing two tires of de Gaulle's Citroën, but his driver skillfully steered to safety. Even as the *Mona Lisa* is unveiled in America, the leader of the assassination plot is on trial in Paris. Jean Bastien-Thiry, a disgruntled former air force lieutenant colonel, will be found guilty and become the last man in French history to be shot by a firing squad.

To prevent an American version of Bastien-Thiry from getting to President Kennedy, eight Secret Service agents travel ahead to survey his upcoming location anytime he leaves the White House. Once the president is out of the White House, eight agents form a human shield around him as he moves.

For those protecting the president, JFK's almost manic activity is the toughest part of the job.

John Kennedy likes to appear vigorous in public and often risks his life by wading deep into crowds to shake hands. These forays terrify his security detail. Any crazed lunatic with a gun and an agenda can easily take a shot during moments like those. Should that happen, each agent is prepared to place his body between the bullet and the president, sacrificing his own life for the good of the country.

It helps that the agents truly like JFK. He knows them by name and is fond of bantering with them. Despite this familiarity, the men of the Secret Service never forget that John Kennedy is the president of the United States. Their sense of decorum is evident in the respectful way they address Kennedy, a man whose intimate life they well know. Face-to-face, they call him "Mr. President." When two agents talk about him, he is known as "the boss." And when speaking to visitors or guests, the detail refers to him as "President Kennedy."

These Secret Service agents are no less fond of Jackie. The agent in charge of her detail, six-foot-tall Clint Hill (code name Dazzle), has become her close friend and confidant.

Thus it is almost natural that Secret Service protection be extended to the *Mona Lisa*. The passionate crowds who will surround da Vinci's painting are similar to the throngs who scream for JFK and Jackie on their travels around the world.

The painting sails to America in her own first-class suite aboard the SS *France*, where French agents guard her around the clock. She travels by ship rather than plane to safeguard against the possibility of a crash that would destroy the painting forever. Should the luxury liner go down, the special metal case containing the *Mona Lisa* is designed to float. Only the captain of the SS *France* is told that the *Mona Lisa* is on board, and security is so intense as she is brought on that guests speculate that the metal box actually holds a secret nuclear device. But when word finally leaks out about the box's true contents, passengers transform the ship into a nonstop *Mona Lisa* party, complete with special pastry cakes and drinking games.

Upon docking in New York, the *Mona Lisa* is driven to Washington, D.C., by a special Secret Service motorcade that does not stop for any reason. Once again, the four-hour drive is chosen over a simple flight, due to fears of a crash. Secret Service snipers are stationed on rooftops along the way, and Secret Service agent John Campion personally rides next to the *Mona Lisa* in the black "National Gallery of Art" van. The vehicle is equipped with extra heavy springs to absorb road shocks that could chip flecks of pigment from the canvas.

Upon arrival in Washington, the *Mona Lisa* is locked behind steel doors in a climate-controlled vault that keeps the temperature at a perfect 62 degrees at all hours. Should the electricity fail, a backup generator will automatically take over. Even in the vault, the Secret Service maintains its vigilance by monitoring her on closed-circuit television.

Their protection of da Vinci's masterpiece is extraordinary. Yet there is one huge difference between protecting the president and protecting this precious cargo: the *Mona Lisa* is just a painting. Angry citizens have damaged her on at least three occasions—a vandal once tried to spray-paint her, another attacked her with a knife, and a third threw a ceramic mug at her—and, of course, she was once stolen. But Lisa Gherardini herself has been in the grave for almost five centuries. There is no way she can be shot dead.

The same cannot be said of the president.

That is why the Secret Service never lets its guard down.

Not yet, at least.

■ ■ ■

"Politics and art, the life of action and the life of thought, the world of events and the world of imagination, are one," John Kennedy tells the distinguished crowd on hand for the unveiling of the *Mona Lisa*. The words come out as "Moner Liser" in his clipped Boston accent.

The president and First Lady have never been more popular than they are right now, and never more synonymous with America herself.

Also, they are closer than ever as a couple. The Secret Service has noticed that Kennedy seems less interested in other women. Friends have seen the couple shift their relationship from the professional formality that defined the first two years in office. There is a new tenderness to their time together and, in the way they talk to each other, a transformation that has made them history's first power couple. The United States is "the most powerful nation in the world," in the words of fashion designer Oleg Cassini, "represented by the most stunning couple imaginable."

One glance around the packed hall gives evidence to Cassini's words. Everyone from Supreme Court justices to senators to wealthy diplomats and oilmen are here to pay their respects. Even as the president's speech brilliantly links the *Mona Lisa* and the politics of the cold war, it is Jackie who orchestrates every last detail of this very special night. The *Mona Lisa* may be dazzling—hidden though she is behind bulletproof glass— but the average partygoer spends only fifteen seconds staring at the painting, while some spend all night staring at Jackie. Her beauty, poise, grace, and glamour are unmatchable.

On this night, it is the First Lady, not the *Mona Lisa*, who owns the room.

■ ■ ■

Jackie has come to think of the Kennedy White House as a mythical place—what she will later describe as an "American Camelot." The First Lady is referring to the Broadway musical starring Richard Burton as the legendary King Arthur, the lovely Julie Andrews as Queen Guinevere, and Robert Goulet as Sir Lancelot. In the play, Camelot represents an oasis of idyllic happiness in a cold, hard world. A growing number of Americans agree with Jackie that the Kennedy White House is a similarly mythical place and a bulwark of idealism in the midst of the cold war.

Even the president is inspired by *Camelot*. Many nights, Jackie will later admit, he plays the Broadway sound track album on his record player before going to sleep.

But there is a dark side to Camelot, one that JFK's Secret Service detail knows all too well.

There is a flip side to the president's popularity polls: 70 percent of the nation may love JFK, but another 30 percent hate his guts. Castro definitely wants him dead. In Miami, many in the Cuban exile community are bitter about the Bay of Pigs debacle and want revenge. In the Deep South, rage at the president's push for racial equality is so widespread that southern Democrats say that their only smart political choice—if they are to remain in office—is to maintain their firm stand against his domestic policies.

Right here in Washington, the CIA is none too happy about rumors that JFK would like to place the agency under closer presidential supervision by putting Bobby Kennedy in charge. Also, more than a few military leaders at the Pentagon do not trust Kennedy's judgment. The president has stated aloud that he thinks the generals are capable of attempting to remove him from office.

Finally, the Mafia, to whom Kennedy was once so close that mobster Sam Giancana referred to JFK as Jack rather than Mr. President, is angry that Kennedy is repaying their years of friendship by allowing Bobby and the Justice Department to conduct an anti-Mafia witch hunt. "We broke our balls for him," Giancana complains, "and he gets his brother to hound us to death."

JFK is aware of his enemies. And he knows the threats will not go away, no matter how often he shuts out the world at night by dropping the needle on his hi-fi and listening to *Camelot*.

■ ■ ■

If the Secret Service is aware of Lee Harvey Oswald, that fact is nowhere in any record.

Their ignorance is not unusual. Why would the powerful Secret Service be watching a low-level former marine living in Dallas, Texas?

Oswald and Marina are back together again. There is always a heat to their reunions, and their latest is no different. Marina Oswald is now pregnant again.

Despite their very different life circumstances, Jackie Kennedy and Marina Oswald are connected by the fact that they are two young women enjoying the life-changing early days of pregnancy. Jackie is due in

September, Marina in October. And one more thing links them: like Jackie, Marina finds JFK to be quite handsome. Which makes her unstable husband more jealous than he usually is.

■ ■ ■

Lee Harvey Oswald's life continues to be defined by a balance of passion and rage. On January 27, 1963, as crowds ten abreast line the streets of Washington to view the *Mona Lisa*, Oswald orders a .38 Special revolver through the mail. The cost is $29.95. Oswald slides a $10 bill into the envelope, with the balance to be paid on delivery. He keeps the purchase a secret from Marina by having the gun sent to his P.O. box and even uses the alias of "A. J. Hidell."

Oswald has no special plans for his new pistol. Nobody has been making threats on his life, and for now he has no intention to kill anyone. He merely likes the idea of owning a gun—just in case.

■ ■ ■

January comes to an end, and with it the *Mona Lisa*'s stay in Washington, D.C. On February 4 another high-security motorcade drives the painting to New York, where "Mona Mania" reaches even greater heights.

January has been an amazing month for the president and Mrs. Kennedy. The glamour surrounding the *Mona Lisa* has temporarily overshadowed the fear of the cold war. Two years into the Kennedy presidency, and it is clear to the world that John and Jackie are in control of America's fate.

Thus, Jackie Kennedy may be right: this might just be Camelot—or at least part of it. For her there is no dark side to the story—although it definitely exists.

When Jackie thinks of *Camelot*, she focuses on the final act of the play, where King Arthur regains his wonder and hope. But she overlooks the rest of the story. *Camelot* is fraught with tragedy, infighting, and betrayal. There is danger and death. More than half the Knights of the Round Table are slain before the final curtain falls.

And Queen Guinevere, the heroine with whom Jackie so identifies, ends up alone.

9

~~

March 11, 1963
St. Augustine, Florida
8:00 p.m.

The loneliest man in Camelot wants to be president of the United States.

Lyndon Baines Johnson stands bathed in a spotlight. His typewritten speech lies before him on the lectern, but he is not focused on the words. He's more interested in the two tables of voters somewhere out in the audience who might just make that impossible presidential dream come true someday.

What Lyndon Johnson wants, above all else, is a return to power. He adores power. And he will endure anything to know that heady sensation once again.

Anything.

The vice president searches the room for the "Negro tables," desperate to know if his political gamble will pay off.

■ ■ ■

Robert Francis Kennedy also wants to be president of the United States.

With five years to go before the 1968 election, an article by Gore Vidal in *Esquire* magazine's March issue picks him to win the Democratic nomination over Lyndon Johnson.

Bobby Kennedy has become such a political force that even the vice president worries he is powerless to stop Bobby from winning in 1968.

It all seems so easy: JFK until 1968, then Bobby takes the White House, and then wins again in 1972, and then maybe even Teddy in 1976 and 1980. The Kennedy dynasty is poised to control the American presidency for the next twenty years. It's almost a sure thing.

But there are no sure things in politics. And little does LBJ know that insidious forces are possibly targeting Bobby even now—plotting not only the attorney general's downfall, but that of the entire Kennedy family political dynasty.

■ ■ ■

August 5, 1962. Marilyn Monroe lies naked facedown on her bed. She is dead. Police investigators see no sign of trauma. The Los Angeles coroner will later conclude that the actress died from an overdose of barbiturates. Yet her stomach is almost completely empty, with no pill residue whatsoever.

The public instantly chalks up Marilyn's death to a life of excess. The tabloids have firmly established that she is a substance abuser. So there is little public outcry for a closer look at what happened to the glamorous actress.

But there is a darker theory circulating in the precincts of organized crime. Mafia lore suggests that the old Sam Giancana–CIA connection from the Operation Mongoose days is still quietly active. The theory holds that Giancana conspired to have Monroe murdered by a team of four hit men who entered her home, taped her mouth shut, and injected a lethal suppository of barbiturates and chloral hydrate into her anus. This was done to prevent the vomiting that often accompanies an oral drug overdose. The tape was removed from her mouth once she was dead, and Monroe's body wiped clean.

Giancana's motivation was revenge for Bobby Kennedy's ongoing Justice Department investigations into organized criminal activity. The intent of the killers, according to that same Mafia legend, was to implicate Bobby in the murder. However, their plans went awry when Bobby was tipped off by anonymous sources that Marilyn Monroe had unexpectedly died. The attorney general then ordered Peter Lawford to arrange for a private eye named Fred Otash to go over Marilyn's home with a fine-tooth comb to ensure there was absolutely no evidence of her involvement with the president or the Kennedy family. The two men cleaned up well, even taking Marilyn's diary.

There was also, however, the issue of Marilyn's phone records. These would show whom she was talking to in the last forty-eight hours of her life. The story goes on to say that Bobby Kennedy appealed to J. Edgar Hoover and the FBI to expunge those records. Not wanting to lose the chance to use Monroe's death for political gain, the legend continues, Los Angeles police chief William Parker obtained a copy of those records and kept them in his garage for years, as blackmail evidence. The tapes, Parker would say, are "my ticket to get Hoover's job when Bobby Kennedy becomes president."

Peter Lawford will later claim that Bobby was in Monroe's home that night, having flown down from the Bay Area, where he was staying with Ethel and four of their children. Lawford's story, not confirmed by anyone, alleges that Marilyn was going to reveal her former relationship with JFK to the press and that Bobby was present in Los Angeles trying to do damage control.

The recollections of both Lawford and Mafia members have been dissected thoroughly. Neither has been proven true. Nor have the rumors that Bobby and Marilyn were having an affair of their own.

The facts are that Marilyn Monroe phoned Bobby several times throughout the summer of 1962. She was distraught over the end of her affair with JFK and was openly gossiping about it in Hollywood. The press had begun asking questions about the alleged affair, and it appeared that the matter might surface during the 1964 election. Yet the Northern California ranch where Bobby and his family were staying on the night of Marilyn's death was an hour from the nearest airport and a five-hour drive from Los Angeles. That makes it highly unlikely that RFK could have slipped away without being noticed.

Any involvement by Bobby Kennedy in Marilyn Monroe's death, whether it was suicide or murder, makes it a conspiracy theory without substance to this day.

There is no question, however, that Monroe's going public could have been enough to sink a presidential campaign. JFK was perceived to be a dedicated family man. Details of a sordid affair with the flamboyant Monroe would have ruined the image of Camelot.

With family baggage all over the place, Bobby Kennedy knows he is anything but a sure thing for the presidency. Which means he must work extra hard to discredit his main rival, Lyndon Johnson, before LBJ does the same to him.

Meanwhile, Bobby Kennedy is quietly backing away from his anti-Mafia investigations.

No sense angering old friends unnecessarily.

■ ■ ■

LBJ is making new friends. He is thrilled by the presence of black voters at his St. Augustine dinner speech. It is a Monday evening, and the occasion is the five hundredth anniversary of the city's founding, an event about which LBJ cares little. What matters are the symbolic reasons he flew to Florida in the first place: his courtship of black Americans.

LBJ's brown eyes scan the mostly white audience in the Ponce de Léon Hotel's ballroom. Finally, he locates the so-called Negro tables. The vice president insisted upon this act of integration when accepting the speaking engagement.

Johnson sees both tables right up front, a handful of black faces in a sea of white southerners. The people seated there nod their heads somberly as he speaks, appreciative just to be in the room. Tonight marks the first time that blacks have been allowed to eat in this fabled hotel, all thanks to LBJ. Two tables aren't many, and the change is only for tonight, but at least Johnson can return to Washington bragging that he's on the front lines of the battle for racial equality.

It's a powerful feeling. Yet back in Washington, LBJ has all but forgotten what power feels like. On the road, he's a big deal. People defer to him. He meets with local leaders. He is quoted in the local papers. People want to touch him or enjoy one of his patented high-energy handshakes, the kind where Johnson wraps his meaty fist around another man's, then holds on for as long as they talk, forging a friendship and, in the old days back in the Senate, winning their vote.

But he is now invisible in Washington. For Johnson, the Kennedy White House is not Camelot. He compares the experience with another *c* word: *castration*. LBJ refers to himself as a "steer" or a "cut dog." The president deliberately excludes him from important meetings, makes jokes about him behind his back, and ignores him at White House dinner parties—if he even bothers to invite him at all.

The president isn't the only one treating Johnson with contempt. Bobby Kennedy thinks LBJ is a political charlatan. Jackie Kennedy keeps her distance. And the White House staff can barely conceal their disdain. "The Harvards," as Johnson calls them, make fun of his ill-fitting suits, his slicked-back hair, and the twang of his Texas Hill Country accent. When Johnson commits the faux pas of pronouncing *hors d'oeuvres* as "whore doves" at one party, he instantly becomes the butt of Washington jokes about his hillbilly ways.

One derogatory nickname for Johnson is "Uncle Cornpone," as if he were some irrelevant hick instead of the man who got Kennedy elected in 1960 by carrying the Deep South. Some refer to him as "Judge Crater," for the New York City official who abruptly disappeared in the 1920s and was never seen again. One White House staffer was overheard at a dinner party joking, "Lyndon? Lyndon who?"

But Johnson is anything but gone, and anything but a hillbilly. During his time as Senate majority leader he was masterful at passing difficult legislation. His favorite biblical verse, Isaiah 1:18, exemplifies his passion for building coalitions: "Come now, let us reason together."

Truth be told, the vice president is a complex man, whose tastes run the gamut from spicy deer sausage to Cutty Sark scotch to Viennese waltzes. And he is almost as sexually active as the president—only far more discreet about how he manages his affairs.

This discretion carries over into politics. The gregarious Johnson has stifled his personality, disciplining himself to be completely silent in meetings in order to avoid offending the president. It's killing Johnson that he has to endure a nonstop barrage of insults. The vice president has become anxious, depressed, and overeager to please. He barely eats. He has lost so much weight that his always-baggy suits look enormous on him. Even the vice president's nose and ears appear proportionally larger—like how a political cartoonist might draw him in caricature.

LBJ has almost nothing to do. His phone barely rings. From his office in the Executive Office Building, he can look out the window and see the comings and goings across the street at the White House. Sometimes the vice president will leave his desk to meander through the West Wing hallways, wishing for a meeting to attend or a decision to make. Other times, he'll take a seat outside the door to the Oval Office, hoping to catch John Kennedy's eye and be invited inside.

But those occasions are fewer and fewer. The president and vice president will spend less than two hours alone in the year 1963.

Still, Johnson puts up with the abuse. Because, without the vice presidency, he has nothing. There is no Senate opening in Texas for which he can run. And the former Kennedy insider John Connally filled the governor's seat there just four months ago. But at the end of four more years, Johnson can run for the most powerful job in America.

And why shouldn't LBJ be president? He served twelve years in the House of Representatives, twelve more in the Senate, and ruled for six years as majority leader. He is versed in foreign policy and domestic legislation and can give a tutorial on the subtleties of backroom wheeling and dealing. There isn't a more qualified politician in the land.

LBJ is fighting for his political life as he locates the two token tables of racial integration in that St. Augustine hotel ballroom. And while the occasion may officially be the anniversary of the city's founding, it also marks the day when Lyndon Johnson takes a public stand in favor of civil rights.

The Kennedy brothers have deliberately kept him out of their escalating battle for racial equality. They know that as a southern politician, he could use the issue to gain power.

Johnson understands this as well. And he does everything he can to be at the forefront of JFK's civil rights campaign.

For Johnson, civil rights has nothing to do with right or wrong. Taking this stand just makes good political sense.

So LBJ waits, castrated and emaciated, hoping it will all pay off.

■ ■ ■

On March 4, just one week before Lyndon Johnson's St. Augustine speech, Attorney General Robert Kennedy responds to the *Esquire* story by telling the press, "I have no plans to run at this time"—which the media know to be code for "I'm running."

But is he qualified? Bobby Kennedy is a lawyer who has never tried a case in court, and he's an attorney general who got the job because of his father and brother. Since then, he has often ignored his duties at the Justice Department to serve as JFK's mouthpiece and sounding board. And the CIA certainly doesn't approve of his job performance. One popular bumper sticker at the agency's Langley, Virginia, headquarters reads "First Ethel, Now Us."

But the world is changing drastically, and Bobby Kennedy reflects the youth and vitality of Camelot instead of the stodgy cold war values synonymous with the older Johnson. American culture is under siege by new influences.

A British rock-and-roll band named the Beatles is releasing their first album.

A new comic book character named Iron Man makes his debut.

Writer Betty Friedan ignites a new wave of the women's movement with her book *The Feminine Mystique*.

The draconian U.S. penitentiary on Alcatraz Island is closed for good. As if to mark the event, the CIA expands its powers even further into J. Edgar Hoover's world by creating a domestic operations division.

Bobby Kennedy is aware of his cultural influence; he well understands the Camelot allure. Yet he is still obsessed by his rivalry with Lyndon Johnson. In fact, he hates him. Bobby does such a poor job of hiding his loathing that friends once presented him with a Lyndon Johnson voodoo doll, complete with stickpins.

The one thing Bobby can't stand is a liar, and he believes that Johnson lies all the time.

Still, there is something in Johnson that inspires fear in Bobby. He once told a White House staffer, "I can't stand the bastard, but he's the most formidable man I know."

And so two intense and ruthless politicians are set against each other. But neither one has an inkling about the calamity that is now just eight months away.

■ ■ ■

Lee Harvey Oswald is growing more isolated. He has turned a closet in his home into an office. There he writes angry diatribes about the world around him. Oswald is growing increasingly agitated, and people are beginning to fear him.

On March 12 in Dallas, just one day after Lyndon Johnson's speech in St. Augustine, Oswald decides to buy a second gun to go along with the pistol he keeps hidden in his home. This time it's a rifle, purchased through the February 1963 issue of *American Rifleman* magazine. The Italian Mannlicher-Carcano, model 91/38, was made in 1940 and originally designed for the Italian infantry during World War II. This is not a gun designed for hunting animals, but for shooting men. As a former Marine Corps sharpshooter, Oswald knows the difference, just as he also knows how to clean, maintain, load, aim, and accurately fire such a weapon.

Of all the amazing things happening in the world in March 1963, this simple mail-order purchase would seem to have little significance.

In fact, nothing will have a greater impact on world events than this nineteen-dollar Italian war-surplus bolt-action rifle.

The weapon arrives on March 25. Marina complains that they could have used the money for food. But Oswald is pleased with the purchase and gets in the habit of riding the bus to a dry riverbed for target practice against the levee.

On March 31, while Marina is hanging diapers on the clothesline to dry, Oswald steps into the backyard dressed all in black. His new pistol is tucked into his belt. He brandishes the rifle in one hand and holds copies of two Communist newspapers in the other. He demands that an amused Marina take photographs of him. He plans to send them to the *Worker* and the *Militant* to show that he is prepared to do anything to wage class warfare.

On April 6, 1963, Lee Harvey Oswald is fired from his job at Jaggars-Chiles-Stovall. His Communist rants have grown offensive to his coworkers, and his bosses claim that he has become undependable.

On April 10, 1963, Oswald decides it's time to kill someone.

10

〜

April 9, 1963
Washington, D.C.
Midday

The man with seven months to live is talking to Winston Churchill.

John Fitzgerald Kennedy stands in the White House Rose Garden before a large, warmhearted crowd. Churchill, the ninety-two-year-old former prime minister whose inspirational courage helped save Britain during World War II, watches live by satellite from his home in London. The purpose of this Rose Garden gathering is to make Winston Churchill an American citizen—the only foreign leader since Lafayette to be so honored.

"A son of America though a subject of Britain," Kennedy begins his speech, referring to the fact that Churchill's mother, née Jenny Jerome, was a U.S. citizen, "has been throughout his life a firm and steadfast friend of the American people and the American nation."

Churchill's fifty-one-year-old son, Randolph, stands at JFK's side. Jackie Kennedy stands directly behind her husband. The Rose Garden is filled with diplomats and acquaintances from the United States and

England. The president's father, Joseph, who served as ambassador to Great Britain just prior to the Second World War, watches from a wheelchair inside the White House, the elder Kennedy having experienced a stroke two years prior.

But even as John Kennedy stands before this idyllic gathering, seeing the warmth and smiles that come with honoring such a distinguished and legendary world leader, his thoughts are never far from another "Churchill"—and another war that is gaining steam.

■ ■ ■

It was Dwight Eisenhower who first sent American soldiers to Vietnam to stem the flow of communism in Southeast Asia. But it was John Kennedy who ordered a gradual escalation in the number of troops since taking office, hoping to ensure that Vietnam did not fall to communism and thus perhaps begin a domino effect that would see other Asian nations turn their backs on democracy.

But Kennedy's good intentions have gone awry. The handful of American "advisers" in Vietnam has now swelled to almost sixteen thousand pilots and soldiers. American pilots are dropping napalm firebombs from the sky to destroy the Viet Cong army that is now fighting the U.S.-backed Saigon regime. Thousands of Viet Cong soldiers have been killed—as have thousands of innocent Vietnamese peasants. "The charred bodies of children and babies have made pathetic piles in the middle of the remains of the marketplace," the Associated Press reported after one such bombing incident.

American pilots fly hundreds of missions over Vietnam every month. A systematic process of defoliation has begun, with American airplanes spraying chemicals over the jungle to kill all vegetation that might hide enemy soldiers. Of course, the crops of many innocent farmers are destroyed in the process. This "scorched earth" policy will eventually come back to haunt the United States in a number of ways.

The CIA has joined in the fight in Vietnam, conducting covert search-and-destroy missions in the Communist north. Gunners aboard American helicopters have free rein to open fire on the peasants who turn and run when they see Hueys come sweeping in over the treetops. The assumption is that the farmers run because they are the enemy, not that they might be superstitious and terrified about aircraft that have suddenly invaded the skies above their primitive villages.

John Kennedy believes that America needs to end the Vietnam conflict—though he is not quite ready to go public with this. "We don't have a prayer of staying in Vietnam," he will tell Pulitzer Prize–winning journalist Charles Bartlett off the record. "Those people hate us. They are going to throw our asses out of there at any point. But I can't give up that territory to the Communists and get the American people to reelect me."

To safeguard his chances for reelection, the president cannot, and will not, pull U.S. troops out of Vietnam until after the 1964 election. The war is still popular with voters. In the meantime, he hopes to contain U.S. involvement, reading his briefing books each morning and praying that South Vietnamese president Ngo Dinh Diem doesn't do anything stupid or irresponsible to inflame the situation.

Diem is a Catholic, just like the Kennedys. But his faith is almost fanatical, causing him to lose focus on fighting communism. He is now fighting a war on two fronts. The first is against the Viet Cong; the second is a holy war against Vietnam's majority Buddhist population.

Yet it is Diem whom Vice President Johnson once famously praised as "the Winston Churchill of Asia." The Kennedy brothers hate that gross exaggeration. Unlike the real Winston Churchill, Diem is not a firm and steadfast friend of the American people or the United States of America. He is a mass murderer, concerned only about his own glorification.

And that narcissism will soon doom him.

■ ■ ■

In the Rose Garden, Kennedy concludes his remarks. He now listens as Randolph Churchill reads from a speech his father has prepared. "Our past is our key to our future," says Churchill, in words that make Kennedy and the British icon sound like two very similar statesmen. "Let no one underrate our energies, our potentialities, and our abiding power for good."

■ ■ ■

But not every man believes in an abiding power for good.

John Kennedy is hardly a violent man. He dislikes guns and even abhors hunting animals. The same cannot be said for Lee Harvey Oswald. Now, on a hot April night, Oswald hides in the shadows of a Dallas alleyway. His new rifle is pointed at Major General Ted Walker, an avowed anticommunist.

Walker sits in the study of his Dallas home intently poring over his 1962 tax returns. The fifty-three-year-old West Point graduate is a closeted gay man and a famous opponent of communism. The date is April 10, and he is home alone on this Wednesday night, having just returned from a controversial trip around the country. The desk lamp is the room's only light. A small window looks out into the darkness. Normally, Walker might crack the window to let in the sweet spring air, but it was a record-high ninety-nine degrees today. It's still hot, even at 9:00 P.M. Walker is running the air-conditioning.

Lee Harvey Oswald's hiding spot in the alley is just forty yards away. He watches Walker's every move through the telescopic sight of his Italian Mannlicher-Carcano rifle. The hum of the air-conditioning unit drowns out the sound of Oswald's carefully choreographed movements. He is now concealed behind Walker's back fence, the barrel of his rifle poking through the latticework. There is a church near Walker's home, where the congregants have gathered for a midweek service on this Wednesday evening.

The oppression of the workingman courses through Lee Harvey Oswald's veins. He finds strength in the ideals of communism and socialism. After almost a year back home in America, he has become even more enraged by what he perceives as the injustice of the capitalist system. He is angry enough to kill any man who speaks out against communism.

Which is why he is aiming his brand-new rifle with murderous intent at Ted Walker's head. The former general is at the very top of the list of people whom Oswald despises. Eighteen months ago, Walker was asked to leave the army after telling a newspaper reporter that Harry Truman and Eleanor Roosevelt were most likely Communists. He resigned his post rather than retire, a symbolic gesture of defiance that cost him his pension. Since then, the veteran of World War II and the Korean War has devoted himself to political causes. He ran for governor of Texas as a Democrat—an odd alignment for a man so politically far to the right, especially one living in Dallas, a violent city where Democrats are such a minority that many of them are wary of openly expressing their beliefs.

After finishing last in that election—which was won by John Connally—Walker traveled to Mississippi, attempting to block the integration of the University of Mississippi. Two people were killed and six U.S. Marshals were shot in the ensuing riot, after which Walker was temporarily sent to a mental institution and held on federal charges of sedition. It was Bobby Kennedy himself who ordered that Walker be charged for acts of violence against the civil rights of an American citizen.

But Oswald doesn't care about civil rights. He has come to Walker's home because the *Worker*, the Communist newspaper to which he subscribes, has targeted the general as a threat to its beliefs. And because of Walker's recent participation in Operation Midnight Ride, a Paul Revere–like barnstorming tour to warn Americans about the scourge of communism. The Mississippi grand jury's decision not to press charges against Walker was Oswald's motivation for purchasing a rifle. Since the Mannlicher-Carcano's arrival, Oswald has traveled frequently by bus to the area around Walker's home. He has walked the streets and alleys, studying and sketching and learning the lay of the land, memorizing escape routes and the church schedule. Oswald took several photographs of the area and developed them at work before being fired on April 6. All his intelligence is stored in a special blue loose-leaf notebook.

Oswald knows that Walker spends most evenings in his study. The short distance between the alley and that room makes Walker impossible to miss.

Oswald didn't tell Marina where he was going tonight. But before leaving their apartment, he jotted down a note detailing what she should do if he is arrested. The note contains details about the bills he has paid, how much money he has left to her, and where the Dallas jail is located. Oswald wrote the note in Russian, just to be sure Marina understood every word. He left the note on his desk, in that small closet he's converted into a study. She knows not to go in there, but if he's missing long enough, Oswald is sure she will enter the room.

▪ ▪ ▪

Back in the alleyway, Oswald quietly takes aim. Walker is in profile, viewed from his left side. The general wears his dark hair slicked close to the scalp. Oswald can see every strand through his scope. He has never shot a man before, nor even fired a gun in anger. But he spent hours on the firing range back in his Marine Corps days, and these last few weeks, he has been diligently working on his shot down in the dry bed of the Trinity River, using the levee walls as a backstop. It's almost comical that a man plotting a murder takes the bus to and from target practice, and indeed to and from the murder scene itself. But Lee Harvey Oswald has no choice. He doesn't own a car.

Walker sits, transfixed by the numbers on his tax forms. Oswald takes a deep breath and slowly lets it out. He knows to exhale before firing, and to time the squeezing of the trigger with the end of that breath leaving his body. He also knows to gradually increase pressure on the trigger, squeezing it slowly rather than jerking it.

Back when he was in the marines, he rarely took practice at the rifle range seriously, openly laughing about the red "Maggie's drawers" flag that was raised whenever he missed a target. But he can shoot extremely well when he wants to, as his Marine Corps "sharpshooter" qualification proves.

Now he wants to.

Oswald squeezes the trigger. He fires just one shot. Then he turns and runs as far and as fast as he can.

▪ ▪ ▪

"I shot Walker," Oswald breathlessly tells Marina. It's 11:30 at night. She has already read the note and is worried sick.

"Did you kill him?" she asks.

"I don't know," he replies in Russian.

"My God, the police will be here any minute," she cries. It is an irrational fear, for the police have absolutely no idea who shot at Walker. "What did you do with the rifle?"

"Buried it."

Oswald turns on the radio to see if he's made the news. Marina, meanwhile, is terrified and anxious. She paces and frets, while her exhausted husband finally lies down on their bed and falls into a deep and immediate sleep.

■ ■ ■

The Walker assassination attempt is in the newspapers and on the radio the next morning. Oswald hangs on every word, though he is appalled to learn that he missed Walker completely. Eyewitnesses claim they saw two men fleeing the scene in a car, and Dallas police are looking for a gun that fires a completely different sort of ammunition than the kind Oswald fired. Oswald is crestfallen. He shot at Walker because he wanted to be a hero in the eyes of the Communist Party; he wanted to be special. Now not only has he botched the easiest shot he will ever take but the police are looking for a completely different man. Police will later surmise that the bullet ricocheted off the windowpane, missing Walker's head by just three inches. Oswald's telescopic sight, designed to look far into the distance, would have blurred the windowpane for Oswald, meaning that he didn't even know it was in the way as he took aim and fired.

But none of this matters to Lee Harvey Oswald right now. He is worse than a failure; he is anonymous.

■ ■ ■

Three days later, Lee Harvey Oswald burns his blue loose-leaf notebook. Walker's house is being guarded around the clock, and a second attempt on his life would be almost impossible. Still, Marina knows that her husband is unstable and tenacious. His hatred for those who would oppose communism is powerful and real.

Deeply afraid, she suggests something drastic: she wants to move the family to New Orleans. She believes that the police will come knocking on their door any minute. Having grown up in the repressive Soviet police state, she lives in fear of being marched off to jail in the middle of the night and disappearing forever.

On April 21, Marina spots Oswald getting ready to leave the house with a pistol tucked in his waistband. It's a Sunday. He's wearing a suit. Marina furiously demands to know where he's going. "Nixon is coming," Oswald tells her. "I'm going to go check it out."

The former vice president has just made headlines by demanding the removal of all Communists from Cuba. Like General Walker, Richard Nixon has been making a political name for himself by denouncing Communists.

"I know how you look," Marina says. Her husband's idea of checking out a situation is to fire a shot at a human being. It's quite clear that Lee Harvey needs to be saved from himself.

Then, showing just how powerful she can be when pushed to the limit, Marina Oswald pushes her husband into their tiny bathroom and forces him to remain there. Her husband is a prisoner the rest of the day. By the time she sets him free, it's clear that, for his own good, Lee Harvey Oswald must leave Dallas.

■ ■ ■

Five days after John Kennedy's Rose Garden speech, the president and First Lady formally announce that she is pregnant. This marks the first time that a sitting president's wife will have a baby since Grover Cleveland's spouse gave birth in 1893.

Americans respond with warmth and enthusiasm—and more than a little surprise. For although she is four months along, Jackie still doesn't show the slightest sign of expecting. The baby will sleep in the same white crib that John Jr. used as an infant. Drapes and a new rug will be added to a small room in the residence as it is transformed into a nursery.

With every passing moment, the Kennedys seem to be living an idyllic life, where everything goes right and each day is more glamorous than the one before it. Unlike Abraham Lincoln, whose shoulders sagged and whose face grew lined and weary from the strains of being president, John Kennedy truly enjoys the job—and it shows. Friends have noted how much he has grown as a leader during his time in office, and the vigor with which he tackles his work.

But America is changing rapidly. John Kennedy will soon be forced to use every bit of these hard-won presidential skills to manage turbulent times. The tense challenges that have dogged his presidency—Cuba, Vietnam, Mafia power, civil rights, and even his personal life—have not disappeared.

For now, they are merely simmering—and as spring becomes summer in 1963, these problems will explode.

11

⤳

May 3, 1963
Birmingham, Alabama
1:00 P.M.

"We're going to walk, walk, walk. Freedom . . . Freedom . . . Freedom," the protesters chant as they march out through the great oak doors of the Sixteenth Street Baptist Church. It is a Friday, and these young black students should be in school. Instead, they have gathered to march for civil rights. Some are less than ten years old. Most are teenagers. They are football players, homecoming queens, track stars, and cheerleaders. Most are nicely dressed, in button-down shirts and clean slacks for the boys, and dresses and bows for the girls.

The marchers number more than one thousand strong. All have skipped class to be here. Some of them even climbed over locked gates. Their goal is to experience something their parents have never known for a single day of their lives: an integrated Birmingham, where lunch counters, department stores, public restrooms, and water fountains are open to all.

The Children's Crusade, as *Newsweek* magazine will call it, fans out and marches across acre-wide Kelly Ingram Park. "We're going to walk,

walk, walk," they continue to chant. They are peaceful, almost spiritual. Yet electricity courses through the group, for what they are doing is completely illegal. "Freedom . . . Freedom . . . Freedom."

The protesters plan to march into the white business district and peacefully enter stores and restaurants. More than six hundred students were arrested doing the same thing yesterday. The youngest was just eight years old. This earned the Children's Crusade national recognition. About a thousand miles away, Attorney General Bobby Kennedy actually scolded the black civil rights leaders who had organized the children's march, stating that "schoolchildren participating in street demonstrations is dangerous business. An injured, maimed or dead child is a price that none of us wants to pay."

Even Malcolm X, one of the fieriest black leaders in America, railed against the Children's Crusade, stating that "real men don't put their children on the firing line."

But these kids want to be here. Many have come against their parents' wishes. Nothing can stop them. They know that if their mothers and fathers were to do the marching, their arrests could cause them to lose jobs, or days and weeks of income.

They know that this march is not just about public toilets; this march is an act of defiance. A few days before he took office, just four months ago, Alabama governor George Wallace made one thing crystal clear: "I'm gonna make race the basis of politics in this state, and I'm gonna make it the basis of politics in this country." Later, at his inaugural, he proclaimed, "I have stood where once Jefferson Davis stood, and took an oath to my people. It is very appropriate then that from this cradle of the Confederacy, this very heart of the great Anglo-Saxon Southland, that today we sound the drum for freedom . . . Let us rise to the call of freedom-loving blood that is in us . . . In the name of the greatest people that have ever trod this earth, I draw the line in the dust and toss the gauntlet before the feet of tyranny. And I say, segregation today! Segregation tomorrow! Segregation forever!"

Those words are a call to arms for blacks and whites alike who disagree with Wallace. The Reverend Martin Luther King Jr. traveled to

Birmingham earlier in the spring to fight for integration. Local black leaders, fearing retribution from their white creditors, told King they didn't want him in town. The civil rights leader ridiculed their fears, implying they were cowardly, thus shaming them into joining the fight.

But despite the best efforts of King and his close friend Ralph Abernathy, the fight for Birmingham stalled just a week ago. After months of protests and arrests, the national media lost interest. There was no longer money to pay the bail for the hundreds being arrested. And the size of the protests dwindled. The segregationists, led by Birmingham's public safety commissioner, Eugene "Bull" Connor, were on the verge of winning. Connor, a sixty-five-year-old former member of the Ku Klux Klan, has enjoyed this battle tremendously and takes great delight in the thought of keeping blacks "in their place."

The first children's march, on May 2, altered Connor's plans. When it is done, thousands gather in the Sixth Avenue Baptist Church to hear Dr. Martin Luther King Jr. speak about the courage of the children. And King swears that the demonstrations will continue. "We are ready to negotiate," he tells the press. "But we intend to negotiate from strength."

But Bull Connor has other plans.

■ ■ ■

"We're going to walk, walk, walk. Freedom . . . Freedom . . . Freedom."

The Children's Crusade has now reached the shade of Kelly Ingram Park's elm trees. The temperature is a humid eighty degrees. Ahead, the marchers see barricades and rows of fire trucks. German shepherds, trained by the police to attack, bark and snarl at the approach of the young students, and an enormous crowd of black and white spectators lines the east side of the park, waiting to see what will happen next. The black adults taunt the police, even as the marchers begin singing "We Shall Overcome."

Martin Luther King Jr. spoke to the protesters before they set out from the church, reminding them that jail was a small price to pay for a good cause. They know not to fight back against the police or otherwise provoke confrontation when challenged. Their efforts will be in vain if the march turns into a riot.

Bull Connor can't afford to let these kids get to the white shopping district. He has ordered Birmingham firefighters to attach their hoses to hydrants and be ready to open those nozzles and spray water on the marchers at full force—a power so great that it can remove the bark from trees or the mortar from a brick building. If the protesters reach the shopping district, using the hoses might damage expensive storefronts. The marchers need to be stopped now.

The first children in the group are met with a half-strength blast from the fire hoses. It's still enough force to stop many of them in their tracks. Some of the kids simply sit down and let the water batter them, following orders not to be violent—or to retreat.

Connor, realizing that half measures will not work with these determined children, then gives the order to spray at full strength. Every protester is knocked off his or her feet. Many children are swept away down the streets and sidewalks, their bodies scraping against grass and concrete. Clothing is torn from their bodies. Those who make the mistake of pressing themselves against a building to dodge the hoses soon become perfect targets. "The water stung like a whip and hit like a cannon," one child will later remember. "The force of it knocked you down like you weighed only twenty pounds, pushing people around like rag dolls. We tried to hold on to the building but it was no use."

Then Connor lets loose the police dogs.

A German shepherd's jaws bite down with 320 pounds of pressure— half the force of a great white shark or a lion. But the German shepherd is much smaller than these predators. Pound for pound, the Birmingham police dogs are unmatched in their bite force.

Bull Connor watches with glee as the German shepherds lunge at the children, ripping away their clothing and tearing into their flesh. Connor, a pear-shaped, balding man who wears glasses, appears mild-mannered. But in actuality he is a vicious good old boy whose beliefs are even more racist than those of Governor Wallace. The public safety commissioner wades into the thick of the action, encouraging policemen to open the barricades so that Birmingham's white citizens can get a better view as the police dogs do their worst.

By 3:00 P.M., it all seems to be over. The children who haven't been arrested limp home in their soaked and torn clothing, their bodies bruised by countless point-blank blasts of water cannon. No longer bold and defiant, they are now just a bunch of kids who have to explain to their angry parents about their wrecked clothes and a missed day of school.

Once again, Bull Connor has won.

Or at least it seems that way.

But among those in Birmingham this afternoon is an Associated Press photographer named Bill Hudson. He is considered one of the best in the business, willing to endure any danger to get a great photo. He has ducked bullets during the Korean War and dodged bricks while covering the civil rights movement.

On this day in Birmingham, Bill Hudson takes the best photo of his life. Appropriately, it's in black and white. He snaps it from just five feet away. The photograph is an image of a Birmingham police officer—looking official in pressed shirt, tie, and sunglasses—encouraging his German shepherd to take a chunk out of black high school student Walter Gadsden's stomach.

The next morning that photograph appears on the front page of the *New York Times*, three columns wide, above the fold.

And so it is that John Kennedy, starting his morning as he always does by reading the papers, sees this image from Birmingham. Disgusted by what he sees, Kennedy makes a point to tell reporters that the picture is "sick" and "shameful."

Just one look and JFK instinctively knows that America and the world will be outraged by Hudson's image. Civil rights are sure to be a major issue of the 1964 presidential election. And Kennedy now understands he can no longer be a passive observer of the civil rights movement. He must take a stand—no matter how many votes it might lose him in the South.

Meanwhile, the reputation of Martin Luther King Jr. is on the rise. He will soon see the Birmingham situation resolved in his favor, thanks to the Children's Crusade. After Bull Connor's initial "victory," the public pressure against Alabama authorities becomes so intense that change is inevitable.

This photograph of a nonviolent civil rights protester being attacked by police dogs brought the brutality of Bull Connor's police force to national attention. (Bill Hudson/Associated Press)

Despite the triumph, Martin Luther King Jr. and John Fitzgerald Kennedy are not on the same page. In fact, they are on a collision course.

■ ■ ■

Civil disobedience is not limited to the American civil rights movement.

Five days after the children of Birmingham peacefully march into that wall of water cannons and police dogs, and two days after a U.S. Army lieutenant is killed by the Viet Cong just outside Saigon, a crowd of Buddhists gathers in the South Vietnamese city of Hue. It is May 8, 1963, the 2,527th birthday of the Buddha.

The protesters have come to demonstrate against a new law set forth by President Ngo Dinh Diem that makes flying the Buddhist flag illegal in Vietnam. It is Diem's great desire to convert his country to Catholicism, and vital to that effort is the systematic subjugation of the nation's Buddhist majority. Diem—whose regime President Kennedy has long supported, but whose anti-Buddhist stance is contrary to American foreign policy—denies promotions to officials known to be Buddhist and looks the other way when Roman Catholic priests organize private armies that loot and demolish the pagodas where the Buddhists worship. To give his crusade credibility in the eyes of the American government, Diem insists that Buddhism and communism are the same—a suggestion akin to J. Edgar Hoover's quiet belief that civil rights and communism are synonymous.

Now, as the three thousand unarmed Buddhist protesters gather near the Perfume River to voice their frustrations, government police and troops fire into the crowd. Bullets and grenades scatter the marchers, killing one woman and eight children in the process.

In the ensuing public outrage, Diem blames the deaths on his Viet Cong opponents—even though the police and army were clearly South Vietnamese. The so-called Buddhist crisis escalates when Diem refuses to punish the men who did the shooting.

Tensions grow throughout Vietnam during the month of May. Diem, like Bull Connor in Birmingham, appears to have the upper hand. Nothing can be done to end his reign of terror. On June 3, government troops once again attack Buddhists in Hue, using tear gas and dogs to disperse the demonstrators. But the crowd will not leave and continues to reassemble. Now the Buddhists turn violent, shouting obscenities at their government attackers. Finally, South Vietnamese troops pour an unnamed red liquid on the heads of Buddhists who are sitting in the streets praying. Sixty-seven of these men and women are taken to hospitals with burns covering their scalps and shoulders.

Unable to control the protesters any longer, Diem's soldiers place the entire city of Hue under martial law.

Still, just as the Birmingham integration movement was losing steam before the Children's Crusade gave it new life, so the Buddhist crisis has begun to bore members of the foreign press. Diem's persecution of Buddhists has become old news.

But on June 11, 1963, a seventy-three-year-old Buddhist monk will give those reporters something to write about.

■ ■ ■

It is almost 10:00 A.M. as Thich Quang Duc sits down on a crowded Saigon thoroughfare. He is dressed in a flowing saffron robe. Duc is an ordained member of the Buddhist clergy, a monastic who lives a meditative life of poverty. This morning he has chosen to protest the government crackdown on his beliefs by burning himself to death.

This is not an impulsive decision. Many within the Buddhist community have sought someone who would immolate himself to draw attention to their plight. Such a startling gesture can't help but attract media coverage from around the world. Indeed, the day before, members of the foreign press were told to be in front of the Cambodian legation the next day if they wanted to see something special.

Not many journalists accept the invitation, so few are on hand to witness the gray Austin sedan driving slowly toward the intersection of Phan Dinh Phung Boulevard and Le Van Duyet Street. Three hundred and fifty Buddhist protesters carrying banners in Vietnamese and English that denounce the Diem regime follow right behind.

The Austin stops at the intersection. Thich Quang Duc gets out, gathering his robes about him as he does so. A cushion is placed on the street, and the aging monk sits down. He assumes the lotus position and begins to recite the words "return to eternal earth Buddha" over and over again.

Duc has come to this point in his life willingly, but nothing has prepared him for the moment when a fellow protester pours five gallons of gasoline over his bald head. The fuel soaks his robes and flows down his back until the cushion on which he sits is saturated.

The protesters gather in a circle around Duc to prevent the police from interfering. In one hand the monk holds a string of oak prayer beads. In the other he holds a match.

Duc lights the match.

There is no need to touch the flame to his person, because the fumes are enough to make his body burst into fire. His face, as seen through the flames, is a mask of pure agony. But Duc does not cry out or even make a sound. His skin turns black. His eyelids are fused shut. Yet as one minute passes, and then another, he still does not die.

The police cannot get to him; they are blocked by that protective circle of protesters. When a fire truck tries to get close enough to drench the monk with water, other monks throw their bodies beneath its wheels to stop it.

Finally, after ten agonizing minutes, Thich Quang Duc topples forward, dead.

His fellow monks lift the charred corpse into the coffin they have brought with them for this moment. The destroyed body does not fit, and one of Duc's arms sticks out from the lid as they carry him back to the Xa Loi Pagoda. His heart, they discover later, despite the intensity of the flames, is not badly damaged. The monks remove it from Duc's chest cavity and place it on display in a glass chalice.

In the months that follow, other monks will also martyr themselves. And one South Vietnamese official will even make the mistake of telling a reporter, "Let them burn and we shall clap our hands."

As in Birmingham, this moment is the beginning of the end for those who hold power in Saigon. And once again, an Associated Press photograph will make the difference.

Malcolm Browne, the AP Saigon bureau chief, was one of the few journalists to witness the immolation of Thich Quang Duc. His picture of the burning monk horrifies people around the world. And as with Bill Hudson's photo of police dogs attacking innocent protesters, that shot will become one of the most enduring and iconic images of the 1960s.

And again, John F. Kennedy will read his morning papers horrified by the photograph. Instantly, the president knows that his Vietnam problem has just escalated. He can no longer support President Diem. The world will turn on the Vietnamese leader after such a horrific image.

Diem must go.

The question facing John Kennedy, his fellow Catholic, is how?

This horrifying image of a Buddhist monk self-immolating became one of the most enduring images of protest against the Vietnam War. (Malcolm Browne/ Associated Press)

■ ■ ■

It is 5:45 P.M. on May 29 in Washington, D.C. President John Kennedy has had a busy day of back-to-back meetings in the Oval Office. Yet his burgundy tie is neatly cinched around his neck and his tailored navy blue suit coat looks as immaculate as when he put it on after his 1:00 P.M. nap. Right now, JFK is needed in the Navy Mess, on the lower level of the White House. He rises slowly from his desk, stretching his back as he does so, then begins the short walk downstairs.

The president has no illusions over what is about to transpire. Today is his forty-sixth birthday. His staff has abruptly disappeared, leading him to believe that they have already made their way to the Navy Mess for what is supposed to be a surprise party.

The cares of the world are never far from Kennedy's shoulders, even during a time of celebration. So as he walks to a party in his honor, there is a third incendiary situation looming over his administration. This problem has nothing to do with race or religion or war. Instead, it is about that most primal of all human longings: sex. And it has far more potential to end his presidency than does Birmingham or even Vietnam.

JFK has long been aware that revelations about his philandering would ruin not only that carefully burnished image of him as a family man but also his political future. Now he need look no further than Great Britain to see exactly what that downfall might look like. John Profumo, a dapper forty-eight-year-old British war hero and politician, has been caught having an affair with a twenty-one-year-old call girl named Christine Keeler. Profumo is married, and his wife, former film star Valerie Hobson, has chosen to forgive him. If Profumo were any other man, the embarrassing story might end there.

But John Profumo is also Britain's secretary of war and one of the most powerful men in the government of Prime Minister Harold Macmillan. And not only is Christine Keeler sleeping in his bed, but she is also having sex with a deputy Soviet naval attaché. When first confronted about his affair in the House of Commons, Profumo denied it. On June 5, he will be forced to admit that he lied. A disgraced Profumo will be shunned by his colleagues and forced to resign.

Profumo will disappear from the government and high society. His humiliation will be so complete that he will undertake extraordinary measures to seek redemption. He will volunteer to scrub toilets at a London shelter for the poor—a penance that he will continue to perform long after Queen Elizabeth restores his social status in 1975 by making him a Commander of the British Empire.

Prime Minister Macmillan is not guilty of a single indiscretion, but he is the man ultimately responsible for any secrets Profumo might inadvertently have leaked to his mistress. Seventy-one percent of the British public is in favor of either Macmillan's resignation or the chance to vote for a new prime minister via an immediate general election.

John Kennedy is riveted by the scandal. The similarities between himself and Profumo are too many to be ignored: both are nearly the same age, both have glamorous wives, both are decorated World War II veterans, and both men even go by the nickname Jack.

But there is no comparison in their womanizing. JFK's indiscretions go far beyond those of Profumo. John Kennedy has been extremely fortunate so far that no women have stepped forward to boast about bedding the president. And he has no reason to believe that any of the women who spent the night in the White House were spies. But as his brother Bobby reminds him, even one woman going to the tabloids could ruin him. The damage would go far beyond the innuendos Marilyn Monroe spread around Hollywood before her untimely death.

The irony is that Jackie's pregnancy has made John Kennedy more devoted to his wife and family than ever before. His staff has continued to see the president and First Lady holding hands and spending far more time together—though only Jackie bears witness to the president saying nightly prayers on his knees. Back in March, Secret Service agents were stunned when JFK actually showed up at the airport to greet Jackie, Caroline, and John upon their return from a trip. "The president had clearly missed his family and was eager to see them," agent Clint Hill will later write.

As Jackie's pregnancy becomes more visible, the Kennedys are spending more weekends together at Camp David, the presidential retreat in Maryland that Dwight Eisenhower famously named for his grandson. Situated on 125 acres in the Catoctin Mountains, the thickly forested retreat features miles of trails for walking, a large main cabin known as the Aspen Lodge, a putting green, a driving range, a skeet-shooting facility, horse stables, and a heated outdoor pool. Wire fences patrolled by Marine Corps guards ring the entire facility. Best of all to the Kennedy family, Camp David is one of the only places in the world where a Secret Service agent does not hover nearby every minute of the day. The marines are deemed enough to protect the First Family.

Now, in the Navy Mess, it is Jackie who leads the chorus of "Happy Birthday" the instant her husband enters the room. He feigns surprise as a glass of champagne is slipped into his hand and his staff gathers around to present an array of gag gifts.

But Jackie Kennedy has more surprises up her sleeve. For the party later moves from the Navy Mess to the presidential yacht, *Sequoia*. Only family and a few close friends are invited. As *Sequoia* cruises slowly up

Despite his infidelities, President Kennedy was devoted to his family, shown here on Easter Sunday, 1963. (Cecil Stoughton, White House Photographs, John F. Kennedy Presidential Library and Museum, Boston)

and down the Potomac, the quiet birthday gathering turns into a raging party. Dom Perignon 1955 flows, and music from a three-piece band blares in the aft salon. The Twist has gone out of style, but it's the president's favorite, so the band plays Chubby Checker again and again. Secret Service agent Clint Hill will later say that he's never seen John and Jackie Kennedy having more fun together, "doing the twist, the cha-cha, and everything in between."

The cruise is set to end at 10:30, but JFK is having so much fun that he orders the skipper to take her out for another hour. And another. And yet another, all the while ignoring the lightning and rain that keep Bobby, Ethel, Teddy, and the rest of the party indoors.

It's 1:20 in the morning when the *Sequoia* finally docks. Washington is asleep. John and Jackie Kennedy are awash in the romance of a very special evening. The Birminghams and Vietnams and Profumos will once again confront the president in the morning, but for now those problems are very far away.

The man with six months to live doesn't contemplate it, but those closest to him may remember his last birthday party as his very best.

12

JUNE 22, 1963
WASHINGTON, D.C.
LATE MORNING

"You've read about Profumo?" John Kennedy asks his guest.

The president and Martin Luther King Jr. walk alone through the White House Rose Garden. This is the first time they've met. Kennedy towers over the five-foot-six civil rights leader. Today is a Saturday and the start of a carefully orchestrated series of meetings between the White House and some powerful business groups to mobilize support for the civil rights movement. In a few hours, the president will board Air Force One for a trip to Europe, temporarily leaving the racial inferno behind. This will put control of White House business into the hands of Lyndon Johnson and Bobby Kennedy, whose feuding has reached an all-time high.

Before he goes, JFK has an important point to make to Reverend King. The president has hard evidence, provided by J. Edgar Hoover, that the civil rights leader has something in common with the disgraced British politician John Profumo.

In not so many words, the president is warning King to be smart and control his libido.

For both their sakes.

John Kennedy has thrown the power of his office behind the civil rights movement, but he has done so reluctantly. The president has no black friends. The nearest he comes to indulging in black culture is dancing to Chubby Checker. In John Kennedy's world, blacks are primarily valets, cooks, waiters, and maids. His forefathers were poor immigrants from Ireland who quickly took advantage of America's freedoms to achieve prosperity. JFK takes liberties for granted, even as generation after generation of children descended from slaves have never known such opportunities.

Bobby Kennedy is a driving force behind his brother's new stand. Bobby has become such a zealot for civil rights that his first name is considered an insult in the South. John Kennedy's finally standing up for the black man is a victory for Bobby as well.

May 1963 was a trying month, marked by confrontation after confrontation in Birmingham spurred by the racist Alabama governor George Wallace. The battles rage on. On June 11, after successfully ensuring that the University of Alabama was integrated, JFK delivered a major nationally televised address about civil rights. In a hastily written and partially improvised speech that would one day be counted among his best, the president promised that his administration would do everything it could to end segregation. He pushed Congress to "enact legislation giving all Americans the right to be served in facilities open to the public."

The very next day, civil rights activist Medgar Evers is shot dead in the driveway of his Mississippi home.

Integration, however, is not just a matter of doing the right thing. JFK's commitment has far-reaching ramifications. For instance, some Americans equate civil rights with communism. The last thing Kennedy needs during the height of the cold war is to be branded a Communist *and* a Negro sympathizer—even though he knows that many in the Deep South will immediately make that improbable leap.

And then there is Martin Luther King Jr.'s womanizing. This fact is well-known throughout the civil rights movement. King spends the majority of each month away from his home and from his wife, Coretta, who knows not to question him about his faithfulness. According to FBI surveillance and the admissions of his good friend Ralph Abernathy, King has sex with prostitutes, hangers-on, and even other men's wives. When pressed by friends, he does not deny the indiscretions, explaining that he needs sex to curb his anxiety during intense times when he is often very lonely. (Nearly a decade after Martin Luther King Jr. is assassinated in 1968, the FBI files on his private life will be sealed until the year 2027.)

Because Director Hoover believes King is a Communist, the FBI has been tapping King's phones and bugging his motel rooms for a year and a half. Hoover is obsessed with bringing King down. The FBI chief describes the civil rights leader as a "tomcat with obsessive degenerate sexual urges." Hoover fumes when King is named *Time* magazine's 1963 Man of the Year. (Kennedy won in 1961; Johnson will win in 1964.) J. Edgar Hoover actually spends hours listening to the secret recordings made of King's assignations. The president and attorney general are both informed of what is being recorded. Jackie Kennedy, who thinks King is a phony, will later remember her husband confiding the contents of a tape recording in which King "was calling up all these girls and arranging for a party of men and women, I mean, sort of an orgy in the hotel and everything."

The most infamous King recording will take place on January 6, 1964, at Washington, D.C.'s Willard Hotel. As recounted in Taylor Branch's *Pillar of Fire*, King is caught on tape saying, "I'm [having sex] for God. I'm not a negro tonight!"

None of these shenanigans would normally matter to John F. Kennedy. What King does in private is the good reverend's business. But the president has thrown in with the civil rights movement. Kennedy and King, its most prominent voice, are politically shackled at the wrist—like it or not.

And the president doesn't like it one bit. His alliance with King runs counter to every careful strand of his political DNA. There are enormous parallels between the two men. Kennedy can be impulsive in some aspects of his life, but he is precise and cautious when it comes to preparing for an election. King's infidelities, alleged Communist sympathies, and relentless pursuit of civil rights make their public association an enormous political risk. Even standing here in the relative privacy of the Rose Garden with Martin Luther King makes Kennedy sweat. "King is so hot," an exasperated JFK confided to Bobby before the reverend's arrival, "that it's like [Karl] Marx coming to the White House."

Martin Luther King Jr. could not care less about the president's discomfort. In fact, he's turning up the heat. Dr. King is planning a mass demonstration for August, on the Washington Mall. This moves the civil rights battle from the Deep South and into full view of the Oval Office. "What if they pee on the Washington Monument?" a horrified Kennedy says when he hears the news.

The president's words underscore a painful truth: unlike the Cuban missile crisis or even the failed Bay of Pigs invasion, the civil rights situation is a problem over which John Kennedy has little direct control. Martin Luther King Jr. is on the front lines in this battle. After his victory in Birmingham, it is King who is in command—and both men know it.

Now JFK wants some of that power back. "I assume you know you're under very close surveillance," he warns the civil rights leader.

King does not know. However, he doesn't rattle easily. The reverend is round to Kennedy's lean, and short to Kennedy's tall. Their upbringings couldn't have been more different. But Martin Luther King Jr. is every bit as educated, well-read, and politically savvy as the president. He didn't come this far by buckling to white men.

King laughs off the warning. Kennedy gets even more worried.

But Air Force One is waiting. This will be the president's first visit to Europe since the Cuban missile crisis. The cold war situation is still very tense. JFK will be leaping from one political quagmire and into another.

Before he leaves, JFK needs to know that King understands the problem.

Kennedy counters the reverend's evasiveness. He uses the Profumo affair to explain the potentially volatile link between his presidency and King's crusade.

JFK can be vague when he speaks, diplomatically letting listeners draw their own conclusions. But now he is painfully direct. There can be no mistake: King must sever his ties with Communists and be cautious about his infidelities.

"You must be careful not to lose your cause," the president warns. His point couldn't be clearer. "If they shoot you down, they'll shoot us down, too. So be careful."

The president of the United States has made his point. There is no more time. JFK cuts their conversation short and walks off to catch a plane.

Martin Luther King Jr. has five more years to live.

John Fitzgerald Kennedy has precisely five months.

■ ■ ■

In the meantime, the battle for control of the White House has begun. As the afternoon meeting in the Cabinet Room gets under way, President Kennedy is already on his way to Europe, taking with him most of his top staff. It is left to Lyndon Johnson and Bobby Kennedy to finish the civil rights agenda of June 22.

Lyndon Johnson is holding court. The president has unexpectedly placed him in charge, fearing a confrontation if he did not. The vice president sits in the president's chair at the center of the oblong table in the Cabinet Room. Notable for its headrest among a sea of back-high chairs, this chair is the acknowledged center of power. Bobby Kennedy sits on the far side. Twenty-nine civil rights leaders pack the small room. There aren't enough chairs. Many are forced to stand along the walls. Left unsaid is that there have never been so many black faces in the Cabinet Room.

For Bobby Kennedy and Lyndon Johnson, this is the ideal opportunity to show the gathering just who is boss.

The vice president does so by speechifying, proving to the civil rights leaders that he is their ally. Lyndon Johnson keeps his mouth shut as

Bobby Kennedy was the driving force behind the president's new stance on civil rights. Martin Luther King Jr. and other civil rights leaders are shown here with Bobby and the vice president on an official visit to the White House in 1963. (Cecil Stoughton, White House Photographs, John F. Kennedy Presidential Library and Museum, Boston)

often as possible when the president presides over a meeting. It's his way of keeping a tight rein on his passion for grand speeches. But now that he's in charge, Johnson rambles on and on about civil rights, an issue for which he has become passionate since his speech in St. Augustine. He followed this up with another address, on Memorial Day, at the Gettysburg battlefield in Pennsylvania.

That eloquent speech was a triumph. Coming at the end of May, it had the effect of placing Johnson in competition with the Kennedys for leadership on the civil rights issue. Upon his return to Washington,

Johnson had begged for "fifteen minutes alone with the president," in order to build on that success. Kennedy granted that request. Johnson used that time to wedge himself further into the civil rights battle.

Lyndon Johnson's long-winded Cabinet Room speech does not please Bobby Kennedy. Civil rights are *his* issue, and it was largely at his urging that his brother joined the cause. Bobby doesn't just want Lyndon off civil rights; he wants him out of the White House altogether. With Johnson's political power in the South rapidly declining, the Kennedys might not need him on the ticket in 1964. There is a good chance they can win the state of California, whose thirty-two electoral votes more than make up for losing the twenty-five that Johnson might have delivered with Texas. There is also growing evidence that Johnson has become so weak in his home state that Texas will be lost, even if LBJ remains on the ticket.

There is even talk of a Kennedy-Kennedy ticket in 1964.

So Bobby is fearless as he sits across the Cabinet Room table from Johnson—fearless enough to be rude.

The attorney general crooks a finger, beckoning Louis Martin, a black newspaper publisher. "I've got a date," he whispers as Martin comes to his side. "Can you tell the vice president to cut it short?"

Martin is terrified. He knows both men are capable of great rage. Martin diplomatically returns to his place along the wall.

Bobby doesn't waste any time. He beckons Martin again. "Didn't I tell you to tell the vice president to shut up?"

Now Martin has no choice. He owes Bobby Kennedy a favor—a very big favor. When Louis Martin's good friend Martin Luther King Jr. was jailed for civil rights demonstrations in 1960, Bobby swung support to King's cause by placing a sympathetic phone call to the reverend's wife, Coretta. Of course, that phone call also helped the Kennedys politically, swinging the black vote behind JFK.

The room is not big enough to hide Martin's discomfort. It's obvious to everyone around the table that something is going on. Lyndon Johnson is speaking from his bully pulpit in the chair with the headrest, while Bobby has now twice called the fifty-year-old Martin to his side.

Martin is held in such high esteem that he will one day be known as "the Godfather of Black Politics." So this is not a minor underling whom Bobby has summoned. This is a man known to everyone. And the attorney general has clearly whispered some angry words in Louis Martin's ears.

Martin carefully maneuvers between the many bodies and chairs. Lyndon Johnson pretends not to notice—even though he's a man who notices everything.

Martin is cautious. His progress around the table is not fast, and no one takes his eyes off him.

Lyndon Johnson is speaking as if nothing odd is happening. It's true that all eyes are upon him—but only because Louis Martin is finally standing behind him.

Martin bends over and places his lips near Johnson's ear. The vice president never stops talking.

"Bobby has got to go and he wants to close it up," Martin whispers.

Johnson turns his head so that his eyes bore directly into Louis Martin's. The vice president gazes at him icily but never once stops talking.

In fact, much to the rage of Bobby Kennedy, Lyndon Johnson rambles on for another fifteen minutes.

This battle for control of the White House is not about the ten days JFK will be in Europe but about that all-important spot on the ticket in 1964. And while Lyndon Johnson may have finished his speech, Bobby's move let everyone know who held the real power in the room.

Bobby Kennedy is winning this war. The more Lyndon Johnson realizes this, the sicker and more depressed he will become. Reversing his previous weight loss, LBJ will grow very fat over the course of the summer as a result of this despondence. His face will become mottled, leading some to think he has begun drinking heavily.

The Kennedy brothers have broken the man who once considered himself Washington, D.C.'s ultimate power broker.

■ ■ ■

Lee Harvey Oswald has two passions in the summer of 1963: reading and lying.

He spends the month of June working as a maintenance man for the Reily Coffee Company in New Orleans. Oswald collects unemployment even though he has a job. He writes to the Fair Play for Cuba Committee in New York about all he is doing on its behalf. He prints business cards in the fictitious name of A. J. Hidell that list him as president of Fair Play, and even submits a passport application with false information. Lee Harvey Oswald has become an ardent Communist, with the intention of committing yet another bold act to further that political cause.

Oswald's employers are not thrilled with his job performance, complaining that he spends too many of his working hours reading gun magazines.

Marina lives with him in yet another apartment she can't stand. The family sleeps on pallets, and she sprays a ring of bug repellent on the floor each night to keep away the cockroaches. She knows that her husband is applying for a visa that could return them to the Soviet Union, even though she doesn't want to go. In fact, because he is applying separately for his own visa, it appears he may be trying to send the pregnant Marina and their daughter, June, back to Russia without him.

Lee Harvey Oswald is far from the great man he believes he will one day become. Right now he is a drifter who spends his off time trying to make wine from blackberries, barely clinging to employment, and treating his family like a nuisance.

Reading fuels Oswald's rage. He devours several books a week. The topics range in subject matter from a Chairman Mao biography to James Bond novels. Then, as summer 1963 concludes its first weeks, Oswald chooses to read about subject matter he's never before explored: John F. Kennedy.

In fact, Lee Harvey is so enchanted by William Manchester's bestseller *Portrait of a President* that after returning it to the New Orleans Public Library, he checks out Kennedy's *Profiles in Courage*.

The collection of essays, which won John Kennedy the Pulitzer Prize in 1957, is about the lives and actions of eight great men.

Even in the midst of the squalor and depression that define the Oswalds' New Orleans summer, Lee Harvey Oswald reads JFK's carefully chosen words and is inspired to hope that one day he, too, will exhibit that sort of courage.

■ ■ ■

On day seven of his trip to Europe, John Kennedy rides in an open-air convertible through the narrow, twisting streets of Galway, Ireland. The crowd is manic and presses in close toward the Cadillac. The many tight turns force the president's driver to slow the car to a crawl. Some Secret Service agents believe that seaports such as Galway are higher-risk environments than inland cities because of their large immigrant populations, but as is always the case when a motorcade route causes the president's car to slow down for a turn, the intersection has been thoroughly prechecked by an advance team of agents.

But the tight turns are not the only potential hazard: the buildings lining the route are mostly two stories tall. The distance between their upper windows and the president's motorcade is a third of the distance between General Ted Walker and the alley where Lee Harvey Oswald hid on the night of April 10, 1963.

In fact, John F. Kennedy is traveling through the ideal kill zone. One man with a gun could squeeze off a shot and escape into the throngs in a matter of seconds. And the president is clearly aware that such a thing might happen. He has been thinking quite a bit about martyrs lately and has become fond of quoting a verse by Irish poet Thomas Davis:

> *We thought you would not die—we were sure you would not go;*
> *And leave us in our utmost need to Cromwell's cruel blow—*
> *Sheep without a shepherd when the snow shuts out the sky—*
> *Oh, why did you leave us, Eoghan? Why did you die?*

But today the specter of death doesn't seem to matter. It is Saturday, June 29, 1963. An estimated hundred thousand Irish citizens line the streets of that raucous port city on the west coast of Ireland. Six hundred Gardai, police, are there to hold back the cheering crowds.

Due to Jackie Kennedy's history of troubled pregnancies, she did not make the trip to Europe, as she so famously did two years ago. John Kennedy has the adulation of the crowds all to himself.

Many questioned why the president would go to Europe at such a volatile time. The title of an editorial in last Sunday's edition of the *New York Times* asked, "Is This Trip Necessary?"

"In the face of much adverse comment and good reasons not to go," the editorial went on to say, "President Kennedy is proceeding with his trip to Europe at a most inauspicious time."

But John Kennedy knows the power of good political timing, and the trip has been a smashing success. At a time when the civil rights controversy has threatened to damage his presidency, the European trip proves that he is clearly the most popular and charismatic man in the world. More than a million Germans lined his motorcade route in Cologne when he arrived there a week ago. Twenty million more Europeans watched him on television. And another million greeted him in West Berlin. There, to chants of "Ken-ne-DEE," he won over the crowd with a powerful prodemocracy speech. "All free men, wherever they live, are citizens of Berlin," said the president. "And therefore, as a free man, I take pride in the words, 'Ich bin ein Berliner.'"

The crowd went wild.

JFK's Berlin speech was a security nightmare for the Secret Service. The president stood alone and unprotected on a podium as thousands looked on. The crowd wasn't checked for weapons, and many watched from rooftops or open windows. John Kennedy, in the words of one agent, was a "sitting duck."

Or, in the words of another agent: "All it takes is one lucky shot."

■ ■ ■

In Moscow, Soviet premier Nikita Khrushchev, fearing that Kennedy's popularity would lead to an erosion of support in East Berlin, quickly flew to that divided city to reassert his nation's claims. He and Kennedy did not meet. In fact, crowds a fraction of the size that greeted Kennedy even noticed that Khrushchev was in town, underscoring JFK's amazing popularity and sending a clear message that Khrushchev's power was on the wane.

John F. Kennedy's European presence even affects the arrogant French president, Charles de Gaulle. From his perch in Paris, de Gaulle has become the bully of Western European politics, but he has more than met his match in JFK, prompting an amazed *New York Times* writer to marvel that "for the first time, President de Gaulle had been confronted by a Western leader whose ideas on that future are as firm as his own, whose confidence in the ultimate triumph of his ideas is as great and who, finally, speaks for the most powerful nation in the community."

Kennedy and de Gaulle do not meet on this trip, but the French leader watches every move the president makes.

■ ■ ■

And then comes Ireland.

"If you go to Ireland," Appointments Secretary Kenny O'Donnell pointed out when Kennedy adds it to his European itinerary, "people will just say it's a pleasure trip."

"That's exactly what I want," the president replied. "A pleasure trip to Ireland."

He has been lauded everywhere he has traveled in the small island nation, hailed as a victorious returning son.

Galway comes on his fourth day in Ireland, and it's clear by his easy smile and the playful way he interacts with the locals that the pressures of domestic affairs, foreign problems, and the impending birth of his third child seem a million miles away.

Three hundred and twenty children from the Convent of St. Mercy greet the president's helicopter as it lands on a grassy seaside field at 11:30 A.M. Each of the children is dressed in orange, green, or white, and arranged so that together they form the Irish flag.

Then it is into an open-top limousine for the short drive to Eyre Square, at the center of the city. At one house, Kennedy orders the driver to stop so that he can spend a few minutes talking with the women standing out front.

The speech he gives in Eyre Square is the most heartwarming and personal of JFK's entire presidency, harkening back to the emotional beginnings of his political career in Boston. The president is utterly at ease as he looks out upon the thousands who fill the square, which will one day be renamed in his honor. This visit is not a campaign stop, or a fund-raising dinner, or even one of those significant historical occasions he might mark with a speech filled with gravity and somber words.

This is a visit from a man whose heart has been touched by the people of his homeland at a time when he needs that very much, and who hopes that his words might do the same for them. "If the day was clear enough, and you went down to the bay, and you looked west, and your sight was good enough, you could see Boston, Massachusetts," he tells the adoring crowd.

"And if you could," he continues, "you would see down there working on the docks there some Doughertys and Flahertys and Ryans and cousins of yours who have gone to Boston and made good."

And then the president asks for a show of hands from the crowd, asking the people of Galway if they have a relative in America. The square is instantly filled with hands thrust to the sky. The crowd roars in laughter and recognition, and bursts into applause. The president is truly one of their own.

The impact is overwhelming. Kennedy's words speak to a belief in the American dream. But those words are more than a dream to these people. No child of an immigrant in the history of the world has returned to his homeland and enjoyed this sort of adulation. Just one look at Kennedy as he gazes out over the crowd is proof that a family can come to America with nothing and someday reach the highest level. John F. Kennedy, a son of Ireland, is now the most powerful man in the world.

■ ■ ■

Left unsaid on that day is that black immigrants to America still don't have that opportunity. But Kennedy is working on it.

"If you ever come to America," the president closes, after talking about the bright days he has spent in Ireland, "come to Washington. And tell them, if they wonder who you are at the gate, that you come from Galway. The word will be out and when you do, 'Cead Mile Failte'— One hundred thousand welcomes.

"Thank you and good-bye."

Kennedy is driven back through town and returns to his helicopter just forty-five minutes after arriving. The love of his homeland courses through his veins. The president has nothing to fear in this motorcade, from these people.

Thousands of snapshots are taken of JFK that day. Many of them remain hanging in the pubs and homes of Galway.

13

⌒

AUGUST 7, 1963
OSTERVILLE, MASSACHUSETTS
MORNING

Enjoying the New England summer, a very pregnant Jackie Kennedy leans on a chest-high fence rail watching five-year-old Caroline's horseback riding lesson. The First Lady and the children are spending the summer at a rented cottage named Brambletyde, just a short distance from the Kennedy family compound at Hyannis Port. Normally, the First Family would stay in the house they own adjacent to the compound property.

The president's father and Bobby Kennedy own homes right next door. This enclave has long been the family oasis for planning campaigns, celebrating weddings, or just playing a spirited game of touch football. The Kennedy presence has put Cape Cod, Massachusetts, on the map.

So much so that hordes of tourists now invade the area each summer. The raucous crowds have gotten in the habit of trampling shrubbery and causing traffic headaches on the narrow beachfront streets in their desire to catch a glimpse of JFK and Jackie. The Hyannis Port property is also a security nightmare for the Secret Service, which is why the First Family has rented a more secluded residence for the summer of 1963. Jackie and the children are there all the time, while the president commutes from Washington on weekends.

Brambletyde is concealed by thick woods and is accessible only by driving down a narrow one-lane gravel road. From both a privacy and a security standpoint, renting the home makes perfect sense.

There is another reason Jackie chose Brambletyde: she doesn't want any of the press taking photos of her pregnant. She doesn't even go into town, letting the head of her Secret Service detail, Clint Hill, pick up the tabloids she secretly loves to read.

Today is Wednesday. Hill is taking the day off. The veteran agent is vigilant in his protection of the First Lady. He works six days a week, sometimes sixteen hours a day. But now Special Agent Paul Landis is taking his place. Landis stands near the riding ring, keeping a trained eye on the First Lady while Special Agent Lynn Meredith, of the "kiddie detail," hovers nearby to protect Caroline.

Suddenly Jackie feels a sharp pain in her abdomen. Then another. Soon the pain won't stop. "Mr. Landis, I don't feel well," she says, sensing a crisis. "I think you'd better take me back to the house."

"Of course, Mrs. Kennedy." But there is no urgency in Landis's movements.

"Right now, Mr. Landis," Jackie commands. Her breathy voice has a sharp edge.

Landis rushes to the car and holds open the rear door. Jackie's face has a fearful look as she slides into the backseat. The pain is coming from her womb. Her growing panic is caused by painful memories of the two troubled earlier pregnancies that ended in the loss of children. Jackie miscarried in 1955. Her second pregnancy resulted, on August 23, 1956, in a stillborn baby girl, whom she and her husband christened Arabella. The loss of even a single child is staggering. Losing two, even more so. But to lose a third baby, particularly after delivering two healthy children, would be intolerable for Jackie.

So although the First Lady is just a few short weeks away from a full-term delivery, she takes nothing for granted when it comes to her unborn baby's welfare.

Caroline stays with Agent Meredith as Landis drives eighty miles an hour down the narrow road, at the same time radioing ahead to have a doctor and a helicopter on standby.

The First Lady's anxiety increases as it becomes clearer that she's going into labor. "Please go faster," she commands.

The time has come to get to a hospital—immediately. Should Landis be unable to get there in time, it's very likely that the Secret Service agent will be forced to pull over and personally deliver the president's child in the backseat of a government sedan.

Agent Landis presses down harder on the gas.

■ ■ ■

In Washington, President John Fitzgerald Kennedy confronts a different kind of problem. Polls show that his popularity in the crucial state of Texas has dipped to an all-time low—and continues to drop. The state is growing increasingly conservative and Republican. Lyndon Johnson has lost all political power there. This hurts not just in potential electoral votes, but in the wallet, too. Texas has long been a major source of Democratic campaign funding, thanks to the deep pockets of its wealthy oilmen and other big-business people. And once upon a time, LBJ could be counted upon to deliver that money. But now Texas governor John Connally, a conservative Democrat, holds the purse strings—and behind the scenes, he is not a big Kennedy fan.

Therein lies the problem: JFK has been pushing Johnson to arrange a fund-raising trip to Texas. But Johnson knows that such a trip will reveal his lack of clout, making it obvious to the president that Connally will be the man delivering the big donors to the Kennedy campaign. This will further erode any chance of Johnson remaining on the ticket.

Making matters even more complicated, not only has LBJ deliberately avoided arranging any trip by the president to Texas, but Governor Connally is also trying to prevent Kennedy from coming to the state.

Both are Democrats, but the governor knows that any public appearance he makes with Kennedy will cost him dearly with Texas voters.

But John Kennedy needs Texas and its money. He is determined to make the trip a reality.

That is the problem hanging over the president's head on the morning of August 7. In an instant, it will be almost completely forgotten.

■ ■ ■

Secret Service agent Jerry Behn approaches the desk of Evelyn Lincoln. It is 11:37 A.M.

Special Agent Behn discreetly informs the president's secretary that Jackie is being airlifted to the hospital at Otis Air Force Base, located near Falmouth, Massachusetts, on the western edge of Cape Cod. The agent also tells Lincoln that the First Lady doesn't want her husband to be disturbed, in case the labor pains are a false alarm.

Evelyn Lincoln, knowing the president's deep emotional involvement in Jackie's pregnancy, steps into the Oval Office anyway.

"Jerry tells me that Mrs. Kennedy is on her way to Otis," she says calmly, passing along the message without trying to upset the president or his guests unnecessarily.

It doesn't work. The meeting is immediately adjourned. A hasty series of phone calls confirm that Jackie is being sedated and is about to deliver the Kennedys' new child by Caesarean section. The president summons Air Force One.

But all four of the president's airplanes are unavailable today.

JFK doesn't care. He demands an airplane, any airplane, immediately.

■ ■ ■

One hour later, as the president of the United States, his Secret Service detail, and select members of his staff race to Otis Air Force Base crammed inside a small six-passenger JetStar aircraft, Patrick Bouvier Kennedy takes his first breath. The president's second son weighs just four pounds, ten and a half ounces.

However, there are grave concerns about that breath. It appears shallow and labored. The baby grunts as he exhales. His skin has a bluish pallor, and his chest wall is retracted. The infant is immediately placed in an incubator.

Baby Patrick is assigned a Secret Service agent, even though it's becoming clear that the only direct threat against the newborn's life comes from within his own body. The lungs are among the last organs to develop in the womb, and young Patrick is suffering from hyaline membrane disease, the most common form of death among children born prematurely.

The First Lady is still sedated from her Caesarean and doesn't know of the problem. As soon as the president arrives, he takes command. He huddles with Dr. John Walsh to discuss the status of his new son. The doctor explains that there is a chance Patrick might die. Kennedy immediately summons the base chaplain to baptize Patrick, ensuring that his son will go to heaven, based upon the teachings of the Catholic Church.

Dr. Walsh then makes the suggestion that Patrick be moved to Children's Hospital in Boston, which has state-of-the-art facilities for treating hyaline membrane disease. The president immediately agrees.

At 5:55 P.M., as Jackie is still shaking off the grogginess of her sedation, Patrick Bouvier Kennedy is placed in an ambulance for the hour-long drive to Boston.

This child is precious cargo. Far dearer than the *Mona Lisa*. So like the famous painting, Patrick makes the journey escorted by a full complement of Massachusetts police. Sirens wail as the ambulance pulls away from the air force hospital.

The caravan does not stop. The baby's life must be saved.

■ ■ ■

Now comes the waiting. Jackie Kennedy remains in her ten-room maternity suite, recovering. So it is the president who moves on to Boston to hold vigil at Children's Hospital. This is a far different man from the one who, in 1956, waited three days before returning from Europe to see his wife after her first miscarriage. Now he stares helplessly at the thirty-one-foot-long experimental high-pressure chamber in which the small body of his son gasps for air. Patrick can clearly be seen through the chamber's small windows. The intensive care unit is cleared of all visitors whenever JFK is on the floor, which only adds to the president's solitude.

"How are things with little Patrick?" Evelyn Lincoln gently asks. She has made the trip to Boston to help the president manage the many details of his office that still need his attention.

"He has a fifty-fifty chance," JFK responds.

"That's all a Kennedy needs," she assures him, knowing that her long-time boss will appreciate this sort of encouragement.

World leaders and good friends barrage Kennedy with phone calls and messages, but he never takes the focus off his newborn son. The president has a deep love for children. This baby, conceived in the wake of the Cuban missile crisis, holds special significance. This is the child who would have never entered the world if the crisis had ended in global thermonuclear war. Patrick Bouvier Kennedy, who is named for JFK's paternal grandfather and for Jackie's father, has been a source of pride and concern ever since the day the First Lady announced she was pregnant.

The president has a room at the Ritz-Carlton overlooking Boston Common, where he spends the first night of Patrick's life restlessly passing the hours reading up on documents for a nuclear test ban treaty. But he prefers to spend the second night closer to his ailing son and moves from the luxury of the Ritz-Carlton to an empty hospital room.

At 2:00 A.M. on August 9, Secret Service agent Larry Newman gently awakens him. JFK gets up in an instant and rides the hospital elevator to the pediatric unit on the fifth floor, along with Dr. Walsh and Special Agent Newman. The Secret Service veteran has seen a great deal during his time on the White House detail and knows the president's moods and personal issues intimately. Newman, who admits he doesn't cry easily, has himself been on the verge of tears during this heartbreaking ordeal.

Now Special Agent Newman sees anguish settle upon the president's shoulders. Dr. Walsh is informing JFK that Patrick is in grave condition and is unlikely to survive until the morning. The baby's underdeveloped young lungs aren't functioning properly. He has begun to suffer prolonged periods of apnea, with his body refusing to breathe at all.

The elevator door opens. The hallway is dark and empty at this early hour. John Kennedy begins the slow trek to the intensive care unit to gaze upon his dying son.

Then the president hears the sound of children's laughter. Curious, JFK pokes his head into the room from which it is coming. Two little girls sit up in bed. They are young, just three or four years old. Both have bandages covering large portions of their bodies.

"What's wrong with them?" he asks Dr. Walsh.

They're burn victims, explains the doctor, who goes on to add that one girl may soon lose the use of her hands.

The president pats his pockets, searching for a pen. He doesn't have one. This isn't unusual. The only thing he carries in his pockets is a handkerchief.

Special Agent Newman and Dr. Walsh come up with a pen. A nurse, seeing that the president has no paper, finds a scrap from the nurse's station. Then JFK writes a note to the children, telling them to be courageous, letting them know that the president of the United States cares for their well-being. The nurse assures him that she will give the note to their parents. "Nothing was ever said about it," Newman will later recall. "He just went on to do what he had to do—to see his son. This was part of the dichotomy of the man—the rough-cut diamond."

Patrick Bouvier Kennedy dies just two hours later. "He was such a beautiful baby," the president laments to top aide Dave Powers. "He put up quite a fight."

Kennedy is holding young Patrick's hand as the child breathes his last. As the president absorbs the terrible moment, he is well aware that his grief is not private. The nurses, doctors, and his own staff watch to see how he handles this awful moment. Slowly, JFK leaves the room and wanders the hospital hallway, keeping his pain to himself.

■ ■ ■

In the outside world, there is so much going on. A movie about Kennedy's old boat, PT-109, is a popular summer hit, further burnishing the president's heroic image. The political situation in Texas is a growing mess that the president himself will try to fix by visiting the state in a few short months. In Chicago, mobster Sam Giancana is swearing revenge on the Kennedy brothers for tightening surveillance on his alleged criminal behavior. Ninety miles from Florida, Fidel Castro is in a rage about ongoing American covert activity in Cuba. In the nation's capital, Martin Luther King Jr. is about to direct hundreds of thousands of civil rights protesters onto the Washington Mall. In Vietnam, the chain-smoking Catholic despot Diem is out of control. And, finally, in New Orleans, a ne'er-do-well named Lee Harvey Oswald is under arrest for distributing Communist literature, leading the FBI finally to reopen their investigation into his behavior.

But right now none of that matters to John Fitzgerald Kennedy.

The president's son has died. He lived just thirty-nine hours. The grief is almost too much to bear.

JFK takes the elevator back upstairs to the room in which he had been sleeping. There, he sits down on the bed, lowers his head, and sobs.

"He just cried and cried and cried," Dave Powers will later remember.

■ ■ ■

Sixty-five miles to the south, Jackie is also overcome with agonizing grief. The press swarms outside the hospital at Otis Air Force Base. A few hours later, the president arrives to be with his wife.

Even in the midst of her incredible pain, the First Lady can see how much her husband is also suffering. Gently, she reminds him that they still have each other, as well as John and Caroline.

"The one blow I could not bear," Jackie tells JFK, "would be to lose you."

14

~

August 28, 1963
Washington, D.C.
Afternoon

"Five score years ago, a great American, in whose symbolic shadow we stand today, signed the Emancipation Proclamation," begins Martin Luther King Jr. His words are scripted. His mannerisms are unusually stiff, as befitting a man speaking before such a massive audience for the first time.

Daniel Chester French's iconic white marble statue of Abraham Lincoln looms over King's shoulder. One of Lincoln's fists is curled into the sign language letter A; the other displays the sign language L. The Great Emancipator's shoulders are slumped, and his head is slightly lowered, as if he still carries the great burden of being president. It has been one hundred years since Lincoln freed the slaves, and now King is telling a crowd of hundreds of thousands that black Americans are still not free.

The crowd is silent as he begins his speech. He can hear them fidgeting. The applause is light and polite, when it comes at all. King reminds them that America is still a segregated nation, one hundred years after the slaves were freed. It is a powerful thought, but his matter-of-fact delivery robs the words of their full impact.

King rambles on, the sound system carrying his voice out across the Mall and television cameras transporting his voice and image into homes across the nation.

John Kennedy is considered a great orator for his speeches' carefully chosen words and phrasing, as is Dr. King. But on his best days, Reverend King takes his oration to an even higher level than Kennedy by adding the techniques learned from countless Sunday mornings speaking from the pulpit: thunder and whisper as his voice rises and falls, the changing pace as the reverend speeds up and slows down to make the listener hang on his every word, the stretching or shortening of syllables to accentuate a point. King, in particular, is fond of coming down hard on the letter *t* when he desires emphasis.

Normally, King's delivery is fearless and sure, transforming words of damning rage into a hopeful prayer.

But today his delivery is flat. His long syllables and prepared words sound no different from those of any of the day's other speakers. Martin Luther King Jr., truth be told, is dull.

He talks about poverty and the fact that America separates black from white. Today is the eighth anniversary of Emmett Till's murder. King's words testify that little has changed since then.

Many in the crowd have traveled hundreds of miles to be here today. They are black and they are white. The day has been long, filled with hours of speeches—many of which have been downright boring.

But Martin Luther King Jr. is the man they've waited to hear. And the fatigue and the heat and the claustrophobia are all forgotten as these 250,000 people strain to hear his every word. They have come for the cause of civil rights, but they have also come to hear the great orator shape this day for them. As they listen to the speech, King's mellifluous voice carrying out over the reflecting pools between the Lincoln Memorial and the Washington Monument, the audience knows in their hearts that King will rally them to greatness.

This is their expectation: that before this speech is done, Martin Luther King Jr. will say something so powerful that this day will never be forgotten.

The crowd listens closely, but as King's speech passes the nine-minute mark, he has said almost nothing that excites them.

Two minutes later all that changes.

■ ■ ■

Meanwhile, in the White House, John Kennedy watches King's speech on television. It is exactly three weeks since Jackie went into labor with baby Patrick. She is mourning in seclusion on Cape Cod, her easy smile replaced by a solemn downward gaze and her eyes hidden behind over-size sunglasses. The president has been vigilant about breaking away from Washington whenever possible to be with her.

But today, a Wednesday, is one day he absolutely must be in Washington, D.C. Bobby Kennedy and their brother Teddy, the new senator from Massachusetts, join JFK as he watches King begin speaking.

The attorney general is a major advocate for the civil rights movement, but his relationship with Dr. King is strained. Part of this is because he has heard J. Edgar Hoover's wiretap recordings of King, and part is because Bobby is being protective of the president.

Since King announced the March on Washington three months ago, it is Bobby who has become its reluctant organizer. He knows that his brother's foray into civil rights will fail if the rally at the Lincoln Memorial turns hostile or is sparsely attended. So the attorney general, working closely with his staff at the Justice Department, has quietly guided the march into a shape that can be easily controlled. He made sure that the Lincoln Memorial was the site of King's speech, because it's bordered on one side by the Potomac River and on the other by the Tidal Basin. This would make crowd control smoother in case of riots and also keep marchers away from the Capitol Building and the White House.

Bobby ensured that Washington's police dogs were not on the scene, because dogs would remind people of Bull Connor and Birmingham. He saw to it that all bars and liquor stores were closed for the day, portable toilets were available to avoid his brother's fear about public urination, and that troops were on standby at nearby military bases in case the crowd turned into a mob. To avoid the appearance that the civil rights movement was supported only by blacks, Bobby worked with the United Auto Workers Union to encourage attendance by its white members. And he even arranged for an aide to position himself below the speaker's platform with a copy of Mahalia Jackson's "He's Got the Whole World (in His Hands)" to be played over the sound system the instant one of the day's speakers said something inflammatory or anti-American.

Nothing can be done that reflects poorly on the White House or its belated push for civil rights.

And all this, to support Martin Luther King Jr., a man of whom Bobby acidly commented just last night, "He's not a serious person. If the country knew what we know about King's goings-on, he'd be finished."

Just as the Kennedys would be finished if the country knew about the president's goings-on.

So it is that the president and his brothers watch King's speech with great interest, praying that their unlikely political ally will deliver on the promise of this great march on Washington.

■■■

"We cannot be satisfied as long as a Negro in Mississippi cannot vote and a Negro in New York believes he has nothing for which to vote," Martin Luther King Jr. preaches—and that is exactly what he is doing right now, on the verge of swerving away from his prepared speech to quote from the Old Testament book of Amos.

King's anxiety is so great that he often develops painful stomach problems before a big event. But now his nervousness is gone. His voice begins to rise. His long syllables become staccato. He hits hard on the letter *t* in the word *ghetto*.

Looking out across the Mall, King can see that the weariness of those hundreds of thousands listening to his speech has vanished. His voice rises. He has spoken in paragraphs until now, but, as the words begin to flow, those paragraphs become simple, powerful declarative sentences.

Martin Luther King Jr. has found his rhythm.

Gone is the monotone. Gone is the matter-of-fact delivery. He stands in the pulpit now, a minister exhorting his flock. King's voice turns golden.

And then, for the first time, he belts out the phrase that will come to define this day forever:

"I have a dream!" King proclaims.

Now Martin Luther King owns the crowd. The entire Mall is in a fever pitch.

And then he tells them about that dream. King describes an earthly paradise where blacks and whites are not divided. He dreams that even a hostile southern state like Mississippi will know such wonders.

This dream of King's is a complete and utter fantasy in America right now. But he is putting into words the ultimate goal of the civil rights movement. And for the people in the crowd to hear it stated so powerfully and clearly has them beside themselves with emotion and pride. Black and white alike, they hang on King's every word. In a speech that is just sixteen minutes long, King has proved that today is truly, as he hoped, the greatest day for civil rights in American history.

By the time King winds up for the great finish, he is shouting into the microphone, flecks of spittle bursting from his mouth. The image of Lincoln gazing over his shoulder is profoundly moving as King calls upon the spirit of the Emancipation Proclamation. It is clear to all who stand out on the Mall that King plans to finish what Lincoln began so long ago and that the two men—divided by a century of racial injustice— are forever linked in history from this day forward.

"'Free at last, free at last,'" he quotes from a Negro spiritual, "'thank God almighty, we are free at last.'"

As the crowd on the Mall erupts in applause, knowing they have just seen and heard a profound moment in their nation's history, John Kennedy turns to Bobby and passes judgment on what he has just seen.

"He's damned good."

■ ■ ■

One hour later, an exultant Martin Luther King Jr. meets with John Kennedy in the Oval Office. There are eleven other people in attendance, including Lyndon Johnson, so this visit is not a summit meeting between the president of the United States and the most powerful man in the civil rights movement. But Kennedy makes sure King knows he's been paying attention to the day's events.

"I have a dream," he tells King, adding a nod of the head to show approval—and that his fears about King have been temporarily set aside.

■ ■ ■

But the March on Washington does not change the ongoing racial battle in the American South. At 10:22 A.M. on September 15, 1963, less than three weeks after America listened to Martin Luther King Jr. dream about black boys and girls in Alabama joining hands with white boys and girls, twenty-six black children are led into the basement of the Sixteenth Street Baptist Church for Sunday morning services. They are due to hear a children's sermon on "The Love That Forgives."

The Sixteenth Street Baptist Church is the same congregation that launched the Children's Crusade on Birmingham in May 1963. It stands just across from the park where Bull Connor's police dogs bit into the flesh of innocent black teenagers and elementary school students and has earned a special level of hatred from the white supremacist groups that still battle to block the integration of Birmingham.

The children attending church this Sunday morning cannot possibly know that four members of the Ku Klux Klan have planted a box of dynamite near the basement. So the explosion that shatters the spiritual calm of the church service is completely unexpected. The force of the blast is so great that it doesn't just destroy the basement, but also blows out the back wall of the church and destroys every stained-glass window in the building—all but one. That lone surviving window portrays an image of Jesus Christ ministering to a group of small children.

The window is symbolic in a sense, because almost all of the children in the basement this Sunday morning survive the horrific tragedy. However, four of them—Addie Mae Collins, Cynthia Wesley, Carole Robertson, and Denise McNair—do not.

Their dream has come to an end.

15

～

SEPTEMBER 2, 1963
HYANNIS PORT, MASSACHUSETTS
NOON

"Oh, God," reads a small plaque given to the president, "thy sea is so great and my boat is so small."

On this Labor Day, John Kennedy sees a small boat bobbing in the distance as he removes his American Optical Saratoga sunglasses and eases himself into a wicker chair on the grass of Brambletyde's beachfront yard. Sitting directly across from the president, CBS journalist Walter Cronkite does the same, preparing for one of the biggest TV interviews of his life. Today the subject is the rough waters and turbulent swells being navigated by the president of the United States. Both men wear dark suits, even as the September sun beats directly down on them. Cronkite crosses his legs, while Kennedy's are stretched out in front of him. The wind messes up JFK's carefully combed hair, forcing him to reach up absentmindedly every few minutes to press it back into place. The balding Cronkite has no such problem.

At forty-six, roughly the same age as Kennedy, Walter Cronkite is considered the nation's premier television newsman. He and the president have an easy rapport, and JFK is so comfortable that he leans back in his cushioned chair during parts of the interview, just as he does when thinking over a tough problem in the Oval Office.

The two men casually banter as they are miked for sound and then sit quietly opposite each other as the final ten seconds before taping are counted down. Cronkite acknowledges an off-camera signal, and the interview begins.

The broadcaster aims his questions at JFK in a delivery that alternates between baritone rumble and easy drawl. His interviewing style is disarming and even warm, no matter how sharp his queries. As a result, Kennedy remains completely at ease. The interview sounds like a conversation between two friends well-informed about American politics. And truth be told, that isn't far from Cronkite's mind-set. He is a devoted Democrat, although he skillfully hides that fact from his viewing audience.

"Do you think you'll lose some Southern states in '64?" Cronkite asks.

"Well I lost some in '60, so I suppose I'll lose some in, uh, maybe more in '64," Kennedy smiles wistfully, forced to reveal a painful political weakness. Cronkite is letting Americans in on a secret known only to pollsters and veteran politicians. "I don't know. It's too early to tell, but I would think we were, I'm not sure that, uh, I'm the most popular figure in the country today in the South. But that's all right. I think we're going to have to wait and see a year and a half from now . . ."

There is now a fighting spirit in the president's eyes. The mere talk of the next election excites him. He loves the thrill of the political battle. JFK also loves being president. He is an adrenaline junkie, relishing the rush of competing for power.

Cronkite presses the president. "What do you think the issues might be in '64?"

"Well, of course, abroad would be the security of the United States. Our effort to maintain that security. To maintain the cause of freedom. At home I think it's the economy. Jobs. Opportunity for all Americans."

The president, without consulting notes, then rattles off a long list of statistics. He presses for a tax cut, to ward off a recession, he says, and backs it up with detailed financial specifics about the way in which cutting taxes would stimulate the economy.

Cronkite finally gets around to the touchy subject of Vietnam. With every passing day, Americans are becoming more concerned about U.S. involvement in that troubled nation. The ongoing and well-publicized oppression of the Buddhists has made some Americans forget that communism is the primary reason U.S. troops are in Vietnam. There are growing cries for America to leave Southeast Asia and let the Vietnamese fight their own war.

"Everyone has said the administration would apply diplomacy in Vietnam," Cronkite begins, emphasizing the second syllable with a short letter *a* ("NAM" as in *ram*). "Which I'd assumed we'd been trying all along. What can we do in this situation that seems to parallel other famous debacles of dealing with unpopular governments?"

Cronkite has a soothing on-camera presence that television viewers have grown to trust. The president knows that convincing this newsman of his views on Vietnam is the same as convincing the voters watching at home.

"The war is going better," JFK begins. "But that doesn't mean that the events of the last two months aren't very ominous. I don't think that if greater effort isn't made by the government, that the war can be won out there. In the final analysis, it's their war. They're the ones who have to win it or lose it."

The president stops short of saying that U.S. troops should be removed, despite the fact that dozens of Americans have already been killed fighting another country's battles. He voices his concerns that if Vietnam falls to the Communists, then so will the rest of Asia. JFK lists the countries that will topple, beginning with Thailand and continuing all the way to India. "We're in a desperate struggle with the Communist situation," he insists, "and I don't want Asia to pass into the control of the Chinese."

Kennedy's voice intensifies, showing his disdain for both Vietnam's president Diem and those enemies that would spread communism around the world. This is not the John Kennedy whom some consider to be an affable young man who was elected based on good looks and his father's money. JFK has grown into a true world leader. He combines discipline with a powerful work ethic, knowledge, guts, and compassion.

The interview ends after twenty minutes. The president immediately pulls his sunglasses from his breast pocket and slips them back on. He and Cronkite make small talk about the cost of producing a half-hour television show, but their attention soon turns to a small sunfish sailboat skimming lazily across the water. It is a dot on a sea that stretches endlessly across the horizon. Both men are sailors, fascinated by the water.

The weather in the bay is calm. Turbulence is not far away. Nevertheless, the interview has gone flawlessly. The president can now relax with his family for the rest of the afternoon, enjoying a time of peace amid all the sadness and turmoil of the previous month.

Kennedy and Cronkite shift the conversation to sailing until it is time to remove their microphones. Inside Brambletyde, just a few feet away, a grieving Jackie Kennedy hides from the cameras—and the world. The president has been spending more time not just with Jackie, but with Caroline and John, too, swimming in the ocean, allowing them to ride in the presidential helicopter, and attending Caroline's riding lessons. The president has urged his wife to put on a brave face for the media, but she's just not ready.

However, Jackie will soon break her self-imposed seclusion. She has decided to spend a few weeks in Greece with her sister, Lee Radziwill, in order to ease her mourning. The mere thought of that trip, which is still a month away, brings a rare smile to the First Lady's face.

■ ■ ■

Walter Cronkite and John Kennedy say good-bye. And on this perfect Labor Day afternoon, with the wind blowing in off the Atlantic and the sun warming their faces, neither man can possibly know that it will be Cronkite who will appear on national television in just twelve weeks to make an announcement that will shock the world.

16

✎

November 21 and 22 are looming.

Those dates reside in the back of John F. Kennedy's mind as he stands in the rodeo ring at the Yellowstone County Fairgrounds, addressing an overflow crowd. Billings, Montana, has a population of just fifty-three thousand, and it appears as if every single citizen has come out to cheer on the president. A marching band only adds to the pageantry.

"The potential of this country is unlimited," Kennedy begins, and it's almost as if he is talking about himself. In the past five days alone, he has helped Montana's farmers by approving a massive wheat sale to the Soviet Union, brokered a global ban on the testing of nuclear weapons, cut income taxes, and even stood before the UN General Assembly promising to send men to the moon. JFK's speech that day was so outstanding that even the Soviets applauded.

The sunlight is fading but still warm as the president speaks in the open-air dirt arena, the Rocky Mountains towering in the near distance. The day smells like autumn. Kennedy's coat and tie look stiff compared to the jeans and cowboy boots worn by many in the audience, and his Boston accent is almost jarring in this iconic western setting. And when Kennedy speaks about the wonders of the American West, he quotes Henry David Thoreau—a man from Massachusetts who never crossed the Mississippi.

But the good people of Montana don't mind a bit. They hang on the president's every word, thrilled that John Fitzgerald Kennedy has come to their town as part of his eleven-state swing through the West. The president's focus is on shoring up support for his upcoming campaign. Back in 1960, Nevada was the only western state Kennedy carried. Not only did he lose Montana and its four electoral votes, but Yellowstone County voted against JFK by a margin of 60 percent to 38 percent.

But that was three years ago.

Today, the president was mobbed when Air Force One landed at the Billings airport. Men and women of all ages pressed forward to shake his hand. Kennedy, much to the chagrin of his Secret Service bodyguards, put his life at risk by eagerly wading into the crowd. He knew that nothing would make these people happier than to go home tonight and say they had touched the president. Thousands lined the motorcade route to the fairgrounds, including men on horseback.

It would seem that JFK might just win Montana if the election were held tomorrow. And success in the West is a vital part of Kennedy's reelection strategy. A victory in Texas, for example, would almost guarantee his victory in 1964.

And so Appointments Secretary Kenny O'Donnell has selected November 21 and 22 as the likely dates of Kennedy's eagerly anticipated Texas fund-raising trip.

The president envisions a grand tour of the state, with stops in five major cities: San Antonio, Fort Worth, Dallas, Houston, and Austin. Texas governor John Connally, the conservative Democrat who has been maintaining a discreet political distance from the president, is quietly in favor of a less ambitious itinerary. Dallas, for instance, is not Kennedy territory. It is a city where "K.O. the Kennedys" bumper stickers are displayed. And parlor games about "Which Kennedy do you hate the most?" are commonplace. Children boo the president's name in classrooms, and a popular local poster of Kennedy designed to look like a mug shot bears the inscription "Wanted for Treason. This Man Is Wanted for Treasonous Activities Against the United States."

Even more ominous are the pro-assassination jokes—a situation made all the more troubling by the extraordinary murder rate in Dallas. More murders are committed in Texas than any other state, and more homicides occur in Dallas than anywhere else in Texas. The state does not regulate or register firearms, and 72 percent of the murders are by gunshot.

There is no question that John F. Kennedy's visit to the "Southwest hate capital of Dixie," as Dallas has been called, is fraught with complications.

The president will discuss this issue, along with other details of the trip, with John Connally next week at the White House. In yet another confirmation that Lyndon Johnson has no place in John Kennedy's future plans, the vice president has been neither invited to that meeting nor even told it will take place.

One statistic about the Texas trip is most glaring of all: more than 62 percent of Dallas voters rejected John Kennedy in 1960.

But JFK loves a challenge. If Billings, Montana, can be won over, then why not the "Big D"?

■ ■ ■

Meanwhile, at the exact same time President Kennedy is speaking in Montana, Lee Harvey Oswald is already on his way to Texas—and beyond. Dressed in casual slacks and a zippered jacket, Oswald rides Continental Trailways bus 5121 bound for Houston. From there he will change buses and travel due south to Mexico City. Unlike the American forces (which included among them a young Ulysses S. Grant and Robert E. Lee) that took a year to make that journey during the Mexican-American War of 1846, Oswald will make the trip in just one day.

Oswald is traveling like a man who is never coming back. He has no home, because he has just abandoned his squalid New Orleans apartment. When the landlady came around demanding the seventeen dollars in back rent, Oswald put her off with a lie and later sneaked out in the dead of night.

The sum of Oswald's worldly possessions are now divided among his wallet and the two cloth suitcases stowed in the bus's luggage bay.

As for a family, Oswald no longer has one. Two days ago he sent the very pregnant Marina and their nineteen-month-old daughter, June, back to live with Marina's friend Ruth Paine outside Dallas. Marina has been Oswald's unwitting pawn these past few months, her Soviet citizenship vital to his goal of returning to the Soviet Union. It is unclear if she knows he is traveling to Mexico—or that he had to leave the country to travel at all.

But Oswald has hatched a clever new scheme—one that doesn't require Marina. So just as he abandoned their apartment, now he also abandons his family. Every mile that Trailways 5121 travels past the pine thickets and swampland of the Texas coastal highway puts Lee Harvey Oswald one mile farther away from the shackles of his turbulent and bitter marriage.

Oswald has temporarily abandoned plans to return to the Soviet Union. Instead, he dreams of living in the palm tree–fringed workers' paradise of Cuba. But it's impossible to attain a Cuban travel visa in the United States because the United States and Cuba have severed diplomatic relations. Thus Oswald is taking the bus to Mexico City in order to visit the Cuban embassy there.

Lee Harvey Oswald never fits in, no matter where he goes. He is not an outcast because that would mean allowing himself to join a group before being rejected by it. Instead, he is something far more unpredictable—and ultimately more dangerous: he is a parallel member of society, a thin-skinned loner operating by his own rhythms and rules, constantly searching for that place where he can hunker down, for that identity that will allow him to be the great man he so longs to be.

Oswald believes that Cuba is such a place. And in his mind he has done plenty to impress the Cuban dictator, Castro. Oswald's time in New Orleans passing out leaflets for the Fair Play for Cuba Committee was his way of proving his loyalty to Fidel. Marina Oswald will later claim that Lee Harvey even planned to hijack an airplane that would take him directly to Havana.

At 2:00 A.M. on the morning of September 26, Lee Harvey Oswald changes buses in Houston, switching to Continental Trailways 5133. One day later, he arrives in Mexico City. Throughout the journey he is chatty, even boastful, desperate to impress his fellow passengers. He regales them with tales of his time in the Soviet Union and his work with the Fair Play for Cuba Committee. He even makes a point of showing them the Soviet stamps in his passport. Whenever the bus stops for a food break, the rail-thin Oswald devours heaping platters of Mexican cuisine. He doesn't speak Spanish, which he'll need to learn for his new life in Cuba. So, for now, he orders by jabbing a finger randomly at a menu item and hoping for the best.

In his wallet, Oswald carries close to two hundred dollars, a Mexican tourist card that allows him one fifteen-day trip to that country, and two passports—one from his Soviet days and the other brand-new, recently issued by the U.S. government. In his blue athletic bag, Oswald has wedged a Spanish-English dictionary, newspaper clippings that prove he was arrested while agitating on behalf of Cuba, his Russian-language work permit from his time in Minsk, and proof of his marriage to a Soviet citizen. Oswald also carries a pad containing notes explaining that he speaks Russian and is a devoted friend of the Communist Party.

Like all true Communists, Lee Harvey Oswald is an avowed atheist, so he does not pray for his journey's success. Instead, he puts his faith in that thick stack of documents he now carries.

But Oswald knows that the journey is a gamble. He might get all the way to Mexico City and be denied. If that happens, the precious dollars spent on travel, food, and lodging will have been squandered. But it is a risk he must take.

The bus arrives in Mexico City at 10:00 A.M. Oswald once again drifts, immediately separating himself from his new acquaintances. He checks in at the Hotel de Comercio, just four blocks from the bus station, at a rate of $1.28 per night. And though exhausted after the grueling twenty-hour bus ride, he walks immediately to the Cuban embassy.

■ ■ ■

John Kennedy is traveling west. Lee Harvey Oswald is traveling south. And Jackie Kennedy is traveling east. She and her sister, Lee, are off for Greece. There they will spend two weeks aboard the yacht *Christina*, owned by the shadowy womanizer Aristotle Onassis, a man who has been under surveillance by the FBI for almost twenty years due to his unscrupulous business practices. Among other things, Onassis has been investigated for fraud against the American government and for violation of U.S. shipping laws in the mid-1950s. It's no wonder that, back in 1961, when the First Lady went abroad alone on a goodwill tour, President Kennedy issued very firm instructions to Jackie's Secret Service detail: "Whatever you do in Greece, do not let Mrs. Kennedy cross paths with Aristotle Onassis."

The swarthy Greek shipping magnate is more than twenty years older than Jackie, and three inches shorter. He's also one of the richest men in the world. His yacht has been the scene of many a society function, and men such as JFK and Winston Churchill have been aboard it. The last time the First Lady was on board the 325-foot-long *Christina*, which is renowned for such opulent features as solid-gold faucets, was almost ten years ago, as a guest with JFK. At that time, Jackie Kennedy thought the boat vulgar and was particularly disgusted by the bar stool covers made of whale scrotums. But now her sister is pursuing Onassis romantically, even though the portly Greek is having an affair with opera star Maria Callas. Understanding the situation, Jackie is coming along to offer emotional support.

The First Lady would never dare be photographed in a bikini on U.S. soil. The image of her in a revealing bathing suit would be scandalous, and perhaps even politically damaging for her husband. But Greece is half a world away from the restrictions and cares of being the First Lady.

Jackie needs a break from all that. For the next two weeks she wants nothing more than to be pampered and free-spirited. The First Lady has lost all of her baby weight. It would be a shame not to flaunt her newly slim figure in the privacy of her opulent surroundings. So she makes sure her staff puts a bikini in her suitcase before she boards the TWA 707 for Greece on October 1.

It has been exactly fifty-two days since she endured the tragedy of baby Patrick's death. It is exactly fifty-two days until she will endure another unspeakable tragedy.

17

〰

OCTOBER 6, 1963
CAMP DAVID, MARYLAND
10:27 A.M.

The president of the United States is furious. John Kennedy steers a golf cart to Camp David's military mess hall for Sunday Mass. The paved path meanders through a thick wood, taking him past the Hawthorn, Laurel, Sycamore, and Linden guest cabins on his three-minute journey. With him are five-year-old Caroline and John Jr., who will turn three next month. But it is not politics that is on the president's mind—his trip to Texas is set. (After meeting with Governor John Connally two days ago, the much-needed political foray is a done deal.) Nor is it the pressures of the office. And it is certainly not his children who have JFK annoyed—the president is excited to be spending time alone with Caroline and John. He has even asked legendary *Look* magazine photographer Stanley Tretick to take some informal photos of them at play.

No, what's making the president so angry is the First Lady. She won't come to the phone.

Despite her husband's objections, the First Lady spent two weeks as a guest on Greek shipping magnate Aristotle Onassis's yacht Christina *in 1963.* (Associated Press)

It's bad enough that Jackie Kennedy is cavorting around the Mediterranean with Aristotle Onassis, a man whom the president does not trust. But it's far worse that pictures of her Greek adventures are front-page news around the world, leading many to ask why the president is allowing his wife to spend time with a man who has been investigated for fraud against the U.S. government. Perhaps worst of all, however, Aristotle Onassis is a known philanderer.

A simple phone conversation with Jackie might lessen Jack's tension. But the First Lady is now unreachable. Even when the president plans ahead and accounts for the time change, the most powerful man in the world cannot speak to his wife. JFK doesn't know whether she's avoiding him or if the *Christina* truly lacks modern communication technology.

The situation is not just making Kennedy angry—it's making him jealous.

■ ■ ■

Four months. Four long months. That's how long it will take for Lee Harvey Oswald to obtain a Soviet visa, which it turns out he needs before Cuban officials will grant him travel documents.

But Oswald doesn't have enough money to wait four months. He needs to go to Cuba now.

And so he stands toe-to-toe with consul Eusebio Azcue at the Cuban consulate in Mexico City, arguing with him over the Soviet visa. The conversation long ago stopped being civil. Oswald is "highly agitated and angry," in the eyes of one employee of the Cuban consulate. Instead of being deferential to the man who controls his entry into the Communist country, Oswald is yelling at him.

Finally, Azcue has had enough. The diplomat in him is gone, and he speaks candidly with the American. "A person like you," Azcue tells Oswald in fractured English, "in the place of aiding the Cuban Revolution, are doing it harm."

Azcue concludes by telling Oswald that he will never get the paperwork to enter Cuba.

The consul turns and strides back to his office, leaving Oswald crushed: his dream of escaping to Cuba is over. A consular employee hands Oswald a scrap of paper with her name and the embassy's contact information on it, should he ever want to try again.

A despondent Oswald stays the weekend in Mexico City, loading up on the local food and taking in a bullfight. But his despair is growing.

He then takes the bus back to Dallas, where he rents a room at the YMCA and looks for work. He sheepishly phones Marina, who is still living with family friend Ruth Paine and is due to deliver the Oswalds' second baby any day. Paine is a Quaker housewife who was introduced to the Oswalds by George de Mohrenschildt, the well-educated Russian with possible CIA connections whom Oswald met in the summer of 1962.

Ruth Paine speaks a smattering of Russian, which helps to make Marina feel more at home. All Marina's possessions are stored in Paine's garage. Among them is a green-and-brown rolled blanket in which Lee Harvey Oswald's rifle is concealed. Ruth Paine, being a peace-loving Quaker, would never allow the gun in her garage, but she has no idea it's there.

Oswald regales Marina with tales of Mexico, but also admits that his trip was a failure. Marina listens, and believes that there is a change for the better in her husband. But she refuses to live with him. So, while looking for work, Oswald phones his wife when he can and sometimes hitchhikes from Dallas out to the Paine residence to see her.

Finally, thanks to a kindly reference from Ruth Paine, he finds a job. It is menial labor for a man with Oswald's relatively high IQ of 118, and involves nothing more than placing books into boxes for shipping. But he and Marina are happy nonetheless. Maybe it's a sign of a new beginning.

At 8:00 A.M. on Wednesday, October 16, Lee Harvey Oswald reports for his first day on the job at the Texas School Book Depository. The seven-floor redbrick warehouse is located on the corner of Elm and North Houston and overlooks Dealey Plaza, named for a onetime publisher of the *Dallas Morning News*. Most fortuitously, Parkland Memorial Hospital is just four miles away, should Marina go into labor with the new baby while Oswald is at work.

On October 18, Oswald gets a birthday surprise: the Cuban embassy in Mexico City has inexplicably reversed itself and granted him a travel visa. But it's too late. He has moved on.

On October 20, Audrey Marina Rachel Oswald is born at Parkland Memorial. Lee Harvey doesn't immediately go to see his wife and child, fearful that the hospital will present him with a bill he cannot pay.

This absence from the life of his newborn daughter is something Marina and the baby will have to get used to. Because Lee Harvey will not be around to watch young Audrey Marina Rachel Oswald grow up.

■ ■ ■

Jackie Kennedy is back in Washington. Between her summer on Cape Cod, two September weeks in Newport, Rhode Island, and the two weeks in Greece, she's been gone from the White House for almost four months. The date is October 21, and it's suppertime in the White House. The First Lady has invited *Newsweek* correspondent Ben Bradlee and his wife, Tony, over for a late meal. They will dine in the White House family residence on the second floor, which Jackie renovated in 1961, hand-selecting the antique wallpaper portraying scenes from the American Revolution.

And while tonight's meal will be light and the conversation lively, this room has ghosts. President William Henry Harrison died here in his bed from pneumonia back in 1841. Abraham Lincoln's eleven-year-old son, Willie, took ill and died here in 1862. And Lincoln himself was embalmed in this room after being shot dead. Finally, just before the turn of the century, this high-ceilinged chamber served as the bedroom of William McKinley, who was also killed by an assassin's bullet.

This impromptu dinner is the sort of get-together the First Lady enjoyed so often before baby Patrick's death. It's been a long time since the Kennedys had friends over just for fun. And while Jackie has canceled all formal social obligations until January 1964, this simple supper is an attempt to begin a normal daily life again. She waited until late afternoon to confirm that the president's schedule was clear. The Bradlees received their invitation only at 7:00 P.M. but were more than happy to drop everything and come over.

The president has had a terrible day. The ongoing racial unrest down in Birmingham and the pitched battles over civil rights legislation here in Washington have left him in a foul mood. But the Bradlees are perhaps the Kennedys' closest friends in Washington, and the president knows that, with them, his words are off the record. So Jackie did well by inviting Ben and Tony. JFK sits in his shirtsleeves sipping a drink and blowing off steam by talking politics across the table. Much of the conversation revolves around what he plans to do if he is reelected. "Maybe after 1964," Kennedy repeats over and over. "Maybe after 1964."

But 1964 might not be a year of victory, and John Kennedy knows that. Things are darkening in Camelot. Even Jackie's recent vacation has turned out to be a liability. Her fondness for European culture and fashion have long contrasted with the more down-to-earth sensibilities of the American public. The First Lady's extraordinary popularity once made her impervious to political attacks. This is no longer the case.

Less than two months after she suffered the brutal pain of losing a child, Republicans in Congress have decided that she is fair game. They publicly bash her for the Greece trip, accusing the First Lady of being nothing more than a pleasure-seeker. "Why doesn't the lady see more of her own country instead of gallivanting all over Europe?" wonders Congressman Oliver Bolton of Ohio.

The press is also writing lengthy stories about the frequent parties on the Onassis yacht. Some writers are painting the First Lady as self-indulgent. "Does this sort of behavior seem fitting for a woman in mourning?" asks the *Boston Globe*. One published photograph even shows a carefree Jackie being assisted onto the *Christina* by a strapping, young, bare-chested, and sun-bronzed male crew member. Another image, of Jackie sunning herself in a bikini, was splashed on front pages all around the world. For the first time, the First Family is under siege from the media.

The UPI newspaper syndicate is even questioning the First Lady's morals, suggesting that her sunbathing is too sensual. "Mrs. Kennedy allows herself to be photographed in positions and poses which she would never permit in the United States," reads the story. The writer goes on to add archly that it would be common courtesy for the president and First Lady to reciprocate by inviting Aristotle Onassis to the White House next time he's in the United States.

Now, at the White House dinner table, the First Lady's deep tan is the most obvious reminder of her husband's political fragility. But she seems oblivious to the pain she's causing. Jackie defends Onassis to her husband and the Bradlees, telling them that the Greek is an "alive and vital person"—which, of course, only makes the president angrier.

John Kennedy does not know everything that did, or did not, happen on board the *Christina*. He does know about the massages, caviar dinners, and shots of vodka. He also understands that his wife is drawn to the *Christina's* opulence and to the vast wealth of Aristotle Onassis. What the president doesn't know is whether his wife was unfaithful, though it's most likely that she was not, especially accompanied as she was on board by her sister, who had designs on Onassis. But the president senses that something is troubling his wife, and he has already confided to Ben Bradlee about "Jackie's guilt feelings."

Now he uses that guilt to his advantage.

"Maybe now you'll come to Texas with us next month," the president says with a cautious smile. He is determined that Jackie make this journey. And not just to answer the charges that she has seen more of Europe than of America. The First Lady is far more popular in the South than he is, particularly among female voters. Jackie hasn't made a campaign appearance since 1960, but her presence in Texas might deflect some of the animosity surrounding the president's visit. "Jackie will show those Texas broads a thing or two about fashion," JFK says.

The fact is that Jackie actually *wants* to be at his side—no matter what. She is tired of being away from her husband.

It was in this spirit that Jackie bared her soul to JFK in a handwritten letter on October 5, shortly after the *Christina* put out to sea.

"If I hadn't married you my life would have been tragic, because the definition of tragic is a waste," she wrote in the privacy of her personal stateroom, named for the Greek island Chios. As is her habit, Jackie substitutes dashes for normal punctuation. The First Lady goes on to admit that she's actually sorry for their daughter, Caroline, because it will be impossible for her to marry a man as wonderful as her father.

The Kennedy marriage can be restrained at times; many things are left unsaid. But on other occasions the simmering passion is so palpable that the American people sense it just by watching JFK and Jackie stand side by side. The heat between the president and the First Lady is undeniable, and that sentiment flows through her written words. Jackie writes line after line on the *Christina* that day, until the simple love note stretches to seven pages long.

"I loved you from the first day I saw you," Jackie's letter confesses.

Their ten-year anniversary had been September 12. "Ten years later, I love you so much more."

Now, two weeks later, in the White House, this man whom she so adores wants to take her on a trip to Texas. How can she possibly say no?

"Sure, I will, Jack. We'll just campaign," the First Lady responds. Whatever happened on the *Christina* is in her past. Her future is gazing at her intently with those beautiful greenish-gray eyes of his.

"I'll campaign with you anywhere you want."

The First Lady then reaches for her red appointment book and pens the word *Texas* across November 21, 22, and 23.

PART III

Evil Wins

18

⌒

October 24, 1963
Dallas, Texas
Evening

Jacqueline Kennedy has no clue. If she could see the hell her good friend Adlai Stevenson is enduring in Dallas this balmy evening, she might not be so optimistic about making the upcoming Texas trip with her husband.

Known as "Big D," Dallas is a dusty, dry town, miserably hot in the summer and annoyingly cool in the winter. It is surrounded by some of the most unremarkable scenery in all America. It is a hard city, built on commerce and oil, and driven by just one thing: money. The television series *Dallas* will one day be seen as a caricature of this fixation on garish wealth, but the real Dallas is not that different.

Fifty years from now, Dallas will be a cosmopolitan metropolis, home to a diverse population and a wide range of multinational corporations. But in 1963 the population of 747,000 is overwhelmingly white, 97 percent Protestant, and growing larger and more conservative by the day, as newcomers flood in from rural Texas and Louisiana.

Dallas is a law-and-order town. Sort of. It's the kind of city where heavy fines on sin have driven the prostitutes to nearby Fort Worth, but one where murders are on the rise. Dallas is full of Baptist and Methodist churches, but it's also home to a place like the Carousel Club, a downtown strip joint owned by a fifty-two-year-old suspected mafioso named Jacob Rubinstein—aka Jack Ruby—where cops and newspapermen often drink side by side.

But most of all, Dallas is a city that does not trust outsiders or their political views—particularly those of liberal Yankees. And the local citizens are not passive in their disdain. Jewish stores are sometimes defaced with swastikas.

On this particular night, Adlai Stevenson is experiencing what some have called Dallas's "general atmosphere of hate" firsthand. He is a devoted Democrat who ran against, and was defeated twice by, Dwight Eisenhower. Texas is decidedly not Stevenson country, even though a big crowd is now seated at the Memorial Auditorium. The occasion is United Nations Day. Last night, the right-wing zealot General Ted Walker spoke at the same venue, delivering a rousing anti-UN speech that was attended by the man who once tried to kill him: Lee Harvey Oswald.

Now, as Stevenson tries to speak, he can barely be heard. Time and again he is heckled and booed by a fringe group known as the National Indignation Convention. They intentionally mispronounce the stately diplomat's name, calling him "Addle-Eye."

Stevenson patiently tolerates the abuse, standing still at the lectern, hoping calm will take hold. But this proves impossible. So he finally confronts one heckler: "Surely, my dear friend, I don't have to come here from Illinois to teach Texas manners, do I?"

Then things get worse.

Twenty-two-year-old Robert Edward Hatfield races up to the podium and unloads a violent gob of spit into Stevenson's face. As police seize Hatfield, he spits on them as well. Adlai Stevenson has had enough. Wiping his face, he walks out of the auditorium. But the chaos doesn't end. A waiting crowd of anti-UN protesters confronts him. Rather than let Stevenson walk back to his hotel peacefully, the protesters block his path and jeer at him. One agitator, forty-seven-year-old Cora Frederickson, actually hits the ambassador over the head with her picket sign.

Still, Stevenson tries to be diplomatic. The sixty-three-year-old politician waves off the Dallas police rushing over to make their second arrest of the night. "What is wrong?" Stevenson asks the woman who hit him. "Can I help you in any way?"

"If you don't know what's wrong, I don't know why. Everyone else does," she shoots back with an angry Texas twang.

John Kennedy does not like Adlai Stevenson. But the president is shaken when he hears of the vicious attacks. Now the many negative reports he has heard about Dallas are being confirmed. Trusted friends are warning him to cancel this leg of his Texas trip. As far back as October 3, Senator William Fulbright of Arkansas confided to John Kennedy that he was physically afraid of entering Dallas, calling it "a dangerous place."

"I wouldn't go there," he told JFK. "Don't you go."

Evangelist Billy Graham is also warning the president to stay away from Dallas. Henry Brandon of London's *Sunday Times* is so sure Kennedy's visit will be volatile that he himself is making the trip just to chronicle the tension. Texas congressman Ralph Yarborough's two brothers live and work in Dallas, and both make a point of telling him that the city hates Kennedy. And in early November, Byron Skelton of the Texas Democratic National Committee will have a premonition that JFK may be placing himself in grave danger by coming to Dallas. Skelton will repeatedly warn the president to stay away.

But John Kennedy is the president of the United States of America— all of them. There should be no place in this vast country where he has to be afraid to visit.

As he is fond of saying before attempting a hard golf shot: "No profiles, only courage." So it is with Dallas. JFK has decided to visit Big D. There is no backing down.

■ ■ ■

Half a world away, it is All Souls' Day in Saigon. This is a time of prayer in the Roman Catholic Church. So it is that Ngo Dinh Diem, president of Vietnam, receives Holy Communion alongside his brother, Ngo Dinh Nhu.

But there is another reason the brothers are praying, and John Kennedy should know why. A U.S.-backed coup has overthrown the Diem government. As the military action was unfolding, JFK met with his top advisers to discuss the future of Vietnam—and the fate of Diem and his brother. The meeting dragged on so long that Kennedy even sneaked out halfway through to attend Mass, before returning for the meeting's conclusion.

In a far more frantic manner, President Diem and his brother sneaked out of the presidential palace during the coup, literally running for their lives. Like JFK, they went to Mass. Now the brothers are taking refuge inside the sanctuary of Saigon's St. Francis Xavier Catholic Church.

Shortly after 10:00 A.M. they are recognized, and the president and his brother prepare to be arrested and deported from the country. Diem has readied himself for this moment by stuffing a briefcase with U.S. banknotes.

General Mai Huu Xuan of the Army of the Republic of Vietnam (ARVN) leads a convoy consisting of an armored personnel carrier and two jeeps into the church courtyard. Diem surrenders, asking only that the convoy stop at the palace before taking him and his brother to the airport. General Xuan refuses and orders that his captives be immediately taken to army headquarters. Soldiers then tie the hands of the president and his brother behind their backs, and the two are placed inside an armored personnel carrier—ostensibly for their own protection. Two ARVN officers join them in the back of the vehicle before the heavy steel door is closed.

The convoy stops at a railroad crossing. One of the ARVN officers then calmly places his finger on the trigger of his semiautomatic weapon and fires a bullet into the back of President Diem's skull.

19

NOVEMBER 1, 1963
IRVING, TEXAS
2:30 P.M.

It is Friday afternoon, and a weary James Hosty Jr. rings the bell at Ruth Paine's home. The burly thirty-five-year-old FBI agent has spent the day investigating cases in nearby Fort Worth. He is juggling almost forty investigations right now, taking small bites out of each one. But any case involving J. Edgar Hoover's battle against communism gets top priority, which is why Hosty is stopping at Mrs. Paine's rather than driving straight back into Dallas to start his weekend. The agent is looking for Lee Harvey Oswald. The bureau has received a tip from the CIA about Oswald's visit to the Cuban embassy in Mexico City last month, and the Feds are now anxious to find him.

Mrs. Paine opens the door. Hosty flashes his badge, explaining that he's a special agent of the FBI, and asks if they can talk.

These are hard times for Ruth Paine. Her husband of five years has left and is filing for divorce. Perhaps to mitigate her loneliness, Ruth invited Marina Oswald to live at her home, despite knowing that the young mother has no money to contribute. But the minor financial burden is nothing compared with the quirky behavior of Marina's husband, Lee Harvey, who comes to visit on the weekends. Ruth Paine refuses to let him live in her house. She doesn't trust him.

Yet Mrs. Paine is very warm to James Hosty. She invites him inside and gushes that this is the first time she's ever met an FBI agent.

But Hosty isn't just any agent. He's a Notre Dame graduate and former banker who has worked in the Dallas branch office for almost ten years. He knows his way around Dallas and its growing suburbs. He is also a diligent investigator and thinks nothing of going out of his way to visit the home of Ruth Paine even as his Friday shift comes to an end.

But most of all, Special Agent Hosty is the FBI's expert on Lee Harvey and Marina Oswald. Back in March, he opened a file on Marina in order to keep tabs on the Soviet citizen. Later that month, Hosty requested that Lee Harvey's file be reopened due to Oswald's obvious Communist sympathies. The agent has tracked the Oswalds from apartment to apartment, from Dallas to New Orleans and back again. The New Orleans FBI office has kept Hosty apprised of Oswald's arrest and pro-Cuba behavior. But now the Oswald trail has grown cold.

Hosty asks Ruth Paine if she knows where he can find the man.

Paine admits that Marina and her two girls live in her home. After a moment's hesitation, she puts forth that she doesn't know where Oswald lives, though she does know that he works at the Texas School Book Depository in downtown Dallas. Paine gets a phone book and looks up the address: 411 Elm Street.

Hosty writes all this down.

Marina wanders into the living room, having just awakened from a nap.

Speaking in Russian, Ruth Paine informs her that Hosty is an FBI agent. Marina's face takes on a wild, fearful look. Hosty commonly sees this sort of behavior from people raised in Communist countries and knows that Mrs. Oswald thinks he's some sort of secret police who has come to take her away. He immediately instructs Paine to tell Marina that he's not there for the purpose of "harming her, harassing her, and that it isn't the job of the FBI to harm people. It is our job to protect people."

Ruth Paine translates. Marina smiles and calms down.

Hosty stands to leave. The interview has lasted almost twenty-five minutes. Hosty has a couple more cases he wants to follow up on before going back to Dallas. But even as he writes down his name and phone number for Paine, just in case she has any more information about Oswald's whereabouts, Special Agent Hosty now mentally assigns a low priority to the Oswald investigation. He's concluded that Lee Harvey Oswald is just a young guy with marital problems, a fondness for communism, and a habit of drifting from job to job.

There's no need for urgency. Lee Harvey Oswald is bound to show up sooner or later. Special Agent Hosty is sure of that.

■ ■ ■

On November 11, the Monday after Hosty's visit to Ruth Paine's home, Special Agent Winston G. Lawson of the Secret Service's White House detail is informed of the president's upcoming trip to Dallas.

Lawson, a Korean War veteran in his early thirties, specializes in planning Kennedy's official travels. As with all such visits, his primary responsibilities are to identify individuals who might be a threat to the president, take action against anyone considered to be such a threat, and plan security for the president's speeches and motorcade route.

There is still discussion over whether there is to be a motorcade through downtown Dallas, which will be a security nightmare, thanks to the more than twenty thousand windows lining the city's major thoroughfares. The more windows, the more places for a gunman to aim at the president's limousine.

But Lawson temporarily sets that question aside. He begins his investigation of potential threats by combing through the Secret Service's Protective Research Section (PRS). These files list all individuals who have threatened the president or may be potentially dangerous to him. A check of the PRS on November 8 by Lawson shows that no such person exists in the Dallas area.

Lawson then travels to Texas from Washington and interviews local law enforcement and other federal agencies, continuing his search for individuals who might be a threat to the life of John F. Kennedy. Of particular interest are the protesters involved in the Adlai Stevenson incident just a few weeks ago. Lawson obtains photographs of these people, which will be distributed to Secret Service and Dallas police on the day of the president's visit. People who resemble those individuals will be instantly scrutinized should they come anywhere near the president.

Lawson's diligence is soon rewarded when the FBI comes forth with the name of a Dallas-area resident who might be a serious threat to the life of John Fitzgerald Kennedy.

Special Agent James Hosty Jr., however, does not provide that name, and it is not that of Lee Harvey Oswald. Instead, it is of a known local troublemaker who has absolutely no plans to kill the president of the United States.

■ ■ ■

Back in the nation's capital, November 11 is a brisk day, marked by pale sunlight and a wind that straightens the many flags flying at Arlington National Cemetery, across the Potomac River from the District of Columbia. A crowd of hundreds of soldiers and civilians looks on as the president of the United States celebrates Veterans Day by placing a wreath at the Tomb of the Unknowns. John Kennedy, a decorated war veteran himself, stands at attention as a bugler blows taps, traditionally the final musical movement at all military ceremonies. The bugler's name is Sergeant Keith Clark. He is the principal trumpeter of the U.S. Army Band and knows this sad song all too well. Clark plays the solo beautifully, the lonesome notes echoing mournfully across the sea of white tombstones and green grass.

President Kennedy is touched by the history and drama of this setting. Arlington was once home to the family of Robert E. Lee and was turned into a cemetery during the Civil War by Union troops so that the Confederate general might never again be tempted to live in the family mansion that still dominates the grounds. Kennedy can see why this was such a great loss to Lee, for the rolling hills look out over the river to Washington, where the fast pace and backroom deals are a drastic contrast to the quiet and peace of the cemetery.

"This is one of the really beautiful places on earth," the president later tells Congressman Hale Boggs. "I could stay here forever."

That thought is not fleeting. Kennedy repeats the sentiment to Secretary of Defense Robert McNamara. "I think, maybe someday, this is where I'd like to be."

20

November 13, 1963
The White House
Late evening

The man with nine days to live admires Greta Garbo as she takes off her shoes and lies down atop the mattress in the Lincoln Bedroom. There is a dinner party in Camelot tonight, and the famously reclusive Swedish actress is the guest of honor. Jackie Kennedy is self-admittedly "obsessed" with Garbo, in whom she sees a kindred spirit. But it is the president who has offered to take the fifty-eight-year-old beauty on a tour of what his schedulers simply call "the Mansion."

At dinner, a nervous Garbo has knocked back glass after glass of vodka. But the president has been the picture of abstinence, neither smoking a cigar nor taking a sip of alcohol. "I felt like one of the damned when I lit a cigarette," Garbo will later remember.

John F. Kennedy is enchanted by Garbo, as she is by him. Rather than sneak away from the party right after dinner to enjoy a few quiet moments alone before bed, as is often his habit, JFK lingers for "longer than I have ever done since I became President."

Kennedy and Garbo have never met before tonight but have quickly become fast friends, thanks to a practical joke at the expense of Kennedy's roommate from his teenage years at Choate prep school. Lem Billings is JFK's best friend in the world. The two men are as close as brothers, and Billings spends the night at the White House so often that he keeps a set of clothes in a third-floor bedroom. In 1960 the forty-four-year-old advertising executive voluntarily took a sabbatical from his career to help Kennedy run for president, asking nothing in return. But JFK offered him a job anyway, as head of the brand-new Peace Corps. Billings declined, fearing it would alter their friendship.

Billings met Greta Garbo over the summer, while vacationing in the south of France. Upon his return home, the unmarried Billings boasted so frequently about how well he and Garbo had gotten along that even Jackie told him to stop talking about the movie star.

The president couldn't resist. A friendly practical joke at Billings's expense would only add to the thrill of Garbo's visit. He called the actress, making her a proposition: "My friend Lem boasts how well he knows you. So when he comes in, pretend you've never met him before." JFK persuaded Garbo to arrive early to the White House dinner party in order to rehearse her lines for Kennedy's elaborate ruse.

"Early" in Camelot usually means sometime around 8:30 P.M. Tonight is no exception.

This is because the president has worked yet another typically exhausting day. His schedule began with a 9:45 A.M. meeting with columnist Ann Landers about the 1963 Christmas Seal campaign and ended with a 6:30 P.M. meeting with John A. Hannah, head of the U.S. Commission on Civil Rights. In between there was a meeting with the president of Czechoslovakia; a South Lawn pipe and drums performance by the Black Watch (Royal Highland Regiment), from Great Britain; a fifteen-person meeting about the poverty in eastern Kentucky; and a smaller foreign policy meeting with Dean Rusk, McGeorge Bundy, and former secretary of state Christian Herter in the early evening.

The president took his usual midafternoon swim at 1:10 and had lunch at 1:40, but otherwise the pace never slackened. Meeting followed meeting, with Kennedy expected to be not just in attendance, but also knowledgeable about and decisive on each of the many varied subjects presented to him. All the while, in the back of the president's mind, was the thought of next week's trip to Texas.

When JFK hit the pool for his second swim of the day, it was 7:15. By the time he toweled off and went up to his bedroom, it was 8:03 P.M. Garbo had already arrived. Kennedy took his time showering and changing, knowing Jackie would explain to the actress that he'd been delayed.

Lem Billings was ecstatic when he saw Garbo. "Why, Greta! Oh, my gosh. How are you?" he exclaimed.

Garbo stared at him with a blank expression, then turned her gaze to Jackie. "You must be mistaken. I do not recall that we have ever met before," she said.

When the president arrived, Garbo repeated her assertion that she didn't know Billings. The president's old friend grew more and more dismayed, ignoring JFK to remind Garbo over and over about where they'd met and some of the same people they knew. The more Billings talked, the more obvious it seemed that Greta had never met him before. Throughout it all, JFK unwound, setting aside the cares of the office as he reveled in the easy banter of this lighthearted dinner and his practical joke. Lem Billings will not realize he's been had until tomorrow morning.

Soon after dinner ended, JFK took the entire group on a private tour of the White House. Now a tipsy Greta Garbo doesn't want to soil the bedspread in the Lincoln Bedroom, so takes off her shoes before lying down atop the mattress. The tour ends in the Oval Office. Unbeknownst to most Americans, JFK has a habit of collecting scrimshaw and often bids anonymously for these pieces of inscribed whale's teeth. They are on display in a case in his office. When Garbo admires the collection, the president opens the case and offers her a piece as a gift. The actress gladly accepts.

This is life in Camelot: a day spent solving the world's problems, two therapeutic nude swims, celebrities at the table for a late-night dinner, and a tour of America's most famous residence with a glamorous former movie star. Where else would such a thing happen?

But the evening ends abruptly. "I must go. I am getting intoxicated," Garbo proclaims before disappearing back to her hotel.

Thus ends the last dinner party ever held in Camelot.

But the memory of this magical evening will linger, and even someone as famous as Greta Garbo is not immune to Camelot's allure: "It was a most unusual evening that I spent with you in the White House," she writes in her thank-you note to Jackie Kennedy. "It was really fascinating and enchanting. I might believe it was a dream if I did not have the president's 'tooth' facing me."

But Camelot is not a dream. It is reality—and that reality is about to take a turn that will alter America forever.

21

Thirteen-year-old Sterling Wood aims his Winchester 30-30 rifle at the silhouette of a man's head. He exhales and squeezes the trigger, then squints downrange at the target. It is Saturday. Sterling and his father, Homer, have come to the Sports Drome Rifle Range to sight their guns for deer season.

Young Sterling notices a young man standing in the shooting booth next to him. He is aiming at a similar silhouette. The teenager reads a lot of gun books and is pretty sure that the guy is firing an Italian carbine. It appears that the rifle's barrel has been sawed off to make it shorter, but it's still longer than Sterling's Winchester, by a few inches. Judging from the number of scratches on the stock, the precocious Dallas teenager suspects that the weapon is army surplus. It's even got a sling to make it easier for an infantryman to carry and a four-power telescopic sight to make the target seem closer and easier to shoot with pinpoint accuracy.

"Daddy," Sterling whispers to his father. "It looks like a 6.5 Italian carbine."

The man shoots. Flame leaps from the end of the gun, thanks to its shortened length. Sterling can actually feel the heat from the blast. The gunman removes the spent cartridge and places it in his pocket as if he doesn't want to leave behind evidence that he's been there. Sterling finds it unusual that the shooter does this after each and every round.

The teenager is impressed that almost all of the shooter's bullet holes are clustered around what would be the eye if the paper target were a real man.

"Sir, is that a 6.5 Italian carbine?" Sterling asks the stranger.

"Yes, sir," the man responds.

"And is that a four-power scope?"

"Yes, it is."

The shooter stays just long enough to fire only "eight or ten" shots, in Sterling's estimation—just enough rounds to ration his ammunition while ensuring that his rifle and scope are accurate.

Sterling will later testify that this man is Lee Harvey Oswald.

■ ■ ■

On that November Saturday, the front page of the *Dallas Morning News* features a story on President Kennedy's visit to Dallas, which is just six days away. The paper speculates on the route Kennedy's motorcade will follow through the heart of the city. Air Force One will land at the Love Field, and from there the president will travel to a large commercial center known as the Trade Mart, where he will give a speech. On the way, he will pass the Texas School Book Depository, the workplace of Lee Harvey Oswald.

Oswald is an avid newspaper reader and has known for quite some time that John Kennedy is coming to Dallas. On this day, Oswald has decided to spend the weekend in the city rather than journey out to the suburbs to see Marina and their daughters.

Oswald turned twenty-four just one month ago. He has little to show for his time on earth. He is losing his wife and children. He works a menial job. And despite his keen intellect, he has no advanced education. He doesn't know whether he wants to be an American, a Cuban, or a Russian.

Still, he longs to be a great man. A significant man. A man whose name will never be forgotten.

John Wilkes Booth, in the days before he shot Abraham Lincoln, also longed to be such a man. And just as Booth practiced his marksmanship at a shooting range days before the assassination, so, too, does Lee Harvey Oswald.

Thirteen-year-old Sterling Wood is the first person impressed by Oswald in a long time. For today, Oswald *was* truly great—great at firing several shots through the silhouette of a man's head.

■ ■ ■

The destruction of Camelot might have begun with the Bay of Pigs, when John F. Kennedy made a permanent enemy of Fidel Castro and infuriated his own Central Intelligence Agency.

Or it might have started that October night in 1962 when JFK severed his ties with Sam Giancana, Frank Sinatra, and the Mafia, then stood back and did nothing as his brother Bobby zealously prosecuted organized crime.

Camelot's demise could have originated during the Cuban missile crisis, when JFK scored a decisive public relations victory over Nikita Khrushchev and the Soviet Empire, while at the same time frustrating his top generals and what Dwight Eisenhower called "the military-industrial complex" for refusing to launch a war.

The destruction of Camelot could have begun in any number of ways.

But in fact, it begins on November 18, when Special Agent Winston G. Lawson of the Secret Service advance team, Forrest V. Sorrels of the Secret Service's Dallas office, and Dallas police chief Jesse Curry drive ten very carefully selected miles from Love Field to the Trade Mart. "Hell," says Special Agent Sorrels, glancing up at the thousands of windows looking down on them, "we'd be sitting ducks."

Nevertheless, the agents decide that this will be the presidential motorcade route.

Anytime the president of the United States drives through a crowded city, there is a careful balance between protecting his life and ensuring the spectacle of the chief executive intermingling with the American people. Security is the act of getting him through the crowds alive, which is difficult on those days when the bubble-top roof is not buckled onto his convertible. A perfect motorcade route is devoid of the high windows from which a sniper can poke a gun, offers alternative routes in case something goes wrong, features wide streets that keep crowds far back from the vehicle, and has few, if any, tight turns.

The Dallas motorcade route violates every one of these principles.

The process of turning the presidential vehicle forces William Greer, the Secret Service agent who most often serves as JFK's driver, to slow the limousine down considerably. This makes the president an easier target for a marksman to hit. Secret Service protocol stipulates that whenever a motorcade must slow down for a turn, agents must do a security check of the entire intersection ahead of time. Something as simple as a ninety-degree turn, which the Dallas motorcade route features at the corner of Main and Houston, can cause Greer to step hard on the brakes. A sweeping 120-degree turn, such as the one at the corner of Houston and Elm, can slow Kennedy's Lincoln down to just a few miles per hour.

That is the pace of a brisk walk, and, through the high-powered scope of an assassin's rifle, such a slow speed can turn the president's body into a very attainable target. When this happens, Secret Service agents are trained to position their bodies between the president and the crowd, acting as human shields. While doing so, they are to study the landscape and look up at building windows for signs of a gunman or rifle barrel. The president's limousine has running boards on both sides that allow the agents to shield the president while also performing this scan. They hold on to metallic handles for balance. However, JFK does not like the the agents to stand on the running boards because this blocks the crowd's view of him, so they often ride one car behind.

But all of this protection can be circumvented once a gunman knows the precise motorcade route. Thus, once Secret Service special agents Sorrels and Lawson choose the president's path on November 18, and then release that information to the public, anyone who wants to harm the president can begin planning the precise place and time of the attack. To put it another way: Many people would like to see John F. Kennedy dead. But before Monday, November 18, there existed no field of fire in Dallas.

Now there does.

22

∽

In the final hours of his life, President John F. Kennedy is flying in style aboard Air Force One. He pores over the "Eyes Only, President" intelligence documents overflowing from his battered black alligator-skin briefcase. JFK speed-reads at his normal 1,200 words per minute, glasses perched on the end of his nose, a study in focus. On the couch against the opposite wall of JFK's airborne office, Jackie Kennedy speaks softly in Spanish, practicing a speech she will give tonight in Houston to a group of Latin American women.

The First Lady's Castilian purr is a welcome addition to the president's private in-flight sanctuary. John Kennedy is so glad Jackie is traveling to Texas with him that he took the unusual step of helping her select the clothes she will wear at her many public appearances. One outfit, a pink Chanel wool suit with a matching pillbox hat, is his personal favorite.

Fashion might not normally interest JFK, but the design and décor of Air Force One has received plenty of his attention. There were three presidential airplanes available to him when he first took office. Any one of them could be dubbed "Air Force One" whenever he is on board. Yet these airplanes looked more air force than presidential. Indeed, the words *Military Air Transport Service* were emblazoned on the sides. The predominant fuselage characteristic was unpainted metal.

But the craft possessing tail number 26000, in which John Kennedy now flies, is a distinct upgrade. The president took delivery of this new presidential version of the Boeing 707 in October 1962. And just as Jackie has overseen the redecoration of the White House—one fine detail is now taking place even as the Kennedys fly to Texas: upon their return, JFK will enjoy new drapes in the Oval Office—so John Kennedy has overseen the redecoration of Air Force One. The fuselage and wings, for instance, feature a bold new pale-blue-and-white color scheme, with the words *United States of America* proudly displayed above the row of forty-five oval passenger windows. Inside, the carpeting is lush and the creature comforts many, including a private office, a conference area, and a bedroom where a painting of a French farmhouse hangs over the president's rock-hard mattress. The presidential seal seems to adorn every fixture. JFK enjoys this new airplane so much that he has flown seventy-five thousand miles aboard 26000 in just thirteen months.

Today's journey began at 9:15 A.M., when John Kennedy said good-bye to Caroline as she set off to the third floor of the White House for school. John Jr., who will be three years old next week, got the privilege of riding with his parents in the presidential helicopter as they flew from the White House to Air Force One. The young boy wore a London Fog coat to keep away the November chill and enjoyed the trip immensely.

But as Marine One set down on the runway next to the presidential plane, young John pleaded for his journey to continue. "I want to come," he said to his father.

"You can't," the president replied softly.

"It's just a few days," the First Lady reminded the crying child. "And when we come back, it will be your birthday."

John Jr. began to sob. "John, like Mummy said, we'll be back in a few days," the president explained. JFK then kissed his son and turned to the Secret Service agent in charge of the boy's protection: "You take care of John for me, Mr. Foster," he ordered gently.

Bob Foster thought this unusual. President Kennedy normally never made such statements, no matter how much his son cried when it was time to say good-bye.

At 11:00 A.M., the president gave John Jr. one last hug and stepped onto the tarmac before climbing the steps up into Air Force One. The First Lady was at his side. Five minutes later, the plane went wheels-up out of Andrews for the three-and-a-half-hour flight to Texas. John Kennedy Jr. watched the great jet rise into the sky and disappear into the distance.

Air Force One will land first in San Antonio. Then it's on to Houston and then Fort Worth, where the president and First Lady will spend the night. Dallas will come tomorrow. JFK's personal pilot, Colonel Jim Swindal, will fly the Kennedys from Fort Worth into Dallas's Love Field. The flight will be short, just thirteen minutes. But the symbolic image of Air Force One descending from the heavens to land in that troubled city will be a far more powerful sight than John Kennedy driving thirty-five miles across the prairie in a limousine.

Now the president takes a break from his reading to light a cigar. Jackie has gone into their private cabin to change clothes. JFK smokes thoughtfully. Texas will be tricky politically. There's no telling if the crowds will be hostile or receptive, and he's concerned about Jackie enjoying herself. This could be a big test of whether she will be eager to campaign with him in 1964.

JFK gets up and makes his way back to the First Family's quarters.

The president taps lightly on the door and pokes his head in. "You all right?" he asks Jackie. They will be landing soon. His wife is slipping into a crisp white dress.

"Fine," the First Lady responds, looking in the mirror to adjust the beret that accessorizes the dress and its black belt.

"I just wanted to be sure," he tells her, closing the door.

The president feels a slight dip as Air Force One begins to descend.

He looks out the window. Five miles below and slowly rising up to greet him lies the barren and flat landscape of Texas.

■ ■ ■

On the ground in Dallas, Lee Harvey Oswald stuffs cardboard shipping boxes with books as he fills orders at the Texas School Book Depository. But today he is easily distracted, and a map of the motorcade route printed on the front page of the *Dallas Times Herald*'s afternoon edition soon catches his attention. Oswald need look no farther than the nearest window to see precisely where President Kennedy's limousine will make a slow right turn from Main Street onto Houston, then an even slower left-hand turn onto Elm, where it will pass almost directly below the windows of the depository. Getting a good glimpse of the president will be as simple as looking down onto the street below.

But Lee Harvey Oswald is planning to do much more than catch a glimpse. In fact, he is quietly plotting to shoot the president. Just a month ago, mere days before the birth of their second child, Marina noted his fascination with the movies *Suddenly* and *We Were Strangers*, both of which deal with the shooting of a government official—in the case of *Suddenly*, the president of the United States. The couple watched the films together, and Oswald even told Marina that the films felt authentic. She thought that a strange remark.

Oswald does not hate the president. He has no reason to want JFK dead. He is, however, bitter that a man such as John Kennedy has so many advantages in life. Oswald well understands that it's easier for men born into privilege to distinguish themselves. But other than that small amount of envy, he does not speak unfavorably about the president. In fact, Oswald would very much like to emulate JFK.

Above all, he wants to be a great man.

■ ■ ■

"Can I ride home with you this afternoon?" Oswald casually asks coworker Wesley Frazier. The nineteen-year-old's home is a half block from where Marina Oswald lives with Ruth Paine. Oswald often catches a ride out to

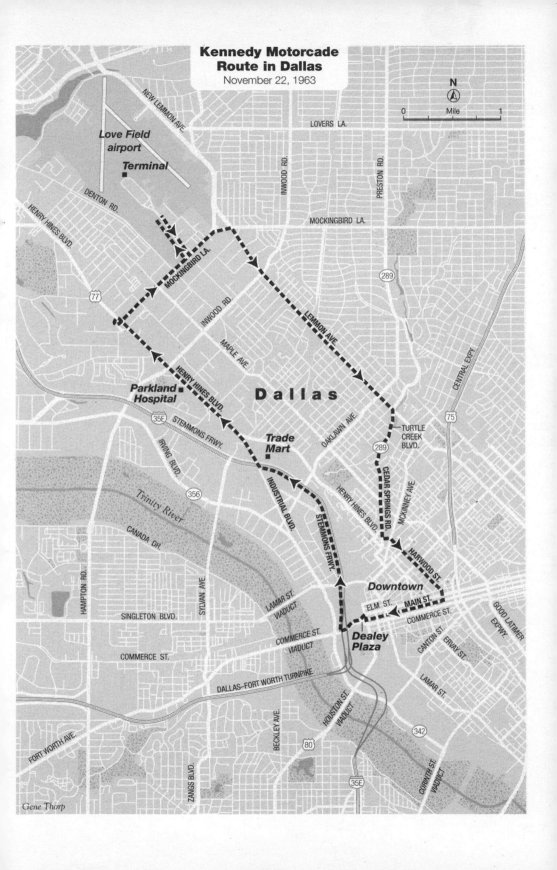

Kennedy Motorcade
Route in Dallas
November 22, 1963

the suburb of Irving on Friday in Frazier's nine-year-old black Chevy four-door and then makes the return trip back into Dallas with him on Monday.

"Sure," Wesley replies. They are standing on the first floor of the Texas School Book Depository, next to a large table. "You know, like I told you, you can go home with me anytime you want to, like I say, anytime you want to go see your wife that is all right with me."

But then Frazier realizes that today isn't Friday. It's Thursday—and Oswald never rides to Irving on Thursdays. "Why are you going home today?" Frazier asks him.

"I am going home to get some curtain rods," Oswald replies.

Oswald then steals a length of brown wrapping paper from the depository's shipping department. He spends the rest of his workday fashioning a bag in which to conceal his "curtain rods."

Through it all, as he folds the paper to form the best possible sheath in which to hide his rifle, Lee Harvey Oswald is unsure that he will actually kill President Kennedy. What he really wants is to be permanently reunited with Marina and the girls. Tonight, he will beg his wife to take him back.

But if she doesn't, Oswald will be left with no choice.

That is how delusional Lee Harvey Oswald's world has become. He now deals only in absolutes: either live happily ever after—or murder the president of the United States.

23

November 22, 1963
Irving, Texas
6:30 a.m.

The Oswalds have been fighting. Again. But this time is different. This time it's over. Lee Harvey stands at the foot of the bed in their cramped room at Ruth Paine's house, dressed for work in gray pants and an old shirt. He twists the wedding band off his left hand and drops it into a china cup on the dresser. It was once a symbol of his love for Marina, but now it is yet another confirmation of the failure that envelops his life.

Today Oswald will do something to change all that. Today he will prove that he is not a failure, even if it means losing his own life in the process.

He drops $187 in cash onto the dresser as a going-away present to his wife and daughters. After all, it's not as if he has a future.

Marina lies on the bed, half awake. Hers and her husband's last night together was not romantic. Oswald tossed and turned while Marina was up with the baby twice. They did not make love, although Marina made a 3:00 A.M. attempt at tenderness. He responded by angrily kicking her away.

Oswald's trip home was primarily to get his rifle. But he was willing to set aside his dark plan if Marina agreed to live with him. All evening long he pleaded with his wife to reconcile. He told her how much he missed his girls, and even promised to buy Marina a washing machine because he knew how much she wanted one.

But Marina was furious that he had come to see her on a Thursday, which was against Ruth Paine's house rules. So Oswald's pleas turned into yet another round of bickering. But still he didn't give up.

Marina, however, doesn't seem to want him back. They spent the evening outside, playing with June and Audrey on the dying autumn grass of Ruth Paine's lawn. Oswald pleaded with Marina to become his wife again. She wavered, because Lee Harvey Oswald had once been the love of her life. But she did not give in.

Oswald went to bed early. He lay there thinking. Even when Marina came to bed, her body warm and smelling like soap from a late-night bath, he pretended to be asleep. The hours passed. Over time he found his courage. He had nothing left in the world. He would go forward with his plan.

Now, at dawn, after dressing for work and leaving his worldly possessions on the dresser, Lee Harvey Oswald hears Marina stir behind him.

"Don't get up," he tells her. "I'll get breakfast myself."

She's exhausted and has no intention of getting up. Audrey fusses, and Marina reaches for her to nurse her. Oswald softly lets himself out of the room without saying good-bye.

The assassin fixes himself a cup of instant coffee in the kitchen, then steps into Ruth Paine's crowded garage to retrieve his rifle. He unrolls the blanket lying next to his olive-green Marine Corps seabag, revealing the 6.5-millimeter Mannlicher-Carcano infantry carbine. He lays the gun in the brown paper wrapping he stole from work yesterday.

Holding the "curtain rods" by the barrel, he steps out of the garage, forever leaving his old life behind.

By 8:00 A.M., Oswald and Wesley Frazier are pulling up for work at the Texas School Book Depository. Oswald is out of the car before Frazier cuts the engine. He has grabbed his brown package and raced inside the building before Frazier can catch up and ask him why he's in such a hurry.

■ ■ ■

"It's raining," says George Thomas, stepping inside John Kennedy's Fort Worth hotel suite. The president's valet rouses him at precisely 7:30 A.M. A crowd is already gathering in the parking lot eight floors below, waiting to hear Kennedy speak to them from the back of a flatbed truck. The audience of nearly five thousand is mostly male, and primarily union workers. Many have been standing in the rain for hours.

"That's too bad," Kennedy replies to his valet. He rises from bed and heads for the shower. Rain means that the bubble-top roof will be buckled onto his limousine for the Dallas motorcade. Not only will the local citizens be upset by having to wait in the cold and rain for hours until he passes by, but their inability to get a clear glimpse of the president and First Lady inside the bubble will do little to sway their votes come next November.

The president wraps himself in his back brace, tightly adjusting the straps. He then dresses in a blue two-button suit, a dark blue tie, and a white shirt with gray stripes from Cardin's in Paris. He reads the CIA situation reports, paying close attention to the casualty count from Vietnam. After that, he scans several newspapers. The *Chicago Sun-Times* is reporting that Jackie just might be the pivotal factor in helping him get reelected in 1964. That's the best news of this trip so far: everyone loves the First Lady. The uproar over her bikini photos has clearly been forgotten.

The people of Texas screamed and cheered for JFK on the first day of the Texas trip. But as big as his ovations are, and as intently as the audiences hung on every word of his speeches, the reception John Kennedy received was nothing like what his wife is experiencing. Jackie is the talk of Texas, and bringing her along may just be the smartest political move the president has ever made.

By 9:00 A.M., John Kennedy is standing on the back of the flatbed truck, looking upbeat and triumphant. "There are no faint hearts in Forth Worth," he says approvingly to the crowd. He has a well-deserved reputation for not giving in to the elements. The union workers knew their waiting in the rain would be rewarded and that the speech would not be canceled.

"Where's Jackie?" someone shouts.

"Where's Jackie?" yells another voice.

John Kennedy smiles and points up to her hotel room. "Mrs. Kennedy is organizing herself," he jokes. On the eighth floor, sitting before her vanity, Jackie can hear the speech rising up from the parking lot. She enjoys hearing her name and how easily her husband banters with the crowd.

"It takes her a little bit longer," the president adds. "But, of course, she looks a little bit better than we do when she does it."

The crowd roars in laughter, as if the president is their coolest drinking buddy and he's sharing some juicy tidbit about his personal life.

But the truth is that, today, Jackie doesn't just need a little extra time to get ready—she needs a lot of time. The First Lady looks visibly exhausted as she primps before the mirror. Campaigning is hard work. Yet she is determined to stick this out. There is to be another swing through California in two weeks, and she wants to make that trip, too. In fact, Jackie Kennedy is determined to be at her husband's side from now until he is reelected next November.

But all of that is in the future. What matters now is that the Texas trip is halfway done. All Jackie has to do is make it through this day, and then she can relax. "Oh, God," she says, looking at her frazzled image in the mirror. "One day's campaigning can age a person thirty years."

The First Lady has no idea that today will age her like no other day in her young life.

■ ■ ■

The energy in the Fort Worth parking lot fuels the president, who delivers a powerful and impassioned speech. "We are going forward!" he exclaims in closing, reminding his audience that he is keeping the promises he made in his inaugural address less than three years earlier. The cold war is behind us, he's saying, all the while implying that the future is a Camelot for all Americans.

The earsplitting cries of approval from those thousands of hardened union men is all the proof John Kennedy needs that Texas really isn't such a bad place after all.

The president rides a wave of adrenaline off the stage and back into the hotel. Campaigning revitalizes him, even in an early-morning Texas drizzle.

But as good as he feels, the president knows that the rest of Friday, November 22, is not going to be easy. From both a political and a personal standpoint, he must be at the top of his game if he is going to win over the hardened people of Dallas.

Or, as the president warns Jackie, "We're heading into nut country today."

24

~

November 22, 1963
Texas School Book Depository, Dallas
9:45 A.M.

Crowds of eager Dallas residents stand on the curb in front of the Texas School Book Depository. The president won't pass by for three hours, but they've come early to get a good spot. Best of all, it looks like the sun might come out. Maybe they'll get a glimpse of John F. Kennedy and Jackie after all.

Lee Harvey Oswald peers out a first-floor window of the depository building, assessing the president's route by where the crowds stand. He can clearly see the corner of Elm and Houston, where John Kennedy's limousine will make a slow left turn. This is important to Oswald. He's selected a spot on the depository's sixth floor as his sniper's roost. The floor is dimly lit by bare 60-watt lightbulbs and is currently under renovation, and thus empty. Stacks of book boxes near the window overlooking Elm and Houston will form a natural hiding place, allowing Oswald to poke his rifle outside and sight the motorcade as it makes that deliberate turn. The marksman in Lee Harvey Oswald knows that he'll have time for two shots, maybe even three if he works the bolt quickly enough.

But one should be all he needs.

■ ■ ■

Air Force One crabs into the wind as Colonel Jim Swindal eases her down onto the runway at Dallas's Love Field. John Kennedy is ecstatic. Peering out the windows of his airplane, he sees that the weather has turned sunny and warm and that yet another large Texas crowd is waiting to greet him. "This trip is turning out to be terrific," he happily confides to Kenny O'Donnell. "Here we are in Dallas and it looks like everything in Texas will turn out to be fine for us!"

Police cars circle the field, and officers are even stationed on rooftops. But these are the only ominous sights at the airport. For the estimated welcoming party of two thousand are overjoyed to see Air Force One touch down, marking the first time a president has visited Dallas since 1948. Grown men stand on their tiptoes to see over the throngs in front of them. Airport personnel leave their desks inside the terminal and jostle into position near the chain-link fence separating the runway from the parking lot. The U.S. Air Force C-130 carrying the president's armored limousine lands and opens its cargo ramp. The bubble top remains on board the plane. The convertible top is completely down. A local television newsman, who is covering the spectacle live on air, enthusiastically reports that the bubble top is nowhere in evidence and that people will be able to see the president and First Lady "in the flesh." The reporter also reminds his audience that the president will be returning to Love Field between "2:15 and 2:30" to depart for Austin.

Lyndon Johnson and his wife, Lady Bird, await the president on the tarmac, as they have on every leg of the Texas trip. The vice president's job is to stand at the bottom of the ramp and greet the president. Johnson is not happy about this assignment, but he puts on a good face as Jackie emerges from the rear door of the plane, radiant in the pink Chanel suit with the matching pillbox hat. Two steps behind, and seen in person for the first time by the people of Dallas, comes John Kennedy.

"I can see his suntan from here!" the local TV reporter gushes.

The official plan is for JFK to head straight for his limousine to join the motorcade, but instead he breaks off and heads into the crowd. Not content with merely shaking a few hands, the president pushes deep into the throng, dragging Jackie along with him. The two of them remain surrounded by this wall of people for more than a full minute, much to the crowd's delight. Then the president and First Lady reemerge, only to wade deep into another section of crowd.

"Boy, this is something," enthuses the local reporter. "This is a bonus for the people who have waited here!"

The president and First Lady shake hands for what seems like an eternity to their very nervous Secret Service detail. "Kennedy is showing he is not afraid," Ronnie Dugger of the *Texas Observer* writes in his notebook.

Finally, John and Jackie Kennedy make their way to the presidential limousine. Awaiting them are Governor John Connally and his wife, Nellie. There are three rows of seats in the vehicle. Up front is the driver, fifty-four-year-old Bill Greer. To his right sits Roy Kellerman, like Greer, a longtime Secret Service agent. Special Agent Kellerman has served on the White House detail since the early days of World War II and has protected presidents Roosevelt, Truman, Eisenhower, and now Kennedy.

JFK sits in the backseat, on the right-hand side, patting his hair into place after his foray into the crowd. Jackie sits to his left. The First Lady was handed a bouquet of red roses upon landing in Dallas, and these now rest on the seat between her and the president.

Governor Connally sits directly in front of the president, in the middle row, known as jump seats. Connally takes off his ten-gallon hat so that the crowds can see him. Nellie sits in front of Jackie and right behind the driver, Special Agent Greer.

As the motorcade leaves Love Field at 11:55 A.M., the presidential limousine—Secret Service code name SS-100-X—is the second car in line, flanked on either side by four motorcycle escorts.

Up front is an advance car filled with local police and Secret Service, among them Dallas police chief Jesse Curry and Secret Service special agent Winston Lawson.

Behind John Kennedy's vehicle is a follow-up convertible code-named Halfback. Kennedy's two main members of the Irish Mafia, Dave Powers and Kenny O'Donnell, sit here, surrounded by Secret Service agents heavily armed with handguns and automatic weapons. Clint Hill, head of the First Lady's Secret Service detail, stands on the left running board of Halfback. Special agents Bill McIntyre, John Ready, and Paul Landis also man the running boards.

Car four is a convertible limousine that has been rented locally for the vice president. Even as the vehicles pull away from Love Field, it is obvious that LBJ is angry and pouting. While every other politician in the motorcade is waving to the crowds, he stares straight forward, unsmiling.

Bringing up the rear is car five, code-named Varsity and filled with a Texas state policeman and four Secret Service agents.

Way up at the front of the motorcade, driving several car lengths in front of SS-100-X, Dallas police chief Jesse Curry is committed to making the president's visit as incident-free as possible. The fifty-year-old chief is a lifetime law enforcement officer. In addition to working his way up through the ranks of the Dallas police, he has augmented his knowledge by attending the FBI Academy. Curry has been involved in almost every aspect of the planning for John Kennedy's visit and is dedicating 350 men—a full third of his force—to lining the motorcade route, handling security for the president's airport arrival, and policing the crowd at the Trade Mart speech.

However, Curry has chosen not to position any men in the vicinity of Dealey Plaza, thinking that the main crowd-control issues will take place prior to that destination. Once the motorcade turns from Houston Street and onto Elm, it goes under an overpass, turns right onto Stemmons Freeway, and through a relatively uncrowded area to the Trade Mart. Better to focus his officers on the busiest thoroughfares along the route, rather than waste them in a place where few people will be standing.

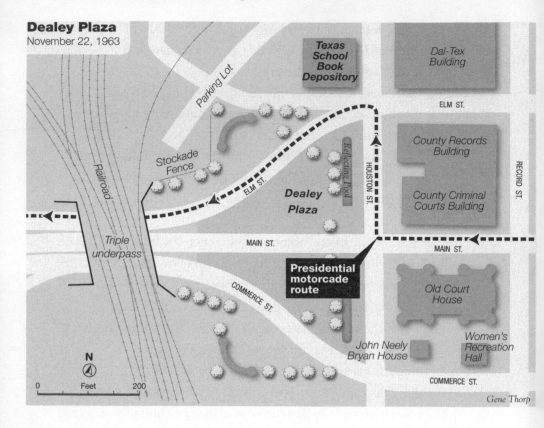

Dealey Plaza
November 22, 1963

Parking Lot

Texas School Book Depository

Dal-Tex Building

ELM ST.

Stockade Fence

Railroad

Reflecting Pool

ELM ST.

Dealey Plaza

HOUSTON ST.

County Records Building

RECORD ST.

County Criminal Courts Building

MAIN ST.

MAIN ST.

Triple underpass

Presidential motorcade route

COMMERCE ST.

Old Court House

John Neely Bryan House

Women's Recreation Hall

N

COMMERCE ST.

0   Feet   200

Gene Thorp

Curry has also ordered his men to face toward the street, rather than toward the crowd, thinking it wouldn't hurt for them to see the man they're protecting as a reward for the many long hours they will be on their feet. This ignores the example of New York City, where policemen stand facing *away* from the street, so they can better help the Secret Service protect the president by scanning the city's many windows for signs of a sniper's rifle.

But it doesn't matter during the motorcade's first easy miles. There is so little to do and so few people to see that a bored Jackie puts on her sunglasses and begins waving at billboards for fun. The white-collar workers along Lemmon Avenue are few in number and unexcited. They'd rather enjoy their lunch break from the IBM factory.

■ ■ ■

At the exact same moment, it's also lunchtime at the Texas School Book Depository. Most of Lee Harvey Oswald's coworkers have left the building, hoping to get a glimpse of the president.

Just down the block, FBI special agent James Hosty has forgotten all about investigating Lee Harvey Oswald and is just trying to make sure he gets a look at his hero, President Kennedy.

Lee Harvey Oswald didn't bring a lunch to work today. And he doesn't plan on eating. Instead, he moves a pile of boxes into position on the grimy sixth floor of the depository building, fashioning a well-concealed shooting nest.

At 12:24 P.M., nearly thirty minutes into the motorcade, the president's car passes Special Agent James Hosty on the corner of Main Street and Field. The G-man gets his wish and sees Kennedy in the flesh, before spinning back around and walking into the Alamo Grill for lunch.

At 12:28 the motorcade enters a seedy downtown neighborhood. Straight ahead, the beautiful green grass of Dealey Plaza is clearly visible. The Secret Service agents are stunned by the reception the president is now receiving, with people everywhere cheering and applauding.

At 12:29 the motorcade makes the crucial sharp right-hand turn onto Houston Street. From high above, in his sixth-floor sniper's lair, Lee Harvey Oswald sees John F. Kennedy in person for the first time. He quickly sights the Mannlicher-Carcano, taking aim through his scope as the motorcade skirts the edge of Dealey Plaza.

The crowds here are still large and enthusiastic, despite Chief Curry's prediction that they would have thinned by this point. The people shout for Jackie and the president to look their way. As per agreement, JFK waves at the people standing in front of buildings on the right side of the road, while Jackie waves at those standing along grassy Dealey Plaza, to their left. This ensures that no voter goes without a wave.

The motorcade is just five minutes away from the Trade Mart, where Kennedy will make his speech. Almost there.

Inside the presidential limousine, Nellie Connally stops waving long enough to look over her right shoulder and smile at John Kennedy. "You sure can't say that Dallas doesn't love you, Mr. President."

Ironically, at that very moment, if JFK had looked up to the sixth floor of the Texas School Book Depository, he would have seen a rifle barrel sticking out of an open window, pointed directly at his head.

But Kennedy doesn't look up.

Nor does the Secret Service.

It is 12:30 P.M. The time has come for Special Agent Bill Greer to steer SS-100-X through the sweeping 120-degree left turn from Houston and onto Elm.

■ ■ ■

Most people live their lives as if the end were always years away. They measure their days in love, laughter, accomplishment, and loss. There are moments of sunshine and storm. There are schedules, phone calls, careers, anxieties, joys, exotic trips, favorite foods, romance, shame, and hunger. A person can be defined by clothing, the smell of his breath, the way she combs her hair, the shape of his torso, or even the company she keeps.

All over the world, children love their parents and yearn for love in return. They revel in the touch of parental hands on their faces. And even on the worst of days, each person has dreams about the future—dreams that sometimes come true.

Such is life.

Yet life can end in less time than it takes to draw one breath.

25

November 22, 1963
Dealey Plaza, Dallas, Texas
12:14 P.M.

Anticipating the arrival of the president of the United States, a married high school student named Aaron Rowland stands with his wife, Barbara, along Dealey Plaza. Looking up at the Texas School Book Depository, he sees a man silhouetted against a corner sixth-floor window. An avid hunter, Rowland recognizes that the man is holding a rifle at port arms—diagonally across his body, with one hand on the stock and the other on the barrel. This is how a U.S. Marine might hold his weapon while waiting to fire at the rifle range.

Rowland is fascinated, but for all the wrong reasons. "Do you want to see a Secret Service agent?" he asks his wife.

"Where?"

"In that building there," he replies, pointing.

Six minutes later, a full ten minutes before the motorcade reaches Dealey Plaza, Ronald Fischer and Robert Edwards, who work in the nearby county auditor's office, look up and see a man standing motionlessly in the sixth-floor window. "He never moved," Fischer will later remember. "He didn't blink his eyes. He was just gazing, like a statue."

At the same time, Howard L. Brennan, a local pipe fitter, uses his khaki shirtsleeve to wipe the sweat from his brow. This makes him wonder how hot it is. And so he glances at the Hertz sign atop the Texas School Book Depository's roof that shows time and temperature. As he does so, Brennan's eyes pick out a stone-still mystery man positioned to fire in the upper window.

But then comes the sound of cheering as the motorcade gets nearer and nearer. Down on Main Street, the crowds are lined up ten to twenty feet deep, and their roar echoes through the window-lined canyons of downtown Dallas. In all the excitement, the sight of a man standing in a window clutching a rifle is forgotten. The president is near.

Nothing else matters.

■ ■ ■

Lee Harvey Oswald would prefer to shoot while in the prone position. That is the optimum for a marksman. In such a position, the rifle is not supported by muscle, which can grow weary or flinch. Instead, when the body is belly-down on the floor, the hard ground and the bones of the right and left forearm form a perfect and stable triangle.

But Oswald does not have that option. He will have to shoot standing up. Yet as a veteran marksman, he knows to keep his body as still as possible. So now he leans hard against the left window jam and presses the butt of his Italian carbine against his right shoulder. The scratched wooden stock of the butt is against his cheek, just as it was for so many hours at the rifle range with the M-1 rifle from his Marine Corps days. His right index finger is curled around the thirty-three-year-old trigger.

Lee Harvey Oswald peers into his four-power telescopic sight, the one that makes John Kennedy's head look as if it is two feet away. Oswald knows time is short. He'll be able to shoot two shots for sure. Three, if he's quick. He has probably nine seconds.

Seeing his target clearly, Oswald exhales, gently squeezes the trigger, and even as he feels the recoil kick the rifle back, hard against his shoulder, he smoothly pulls back the bolt to chamber another round. He can't tell whether the first bullet has done much damage. But that doesn't matter. Oswald must immediately fire again.

The assassin is an impulsive man, and perhaps even more powerless to stop the flood of adrenaline that would course through any man's body after firing a high-powered rifle at the president of the United States. The instant a man commits such an act, his life is changed forever. There is no turning back. From that second on he will be hunted to the ends of the earth. Perhaps he will spend the rest of his life in prison. Perhaps he will be executed.

The smart thing to do after firing a shot at the president is to throw down the rifle and run.

But if the first shot somehow misses, just like that shot missed General Walker back in April, and the president lives, Oswald will look like a fool. And that's the last thing he wants. No, the plan is to kill John Fitzgerald Kennedy. And Lee Harvey Oswald will see that plan through.

He doesn't think twice. Oswald fires again.

The sound of the second shot is not drowned out by the crowd below. It is so loud that pieces of the plaster ceiling inside the Texas School Book Depository fall and the panes of the windows along which Lee Harvey Oswald stands rattle.

At approximately 8.4 seconds after firing his first shot, Lee Harvey Oswald pulls the trigger on the third. And then Oswald is away. He drops his now-unnecessary Italian carbine and steps from the tower of book boxes behind which he's been hiding. He races to get out of the depository.

Dallas motorcycle officer Marrion L. Baker has raced into the building and up the stairs. He stops Oswald at gunpoint on the second floor but then lets him go when it becomes clear that Lee Harvey is a TBSD employee.

Sixty seconds later, Lee Harvey Oswald steps out of the depository building and into the sunshine of a sixty-five-degree Dallas afternoon.

Against all odds, the assassin is getting away.

■ ■ ■

Earwitness testimony in Dealey Plaza will later confirm that three shots were fired from the depository. One of the shots misses the president's car completely, and decades later there is still speculation whether it was the first or third round. But the fact remains that two of the shots did not miss.

The first impact strikes the president in the back of his lower neck. Traveling at 1,904 feet per second, the 6.5-millimeter round tears through the president's trachea and then exits his body through the tight knot of his dark blue tie. No bones are struck, and though his right lung is bruised, JFK's heart and lungs still function perfectly.

The president is badly hurt, but very much alive. He has trouble breathing and talking as blood floods into his windpipe. Otherwise, the rifle shot will most likely not kill him.

The same cannot be said for Texas governor John Connally. His jump seat, immediately in front of the president, is three inches lower than where the president is currently sitting. Therefore, ballistics after the fact show that the bullet that passed through Kennedy then entered Connally's back.

The governor had turned his body just before Oswald fired the shot. He was twisting around, trying to speak face-to-face with the president. Thus, the so-called "magic bullet" (which was traveling at slightly more than 1,700 feet per second) manages to pierce Connally's skin and travel through his body, exiting below the right side of his chest. But the magic bullet isn't finished. It then pierces the governor's wrist and deflects off the bones and into his left thigh, where it finally comes to rest.

The blow knocks Governor Connally forward, bending him double. His chest is immediately drenched in blood. "No, no, no, no," he cries, "they're going to kill us both."

Roy Kellerman thinks he hears the president yell, "My God, I'm hit," and turns to look over his left shoulder at the man whose Boston accent he knows so well.

Kellerman sees for sure that JFK has been shot.

President Kennedy and Governor Connally are just four miles from Parkland Hospital. There, a team of emergency surgeons can save their lives. It's up to Secret Service driver Bill Greer to get them there. But the driver of SS-100-X has also looked back to check on the president's status. This distraction means that the limousine veers slightly from side to side rather than speeding to the emergency room. When Greer turns back to the wheel there's still time to save the president. All he has to do is accelerate.

But the impact of what has happened has not sunk in. Not for Greer. Not for Kellerman. Not even for Jackie, who is now turning toward JFK.

And the presidential limo still travels far too slowly down Elm Street.

■ ■ ■

Secret Service special agent Clint Hill, in charge of the First Lady's detail, hears the shot and leaps into action. Shoving himself away from the running board on Halfback, the vehicle directly behind the president's limousine, Hill sprints forward in an effort to jump on the small step that sticks out from the back of the president's car.

Meanwhile, JFK is leaning to his left, but still upright. Jackie wraps her hands lovingly around her husband's face. The First Lady looks into the president's eyes to see what's wrong with him. The distance between her beautiful, unlined face and that of the tanned and very stunned John Kennedy is approximately six inches.

The torso of a normal man would have been shoved farther forward by the force of a bullet striking his body at nearly twice the speed of sound. This is precisely what happened to Governor Connally. If John F. Kennedy had been knocked forward, he might have lived a long life.

But now the president's long and painful struggle with back problems returns to torture him one last time.

The back brace that he is wearing holds his body erect. The president fortified its rigidity this morning by wrapping the brace and his thighs in a thick layer of Ace bandages.

If not for the brace, the next bullet, less than five seconds later, would have traveled harmlessly over his head.

But it does not. The next bullet explodes his skull.

■ ■ ■

The diameter of the entry wound from the second impact is just slightly wider than that of a number two pencil. The high rate of speed ensures that the shell will travel all the way through the brain and out the front of the skull, rather than lodging inside like the slower bullet that killed Abraham Lincoln. When Lincoln was shot, physicians inserted something called a Nelaton probe into his brain. This slender porcelain stick followed the path of the wound until the tip struck the solid metal ball fired from John Wilkes Booth's pistol. The path of the bullet was all very linear and neat.

But the 6.5-millimeter round fired by Lee Harvey Oswald is a far more vicious chunk of lead. Such a slender bullet might seem insignificant, but it is capable of bringing down a deer from two hundred yards.

This copper-jacketed missile effectively ends John F. Kennedy's life in an instant. It barely slows as it slices through the tender gray brain matter before exploding the thin wall of bone as it exits the front of his skull.

Jackie's arms are still wrapped around her husband when the front of his head explodes. Brains, blood, and bone fragments shower the First Lady's face and that pink Chanel suit; the matter sprays as far forward as the limousine's windshield visors.

As is so often his habit when something messes up his hair, John Kennedy's hand reflexively tries to pat the top of his head.

But now the top of his head is gone.

■ ■ ■

There is no chance for mouth-to-mouth resuscitation, as was attempted when Lincoln lay dying on the floor of his Ford's Theatre box. There will be no overnight vigil, as with Lincoln, so that friends and loved ones can stand over JFK in his final moments, slowly absorbing the pain of impending loss, and perhaps speaking a few honest words about how much they love John Fitzgerald Kennedy.

The man who swam miles to save the men of PT-109, who has

shaken the hands of kings and queens and prime ministers, who inspired the entire world with his bold speeches and deeply held belief in the power of democracy and freedom, who caressed the cheeks of his children, endured the loss of so many family loved ones, and who stood toe-to-toe with men who might otherwise destroy the world, is brain dead.

■ ■ ■

Little do the horrified onlookers know, but historians and conspiracy theorists, as well as average citizens born years after this day, will long argue whether Lee Harvey Oswald acted alone or perhaps had the help of others. Federal authorities will scrutinize ballistics and use a stopwatch to time how quickly a man can aim and reload a 6.5-millimeter Mannlicher-Carcano. A variety of people will become self-described experts on grainy home videos of the assassination, grassy knolls, and the many evildoers who longed to see John F. Kennedy physically removed from power.

Those conspiratorial arguments will become so powerful and so involved that they will one day threaten to overwhelm the human tragedy of November 22, 1963.

So let the record state, once and for all, that at 12:30 P.M. on a sunny Friday afternoon in Dallas, Texas, John Fitzgerald Kennedy is shot dead in less time than it takes to blink an eye.

He leaves behind a beautiful widow.

He leaves behind two adoring young children.

He leaves behind a nation that loves him.

26

November 22, 1963
Dallas, Texas
12:31 p.m.

Inside the presidential limousine, there is chaos.

"Oh, no, no, no. Oh, my God. They have shot my husband. I love you, Jack," Jackie Kennedy cries.

The First Lady will not remember what she does in the seconds after her husband is shot. She is in shock. In the future, she will watch videos of herself and feel as if she is watching some other woman. Her children will protect her by tearing the assassination images out of books before she can see them.

"They've killed my husband," Jackie says to no one and everyone. Up front, driver Bill Greer and Special Agent Roy Kellerman are radioing that the president has been hit. Governor Connally is still conscious, but fading fast. His wife, Nellie, has thrown her body over his. This leaves Jackie alone in the backseat, the president's lifeless body leaning against hers.

"I have his brains in my hand," she yells.

And then Jackie is up and out of the seat. She's on a mission.

Secret Service special agent Clint Hill knows precisely what the First Lady is doing. Rather than sitting with her husband's body, she is crawling onto the trunk of the moving presidential limousine in order to collect pieces of skull and brain that cover the dark blue metal. Some fragments are flesh colored, with the skin still attached. Behind her, the president's body is still upright, though tilted to the left. Blood pours out of his head wound in great torrents, drenching her roses and his clothing and spilling onto the floor of the vehicle.

"Good God, she's going to fly off the back of the car," Hill thinks as he jumps onto the small platform attached to the back of the Lincoln. To Special Agent Hill, the shot that killed the president sounded like "a melon shattering onto cement." Splatter from the president's head covers Hill's face and clothes as he and the fatal bullet reached the kill zone simultaneously.

Terror fills the First Lady's eyes. Her face is covered in blood and gray matter. This is a stark change for a woman so often consumed by appearing nothing less than elegant. But Jackie could not care less. "My God, they have shot his head off," she screams.

Hill is just inches away from Jackie Kennedy as Bill Greer accelerates toward Parkland Hospital. SS-100-X is a behemoth of a vehicle, specially modified for use by the president. In addition to those mid-vehicle jump seats—which stretch the car from the 133-inch wheelbase of a factory Lincoln to 156 inches—the car weighs almost four tons. The 350-horsepower engine is its weak link, making it unable to accelerate quickly. But once the vehicle is up to speed, it hurtles down the freeway like an unstoppable force.

Which is precisely what it's doing now. Scattering the police motorcycle escort, Bill Greer is pressing the accelerator all the way to the floor. Clint Hill, struggling to keep Jackie Kennedy from falling off the vehicle, almost flies off the back bumper himself. His hand clings to a grip on the trunk that has been placed there specifically for the Secret Service to hold on to. Now he grips for dear life with just that one hand, the other reaching for Jackie as the limo rockets down Elm Street. Hill grabs

Jackie's elbow, which allows him finally to get stabilized on the trunk of the presidential limousine.

Hill's first job is to protect Jackie Kennedy. Even as he presses his body flat against the trunk and holds on tight, he shoves her hard back into the backseat. The president's body falls over and onto her lap. She holds his head in her white-gloved hands, cradling him as if he has simply fallen asleep. "Jack, Jack. What have they done to you?"

Up front, driver Bill Greer is depending upon Chief Curry to lead the president's limousine to Parkland Hospital, which is four miles away.

Still clinging to the trunk, Clint Hill turns and looks at Halfback, where Secret Service agents ride on the running boards. He makes eye contact with Special Agent Paul Landis, then shakes his head and holds out his hand in a thumbs-down signal.

Special Agent Emory Roberts sees Hill's gesture and immediately radios to the agents protecting Lyndon Johnson. With one downturned thumb, Clint Hill has confirmed that Lyndon Baines Johnson is now the acting president of the United States. Protecting his life becomes the Secret Service's number one priority.

In the backseat of the Lincoln, Jackie Kennedy holds her husband's head and quietly sobs. "He's dead. They've killed him. Oh Jack, oh Jack. I love you."

■ ■ ■

Lee Harvey Oswald is doing everything right. He's walking east up Elm Street to catch a bus. The panic and chaos that now define Dealey Plaza recede behind him. No one has stopped Oswald. At this point, no one even suspects him.

Meanwhile, his escape plan is coming together slowly. For now, the assassin is on his way to his rooming house to pick up his pistol—just in case.

■ ■ ■

The radio call of "Code 3" means an emergency of the highest importance to Dallas-area hospitals. The term is almost never used. So when

Parkland dispatcher Anne Ferguson requests more details, she is simply told, "The president has been shot."

The time is 12:33 P.M.

Three minutes later, the presidential limousine roars into Parkland, blowing past the sign reading "Emergency Cases Only." Bill Greer parks in the middle of the three ambulance bays.

But there is no stretcher waiting, no emergency team rushing to help the president. Incredibly, a breakdown in communications has stymied the hospital's emergency response. The trauma team has barely been notified.

So those inside the presidential limo simply wait.

Nellie Connally lies atop her husband, even as a moaning Jackie Kennedy holds John Kennedy's head.

Halfback pulls up, right behind SS-100-X. Dave Powers and Kenny O'Donnell, men who have been in the political trenches with JFK since the 1946 congressional campaign, rush to the Lincoln, hoping for the best. The president still has a faint pulse—which continues to push pint after pint of blood out through his head wound.

"Get up," Secret Service special agent Emory Roberts commands Jackie Kennedy.

She doesn't move. She has positioned her arms and jacket so that no one can see JFK's face or head. The First Lady does not want her husband remembered this way.

Roberts delicately lifts Jackie's arm so he can see for himself if the president is dead. One look is all he needs. Roberts backs off.

Dave Powers sees the fixed pupils gazing sightlessly into the distance and breaks into tears. O'Donnell, who served in the Army Air Corps during World War II, reverts to his soldier days and snaps to attention as a sign of numb respect.

Even if Jackie were to try to move right now, she would have nowhere to go. The slumped body of John Connally blocks the car's door, meaning that the governor of Texas must be moved before the president of the United States can be lifted from the Lincoln.

It is Dave Powers, not hospital personnel, who finally sets aside his tears and lifts Connally out by the legs and onto a gurney. The governor is conscious, though just barely. His wounds are life threatening, and the emergency physicians at Parkland will be very busy today trying to save Connally's life. (They will succeed—a rare bit of good news on a brutal day.)

Though Connally has been wheeled inside to Trauma Room Two and no longer obstructs the car door, Jackie Kennedy still refuses to let go of her husband. When she lets go, she knows he's gone forever. This will be the last time she holds him. The First Lady curls her body forward so that the president's blood-soaked face and her breasts come together. She weeps quietly, pushing her body closer and closer to her husband's.

"Mrs. Kennedy," Special Agent Clint Hill says, "please let us help the president."

Jackie doesn't respond. But she knows that voice. It is the soft command of a man who has protected her from danger night and day.

The voice of Clint Hill is the only voice Jackie responds to in her moment of shocked grief.

Hill softly places his hand on her shoulder. The First Lady trembles, in mourning.

The quiet crowd of Secret Service agents and Kennedy staffers around the Lincoln do not speak. The seconds tick past.

"Please, Mrs. Kennedy. Please let us get him into the hospital," Hill implores.

"I'm not going to let him go, Mr. Hill," Jackie says.

"We've got to take him in, Mrs. Kennedy."

"No, Mr. Hill. You know he's dead. Leave me alone."

Jackie sobs. Her body jerks as pain courses through her.

Hill realizes something. It's bad enough that she is seeing the man she loves with his head blown off, but she doesn't want anyone else seeing him like that. And as the media descend onto Parkland Hospital even in the midst of Jackie's lonely Pietà, there is no way in the world Jackie will allow John Fitzgerald Kennedy to be photographed in this state.

Clint Hill is exhausted. He has worked long hours on this trip and gotten by on little food and even less sleep. But there's nothing he won't do for Jackie Kennedy. Knowing in an instant that it is the right thing to do, Special Agent Hill removes his suit coat and sets it gently atop the president's body.

Jackie Kennedy, her pink suit and white gloves now covered in the president's copious blood, wraps her husband's head and torso in Clint Hill's coat.

Then, for the last time, Jacqueline Bouvier Kennedy lets go of the man she loves. The president is placed atop a gurney and hustled down to Trauma Room One, those pushing the gurney following the red line on the floor. The walls are tiled in tan, and atop the president's chest is the bouquet of bloody red roses, which have stuck to his body.

■ ■ ■

About four miles away from the bloody hospital scene, Lee Harvey Oswald boards a bus at the corner of Elm and Murphy and completes his getaway.

■ ■ ■

The assassination of Abraham Lincoln in April 1865 was a spiderweb of conspiracy. On the same evening that Lincoln was shot in Ford's Theatre, there were also plans to kill his vice president and secretary of state. Had those plans succeeded, the top level of American government would have been beheaded.

As soon as the first shot is fired in Dallas, those long-ago events are instantly remembered. Immediate steps are taken to ensure that a possible conspiracy is not completed. Several members of the cabinet are west of Hawaii, en route to Japan. A radio call orders them to turn around and come home.

Vice President Lyndon Johnson is under constant watch the instant his rented limousine arrives at Parkland Hospital. He is hustled into a small white cubicle in Parkland's Minor Medicine section with his wife, Lady Bird. A Secret Service detail guards his life. A patient and a nurse are kicked out to make room for them. There is no word yet on the fate of the president, though everyone knows that surviving such a gunshot wound is just about impossible. The Secret Service wants LBJ flown immediately back to Washington and out of harm's way. Failing that, it would like him relocated to the safest possible security zone in Dallas: Air Force One.

But Vice President Johnson refuses to leave the hospital. He remains waiting for word of President Kennedy's fate. The Secret Service pressures him again and again to depart, but LBJ will not go. Johnson is planning his next steps. Until the presidential succession is official, he will deliver no orders. The oath of office is not necessary to make him officially president. Succession will take place the instant JFK is declared dead. So LBJ stands there in the small cubicle at Parkland Hospital, leaning against the wall and sipping coffee in complete silence, waiting for the official announcement of President Kennedy's death.

In Trauma Room One, the president's body is stripped, except for his underwear. His gold watch is removed from his wrist. He no longer has a regular pulse, but he breathes in short breaths. Blood continues to pour out of his head wound and the hole in his throat; the rest of his body is unscathed. An overhead fluorescent lamp lights the small army of medical professionals at work in the trauma room. The first doctor on the scene is second-year medical resident Charles J. Carrico, who knows what to do and acts quickly. A tube is inserted into John Kennedy's throat to open his airway, and saline solution is pumped into his body through his right femoral vein.

The room slowly fills with surgeons, until there are fourteen doctors standing over the president. Outside the trauma room, Jackie Kennedy sits in a folding chair holding vigil.

Dr. Mac Perry, a thirty-four-year-old surgeon, now steps in to head the team. He uses a scalpel to slice open the president's throat and perform a tracheotomy, while someone else attaches a tube to a respirator to induce regular breathing.

Jackie now rises from her chair, determined to enter the trauma room. She has heard the talk about fluids and resuscitation and is beginning to hope that her husband might just live. A nurse blocks her path, but the demure First Lady can display an iron will when she wants to.

"I'm going to get into that room," she repeats over and over as she wrestles with Nurse Doris Nelson, who shows no signs of backing down. "I'm going to get into that room."

"Mrs. Kennedy, you need a sedative," a nearby doctor tells her.

But the First Lady does not wish to be numbed. She wants to feel every last moment with her husband. "I want to be in there when he dies," she says firmly.

■ ■ ■

Bobby Kennedy gets the bad news from J. Edgar Hoover.

As the head of America's top law enforcement agency, Hoover is informed of the shooting almost immediately. The FBI director is a dispassionate man, but never more so than right now. He sits at his desk on the fifth floor of the Justice Department Building as he picks up the phone to call Bobby Kennedy. It has been fifteen minutes since Lee Harvey Oswald first pulled the trigger. The surgical trauma team at Parkland is fighting to keep the president alive.

Bobby is just about to eat a tuna fish sandwich on the patio of his Virginia home when his wife, Ethel, tells him he has a call.

"It's J. Edgar Hoover," she tells Bobby.

The attorney general knows this must be important. The director knows better than to call Bobby at home. He sets down his sandwich and goes to the phone. It's a special direct government line known as Extension 163.

"I have news for you," Hoover says. "The president has been shot."

Bobby hangs up. His first reaction is one of great distress, and his body seems to go slack. But his next thought, as always, is to protect his older brother. He calls the White House and has all the locks on JFK's file cabinets changed so that Lyndon Johnson cannot go through them. The most delicate files are completely removed from the White House and placed under round-the-clock security.

Bobby then fields phone call after phone call from friends and family. He holds back tears, but Ethel knows that her husband is breaking down and hands him a pair of dark glasses to hide his red-rimmed eyes.

The calls don't stop. In the midst of them all, Bobby realizes that the tables have been turned. And he knows that he will soon get a call from a man he despises.

■ ■ ■

Jackie Kennedy gets the bad news from Dr. William Kemp Clark.

It comes just moments after, against great odds, the First Lady battles her way into the trauma room. She stands in a corner, out of the way, just wanting to be near her husband.

The sight is singularly medical, as tubes now sprout from the president's mouth, nose, and chest. His skin is the palest white. Blood is being transfused into his body. Dr. Mac Perry presses down on the president's sternum to restart the heart, even as the electrocardiogram machine shows a flat line. Dr. William Kemp Clark, Parkland's chief neurosurgeon, assists Perry by monitoring the EKG for even a flicker of deviation.

Finally, Clark knows they can do no more. A sheet is drawn over JFK's face. Dr. Clark turns to Jackie Kennedy. "Your husband has sustained a fatal wound," the veteran surgeon tells the First Lady.

"I know," she replies.

"The president is dead."

Jackie leans up and presses her cheek to that of Dr. Clark. It is an expression of thanks. Kemp Clark, a hard man who served in the Pacific in World War II, can't help himself. He breaks down and sobs.

■ ■ ■

Most people in the United States get the bad news of the president's death from CBS newsman Walter Cronkite.

The most trusted man in America first breaks into the soap opera *As the World Turns* just eight minutes after the shooting, saying that an assassin has fired three shots at the president. Despite the fact that most Americans are at work or school, and not home watching daytime television, more than seventy-five million people are aware of the shooting by 1:00 P.M.

■ ■ ■

Lyndon Baines Johnson gets the bad news from Kenny O'Donnell.

Shortly after 1:00 P.M., John F. Kennedy's appointments secretary marches into the small white cubicle in the Minor Medicine section of the hospital and stands before Lyndon Johnson. O'Donnell is openly distraught. He is not the sort of man who weeps at calamity, but the devastated look on his face is clear for all to see.

Even before O'Donnell opens his mouth, LBJ knows that it is official: Lyndon Baines Johnson is now the thirty-sixth president of the United States.

■ ■ ■

Jack Ruby gets the bad news from television, just like most of America.

The nightclub owner is on the second floor of the *Dallas Morning News* building, just four blocks from Dealey Plaza. He has come to place an ad for his burlesque business, the Carousel Club—"a f---ing classy joint," in Ruby's own words. He pays in person because the *Morning News* has canceled his credit after he fell behind on his payments one too many times. The ad announces his featured performers for the coming weekend and is no different from his usual weekly ads gracing the newspaper.

Ruby is five foot, nine inches and 175 pounds, and is fond of carrying a big roll of cash. He's got friends in the Mafia and on the police force. He is known to like health food and has a lightning-quick temper. But most of all Jack Ruby considers himself a Democrat and a patriot.

The first reports state that a Secret Service man has been killed, but as Ruby and the advertising staff of the *Morning News* gather around a small black-and-white television for more information, the harsh truth is announced.

A despondent Jack Ruby wanders off and sits alone at a desk. After a time, he gets up and announces that he is canceling the club advertisement. Instead, he places another ad. This one tells the good people of Dallas that the Carousel Club will be closed all weekend, out of respect for President Kennedy.

Jack Ruby will not be doing business over the next few days. He will be doing something else.

■ ■ ■

Lee Harvey Oswald is on the move. After his bus stalls in heavy post-assassination traffic, he gets off and walks a bit before finding a cab, which takes him closer to his rooming house at 1026 North Beckley. Upon arriving there, he races to his room, grabs his .38-caliber pistol, and sticks it in his waistband. Then he quickly leaves.

Little does Oswald know, but eyewitnesses at the scene have given the police his description. Now the cops are on the lookout for a "white male, approximately 30, slender build, height 5 foot 10 inches, weight 165 pounds."

At 1:15 P.M., Officer J. D. Tippit of the Dallas Police Department is driving east on Tenth Street. Just after the intersection of Tenth and Patton, he sees a man matching the suspect's description walking alone, wearing a light-colored jacket.

Tippit is a married father of three children. He is thirty-nine years old, earned a Bronze Star as a paratrooper in World War II, has a tenth-grade education, and earns just a little over $5,000 a year. The "J.D." initials do not stand for anything.

Tippit has been with the Dallas Police Department eleven years as he pulls his car alongside Lee Harvey Oswald. He knows to be cautious. But he also knows to be thorough in his questioning.

Oswald leans down and speaks to Tippit through the right front window vent. He is hostile.

Tippit opens the door and steps out of his police cruiser. He walks around to the front of the car, intending to ask Oswald a few more questions. Based on the answers, Tippit will then make a decision whether to place Oswald in handcuffs. But the policeman doesn't get farther than the left front wheel. Lee Harvey Oswald pulls out his .38 and fires four bullets in rapid succession. Tippit is killed instantly.

Oswald, the man who nervously missed General Walker so many

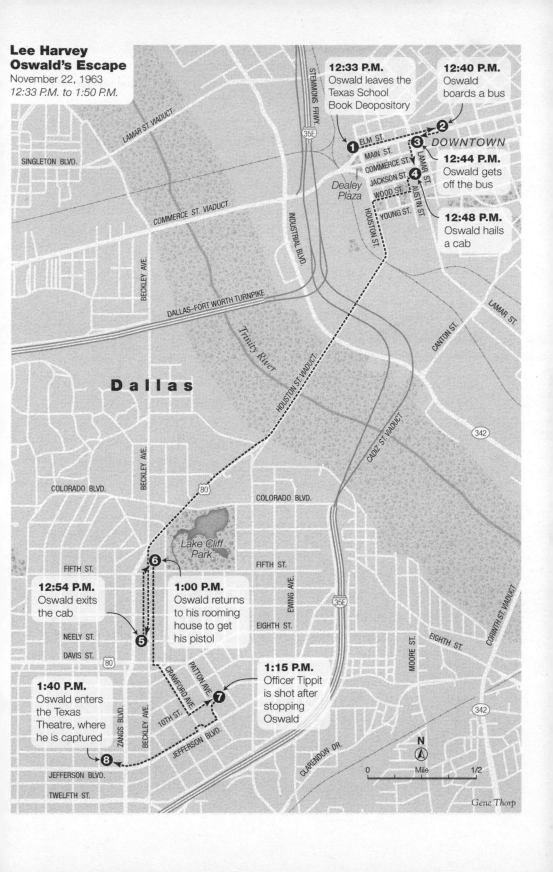

Lee Harvey Oswald's Escape
November 22, 1963
12:33 P.M. to 1:50 P.M.

12:33 P.M. Oswald leaves the Texas School Book Deopository

12:40 P.M. Oswald boards a bus

12:44 P.M. Oswald gets off the bus

12:48 P.M. Oswald hails a cab

12:54 P.M. Oswald exits the cab

1:00 P.M. Oswald returns to his rooming house to get his pistol

1:15 P.M. Officer Tippit is shot after stopping Oswald

1:40 P.M. Oswald enters the Texas Theatre, where he is captured

Dallas

DOWNTOWN

Dealey Plaza

Lake Cliff Park

Trinity River

N

0   Mile   1/2

Gene Thorp

long months ago, has now killed the president of the United States and a Dallas police officer in cold blood just forty-five minutes apart.

But Oswald is running out of options. He is out of money, almost out of ammunition, and the Dallas police know what he looks like. He will have to be very clever in these next few minutes if he is to continue his escape.

The killer quickly reloads and continues his journey, turning down Patton Avenue. But this time he doesn't walk; he jogs. There is no doubt about it: Oswald is being hunted. The police are closing in. He needs to move quickly now. The time is 1:16 P.M.

■ ■ ■

At 1:26 P.M. the Secret Service whisks Lyndon Johnson to Air Force One, where he immediately climbs the steps up to the back door of the plane. There he moves into President Kennedy's personal bedroom, takes off his coat, and sprawls on the bed while he awaits Jackie Kennedy's return to the plane. She has remained behind at Parkland, refusing to leave until the body of her husband comes with her.

And so LBJ waits. Even as he relishes his first moments of power, outside the bedroom, mechanics are removing several of the first-class seats in the rear of Air Force One to make room for John Kennedy's coffin.

LBJ has chosen the bedroom because he wants privacy. He picks up John Kennedy's personal presidential telephone next to the bed and places a call to a man he loathes.

On the other end of the line, Bobby Kennedy picks up the phone and says a professional hello to his new boss.

■ ■ ■

Lee Harvey Oswald hears the sirens and knows they're coming for him.

He races toward the quickest hiding place he can find, a movie house called the Texas Theatre. Oswald has traveled eight blocks in the twenty-five minutes since killing Officer Tippit. He shed his jacket shortly after shooting Tippit, hoping to confuse his pursuers. He runs past the Bethel Temple, where a sign advises "Prepare to Meet Thy God."

But Lee Harvey Oswald is not showing fear.

Foolishly, he runs right past the ticket booth. In the dark of the theater, he finds a seat, trying to make himself invisible. His seat is on the main floor, along the right center aisle. The matinee film is *War Is Hell*, an ironic name for a decidedly hellish day of Oswald's invention.

After seeing the man run inside without paying, and then at the same time hearing sirens as police cars race to the scene of Officer Tippit's murder, ticket taker Julia Postal puts two and two together. Realizing that the man she just saw is "running from them for some reason," she picks up the phone and dials the police.

Squad cars are on the scene almost immediately. Police close off the theater's exits. The house lights are turned on. Patrolman M. N. McDonald approaches Oswald, who suddenly stands and punches the policeman in the face while reaching for the pistol in his waistband. McDonald is not hurt and immediately fights back. Other policemen join the scrum. Thus, screaming about police brutality, Lee Harvey Oswald is dragged out of the theater and taken to jail.

■ ■ ■

Undertaker Vernon Oneal receives the call from Clint Hill personally, ordering him to bring his best casket to Parkland Hospital. Oneal specializes in taking care of the dead, running a fleet of seven radio-equipped white hearses that convey the newly departed to his mortuary, where relatives can sip from the coffee bar before paying their respects in the Slumber Room.

The casket Oneal quickly selects for John Kennedy is the "Britannia" model from the Elgin Casket Company. It is double-walled and solid bronze. The upholstery is satin.

Upon his arrival at Parkland Hospital, Oneal is told that Jackie Kennedy wants one last moment with her husband. That's all. She removes the wedding band from her finger and slides it over the knuckle of Jack's little finger with the help of an orderly, so that it will not fall off during the inevitable embalming. She then smokes a cigarette. Jackie is exhausted and brokenhearted. The mood at Parkland is mournful but slowly returning to normal hospital routine. As doctors and nurses begin attending to other cases, Jackie Kennedy is feeling more and more out of place.

"You could go back to the plane now," she is told.

"I'm not going back till I leave with Jack," she replies.

Meanwhile, Vernon Oneal places a sheet of plastic down on the inside of the coffin, lining the bottom. He then carefully swaddles the body of John Kennedy in seven layers of rubber bags and one more of plastic. Finally, the president's body is laid inside. Oneal is concerned that the president's blood will permanently stain the satin lining.

Almost an hour after being declared dead, John Kennedy is now ready to leave Parkland Hospital and fly back to Washington.

Yet ironically, the city of Dallas, which once wanted him to stay away, now will not let JFK leave.

■ ■ ■

It is a little-known fact that it is not a federal crime to kill the president of the United States. It is against federal law to initiate a *conspiracy* to kill the president, which is why J. Edgar Hoover is now insisting that JFK's murder was the act of many instead of just one. Hoover wants jurisdiction over the case. But at this point, he is not getting it. Jurisdiction falls to the state of Texas and the municipality of Dallas.

Thus Dallas officials won't let John Kennedy's body leave the state of Texas until an official autopsy has been performed. The Dallas medical examiner, who has now arrived at Parkland, will not budge on this matter.

Veteran Secret Service special agent Roy Kellerman, who has now taken charge, is livid. "My friend," Kellerman makes it clear to Dallas medical examiner Dr. Earl Rose, "this is the body of the president of the United States and we are going to take it back to Washington."

"No. That's not the way things are," Rose replies. "Where there is a homicide, we must have an autopsy."

"He is going with us," Kellerman tells Rose.

"The body stays," insists the medical examiner, an upright man fond of wagging his finger in people's faces.

Meanwhile, Lyndon Johnson and Air Force One are stuck on the ground because of this legal wrangling. Jackie Kennedy won't leave without JFK's body, and LBJ won't depart without Jackie, fearing he would be considered insensitive if he did.

The argument now becomes an old-fashioned Texas standoff—a physical showdown between the Secret Service, Dr. Rose, and members of the Dallas Police Department. There are forty men present. Pushing and shoving break out. The Secret Service is determined to have its way, but the Dallas police won't back down. Finally, Kennedy's close friends Kenny O'Donnell and Dave Powers order Secret Service agents to grab JFK's coffin and bull their way through the police. "We're getting out of here," O'Donnell barks as the undertaker's cart on which the casket rests is rolled toward the exit door. "We don't give a damn what these laws say. We're leaving now!"

The president's body is loaded into Vernon Oneal's 1964 white Cadillac hearse. Jackie Kennedy sits in the rear jump seat, next to her husband's body. Clint Hill and other agents jam themselves into the front seat. Bill Greer is still inside the hospital, but Roy Kellerman isn't waiting for him. Secret Service special agent Andy Berger takes the wheel and races for Love Field at top speed. As he watches the hearse peel out, Vernon Oneal wonders aloud how and when he's going to be paid.

There is no stopping when the Cadillac reaches the airport. Tires squealing, Special Agent Berger races the hearse onto the tarmac, ignoring the signs reading "Restricted Area" and "Slow—Dangerous Trucks." He speeds past the Braniff and American Airlines hangars, oblivious to all dangers until the hearse screeches to a halt at the back steps leading up to Air Force One. Kennedy's friends and bodyguards then personally manhandle the six hundred pounds of coffin and president, banging it off the stairwell leading up into the plane and tilting the casket at awkward angles. They load the body onto Air Force One through the same rear door John Kennedy stepped out of three hours

President Lyndon B. Johnson, with Jackie at his side, takes the oath of office on Air Force One following the assassination of President John F. Kennedy. (Cecil Stoughton, White House Photograph, John F. Kennedy Presidential Library and Museum, Boston)

earlier. That moment was ceremonial and presidential. This moment is morbid and ghastly.

Jackie Kennedy waits until her husband's body is on board before climbing up the steps. The inside of Air Force One is like an inferno; the air-conditioning has been off for hours. The blinds are down, and the cabin is dark out of fear that more assassins are on the loose and will shoot through the plane's windows. Yet Lyndon Johnson insists on being sworn in before Air Force One leaves the ground. So it is that the Kennedy staff and the Johnson staff stand uncomfortably next to one another as federal judge Sarah Hughes, who was personally appointed to the bench by LBJ and now has been hastily summoned to the presidential jet of which John F. Kennedy was so fond, administers the oath.

"Do you, Lyndon Baines Johnson, solemnly swear . . ."

"I, Lyndon Baines Johnson, solemnly swear . . ."

LBJ stands tall in Air Force One. To his left, still wearing the blood-stained pink suit, is Jacqueline Bouvier Kennedy. The former First Lady has not changed clothes. She is adamant that the world have a visual reminder of what happened to her husband here.

Standing before Johnson is the judge.

Several feet behind them, in the rear of the plane, lies the body of John F. Kennedy.

After the swearing-in ceremony, Jackie sits down in a seat next to the coffin as the long ride home begins.

■ ■ ■

It is Sunday morning, November 24. The nation is devastated by the assassination of John F. Kennedy and is riveted to the television with depressed fascination as events unfold. Jackie Kennedy is now out of sight, privately mourning her husband's death. So the eyes of America turn to Lee Harvey Oswald. The assassin has become infamous since Friday, particularly after telling a crowd of reporters, "I'm just a patsy."

That impromptu midnight press conference at Dallas police head-quarters was surreal. Reporters were allowed to physically crowd the handcuffed Oswald. Many in Dallas, and across America, are so infuri-ated by JFK's death that they would gladly exact revenge. Yet the Dallas police do little to shield Oswald.

One of those enraged is Jack Ruby, who worked his way into the press conference unmolested, with a loaded Colt Cobra .38 in his suit coat pocket.

The lack of security around Oswald continued throughout the press conference. He told reporters that the police were after him only because he had lived in the Soviet Union. He denied shooting the president. His tantalizing words "I'm just a patsy" hung in the air, suggesting that he was some sort of scapegoat.

To some, those words brought to mind another such incident, thirty years earlier.

On February 15, 1933, in Miami, Florida, Giuseppe "Joe" Zangara emptied a .32-caliber handgun at President Franklin Delano Roosevelt. Zangara missed his target, instead hitting and killing Chicago mayor Anton Cermak. The trial was amazingly quick, and Zangara was executed by the electric chair just five weeks later.

There are some who insist that Roosevelt was not the intended target. Instead, they believe that the point all along was to kill Cermak, as part of a Mafia conspiracy.

In mob slang, Zangara was a "patsy"—someone whose guilt was set up to advance a crime coordinated from behind the scenes.

Lee Harvey Oswald's public statement that he is a patsy fuels the flames that John Kennedy's death is part of a greater conspiracy.

■ ■ ■

There are still Americans who believe Lee Harvey Oswald did not act alone in killing John F. Kennedy. Some came to this belief thanks to Oswald's comments and J. Edgar Hoover's insistence that there was a conspiracy. Even Bobby Kennedy believed that Oswald did not act alone.

The world will never know the answer.

After saying just a few words to the press on Sunday morning, Lee Harvey Oswald is led through the basement of the Dallas Police Department to a waiting armored car, where he will be transferred to the county jail. In actuality, the armored car is a decoy—for security measures, Oswald will be led to a police car instead.

A crowd of journalists watches a handcuffed and smiling Oswald as he makes his way down the corridor, his right arm handcuffed to the left of Detective J. R. Leavelle.

Between forty and fifty journalists and more than seventy policemen are waiting as Oswald is brought out. Three television cameras roll.

"Here he comes!" someone shouts as Oswald emerges from the jail office.

The newsmen press forward. Microphones are thrust at Oswald and

An unrepentant Lee Harvey Oswald. (Associated Press)

questions shouted. Flashbulbs pop as photographers capture the moment for posterity.

Oswald walks ten feet outside the jail office, on his way to the ramp where the police car is waiting.

Suddenly, Jack Ruby emerges from the crowd to Oswald's left. He has come back to see Oswald for a second time, and once again he carries a pistol. Known to policemen and reporters, Ruby had no problem getting close to the perp walk, even though there is absolutely no reason for him to be there.

Ruby has left his dog waiting in the car. But he is an impulsive man, fond of spontaneously beating drunks who make passes at the strippers in his club. He is so devastated by Kennedy's assassination that friends have found him crying. Now, enraged by Oswald's smiling presence, Jacob Rubinstein ensures that he will never see his dog again. He moves fast, aiming his gun at Oswald's abdomen, and fires one shot. The time is 11:21 A.M.

Jack Ruby is set upon by police. Lee Harvey Oswald slumps and is immediately transported to Parkland Hospital. After arriving, he is placed in Trauma Room Two, right across the hall from the emergency room where John Kennedy spent the final minutes of his life. At 1:07 P.M., forty-eight hours and seven minutes after JFK's death, Lee Harvey Oswald also dies.

But unlike Kennedy, Oswald is not mourned.

By anyone.

27

〜

JANUARY 14, 1964
ATTORNEY GENERAL'S OFFICE, WASHINGTON, D.C.

Jackie Kennedy sits in a simple leather club chair before a roaring fire. The flag of the United States can be seen over her left shoulder. Her eyes, once so bright and playful, are dull. She wears black. Across from her as the cameras roll, are Bobby and Teddy Kennedy, there to offer moral support. Bobby, in particular, has become a surrogate parent to Caroline and John, and a constant companion to Jackie.

When her husband died eight weeks ago, Jackie Kennedy had no place to go—protocol mandated that she move out of the White House immediately, which also meant an end to Caroline's special schooling and John's fondness for riding in Marine One. Jackie was hardly penniless, but actually had little cash to her name, a circumstance that will continue until JFK's will is sorted out.

Jackie's whole life was John Kennedy, and even now she sometimes forgets that he's dead. She is filming this spot, which will be shown in movie theaters across the nation as a newsreel, because she wants to give thanks for the tremendous outpouring of warmth from the American people. She's received more than eight hundred thousand letters of condolence. "The knowledge of the affection in which my husband was held by all of you has sustained me," Jackie says firmly to the camera, "and the warmth of these tributes is something we shall never forget."

Jackie's words are scripted, and she reads from cue cards. But they are her own words, chosen specifically to evoke heartfelt emotion. The same American people who elevated a president and his wife to movie star celebrity status have not forgotten Jackie in her time of need. And while she is no longer the First Lady, Jackie Kennedy carries herself with the full weight of that title as never before.

But looks are deceiving: privately she aches, compulsively chain-smoking Newport cigarettes and biting her fingernails to the quick. Her eyes are constantly red-rimmed from crying.

Jackie pauses several times during the filming to catch her breath or flutter her eyes to keep the tears at bay. "All of you who have written to me know how much we all loved him, and that he returned that love in full measure," she tells the world.

And then Jackie Kennedy takes on the same visionary tone of her husband. She speaks of building a John F. Kennedy Presidential Library in Boston, so that people from around the world will know of her husband's legacy.

It is a brave and poignant performance. In less than two minutes, Jackie Kennedy says a heartbreaking thank-you to the American people. Her grief is obvious, as is her elegance. She symbolizes the grandeur of Camelot, for which Americans are already growing nostalgic.

One of the last times Jackie Kennedy saw her husband's face was that afternoon at Parkland Hospital, just before the quiet reverence of Trauma One was turned into an unsightly fracas between Secret Service agents and Dallas police. It was in that quiet moment before she slipped her wedding ring onto Jack's finger. She remembers that moment as if it were yesterday, but prefers to dwell only on the wonderful times. All the indiscretions and controversies of the past are forgotten.

Calm and in command is the way Jackie will always remember Jack. And that's the way she wants history to remember him. "For Jack, history

The end of Camelot. Bobby, Jackie, President Kennedy's sister Patricia, and his children, Caroline and John Jr., in mourning. (Abbie Rowe, National Park Service, John F. Kennedy Presidential Library and Museum, Boston)

was full of heroes," she told Theodore White of *Life* magazine a week after the assassination. "He was such a simple man, but he was so complex, too. Jack had this hero side to history, the idealistic view, but then he had that other side, the pragmatic side. His friends were his old friends, he loved his Irish Mafia."

It was during that interview, which ran in *Life's* December 6 edition, that she first told the world the tale of JFK listening to the Camelot sound track before falling asleep, and how he loved the final line: "Don't let it be forgot, that once there was a spot, for one brief shining moment, that was known as Camelot."

When White dictated the story to his editors in New York, Jackie hovered nearby, listening in. She insisted that the Camelot theme be predominant. This is how she wants her husband's presidency to be remembered.

So as Jackie Kennedy finishes filming the newsreel, and rises from the club chair in Bobby Kennedy's office—he will keep the attorney general title for nine more months—she understands that this is all part of her ongoing obligation to frame her husband's legacy. But she also knows it is time to move on to a more normal life—a life that will be far less magical than the one she wants the world to remember. As she sadly admitted to *Life*'s Theodore White, "There'll never be another Camelot."

And to this day, that statement remains true.

Afterword

Jackie Kennedy's enormous grief, and the grace with which she handled herself after the assassination, only enhanced the public admiration she earned during her husband's presidency. In 1968 she married **Aristotle Onassis**, the Greek shipping tycoon on whose yacht she recovered from the death of her son Patrick. The paparazzi dubbed her "Jackie O," and hounded her constantly, a practice they would continue for the rest of her life. Sadly, the sixty-nine-year-old Onassis died of respiratory failure just seven years after their marriage, making Jackie a widow for the second time at the young age of forty-six. After Onassis's death, Jackie retreated from the public eye, eventually securing a job with Viking Press as a book editor in New York City. She quit that job three years later, angry and embarrassed that the company had published a work of fiction in which Ted Kennedy was the president of the United States and there was an assassination plot against his life. She then moved on to work for Doubleday for the remainder of her nearly two decades in publishing, editing the books of people as diverse as Michael Jackson, Carly Simon, and Egyptian novelist Naguib Mahfouz, a Nobel laureate. In the early 1990s, Jackie's lifetime smoking habit finally caught up with her. She died on May 19, 1994, from non-Hodgkin's lymphoma at the age of sixty-four.

Caroline Kennedy grew up to attend Radcliffe College and later earn her Juris Doctor from Columbia University. She married Edwin Schlossberg, bore three children, and pretty much stays out of the public eye. In December 2011, singer Neil Diamond admitted that Caroline was the inspiration for his multimillion-selling song "Sweet Caroline."

John F. Kennedy Jr. became a symbol for the tragic history of the Kennedy family. The image of him on his third birthday saluting his father's coffin broke hearts worldwide. Erroneously thought to be nicknamed "John-John"—that name was fabricated by the press—John Jr. attended college at Brown and then went on to the New York University School of Law, which eventually led to a short stint in the Manhattan district attorney's office. In 1988, *People* magazine named John Jr. "The Sexiest Man Alive." Like his mother, he was the subject of intense media scrutiny. On July 16, 1999, he was piloting a small plane when it crashed into the Atlantic Ocean off the coast of Martha's Vineyard. The accident killed John Kennedy Jr., his wife, Carolyn Bessette Kennedy, and her sister, Lauren. He was thirty-eight years old. His ashes, and those of his wife, were scattered at sea.

Lyndon Johnson inherited no small amount of unfinished business from the Kennedy administration, most notably the Vietnam War. He masterfully cobbled together coalitions within Congress to help pass the historic Civil Rights Act of 1964. Johnson, working closely with Martin Luther King Jr., framed the issue in terms of JFK's legacy in order to gather support for the act. However, Vietnam was an inherited headache that proved to be his undoing. The Diem assassination was America's point of no return in terms of involvement, and while there are many who debate whether or not the United States had a hand in his death, there's no disputing that the situation only got worse from there. After winning the 1964 election in a landslide over Arizona's Barry Goldwater (a Republican defeat JFK had predicted), Johnson began to mismanage the war in Southeast Asia. As the antiwar movement gained traction, LBJ, fearing defeat, chose not to run again in 1968. Upon leaving Washington, Lyndon Baines Johnson returned to his Texas ranch, where he died of a heart attack at the age of sixty-four on January 22, 1973.

As with the death of John Kennedy, it was **Walter Cronkite** who broke the news of LBJ's death to the nation. Cronkite himself remained a news broadcaster at CBS until 1980. In 2009 he died at the age of ninety-two, still bitter about being replaced by Dan Rather as the anchor of the CBS *Evening News*.

The man who took most advantage of Lyndon Johnson's decision not to run for the presidency in 1968 was **Bobby Kennedy**. The former attorney general had been devastated by his brother's assassination, but overcame his grief to mount a very successful campaign. However, like his brother, Bobby Kennedy was assassinated by a disturbed lone gunman, Sirhan Sirhan, who shot Bobby in a Los Angeles hotel just moments after he had claimed victory in the California primary. He lived for twenty-six hours before dying on June 6, 1968, at the age of forty-two.

Lee Harvey Oswald was buried in Shannon Rose Hill Cemetery in Fort Worth, Texas, on November 25, 1963, the same day that John F. Kennedy was interred at Arlington. In 1967, on the fourth anniversary of Oswald's death, his tombstone was stolen by local vandals. Though it was eventually returned, his mother feared that the grave site would be robbed again, so she replaced the stone with one much cheaper and hid her son's original tombstone in the crawl space beneath her Fort Worth home. After Marguerite Oswald died in 1981 at the age of seventy-three, the house was sold. When the new owners discovered the 130-pound slab in the crawl space, they quietly sold it to the Historic Automotive Attractions

Museum in Roscoe, Illinois, for less than ten thousand dollars. The museum also houses the ambulance that transported Oswald to Parkland Hospital and the Checker Cab he hailed shortly after shooting JFK.

The museum's owners, however, balked at buying Oswald's original pine casket, which was replaced after his body was exhumed in 1981, saying it was too macabre.

One other anonymous individual disagreed, purchasing the coffin at auction for $87,468 in December 2010.

Jack Ruby, aka Jacob Rubinstein, argued that he shot Lee Harvey Oswald to redeem the city of Dallas for the assassination. Legendary San Francisco attorney Melvin Belli defended Ruby for free during his trial, but his arguments about Ruby being insane at the time of the murder did not sway the jury. Jack Ruby was convicted of murder with malice and sentenced to death. After that, Ruby testified before the Warren Commission about the Kennedy assassination and was eventually awarded a new trial by the Texas Criminal Court of Appeals, the judge buying the argument that Ruby could not have received a fair trial in Dallas, due to the enormous publicity surrounding the shooting. But before proceedings could get under way, Ruby was admitted to the now-legendary Parkland Hospital for symptoms of the flu. Instead, he was found to have cancer in his liver, lungs, and brain. He died of a pulmonary embolism on January 3, 1967, at the age of fifty-five. Jack Ruby is buried next to his parents in Westlawn Cemetery, in Norridge, Illinois. It's worth noting that Ruby may have known about his aggressive cancer before he shot Oswald.

Martin Luther King Jr. continued his civil rights crusading and became one of the world's most admired men. On April 4, 1968, King was shot down in Memphis, Tennessee, by an assassin named James Earl Ray, a racist who escaped to Canada, and then to England, before being arrested for the murder of Dr. King. Ray was sentenced to ninety-nine years in prison, a term that was extended to an even one hundred as punishment after he again escaped, this time from the Brushy Mountain State Penitentiary. He was caught three days later. Some believe Ray had help in assassinating King, but this has never been proven. The murders of Martin Luther King Jr. and Robert Kennedy, coupled with the drawn-out American involvement in Vietnam, led to a national sense of disillusionment that was the diametric opposite of Camelot's hope and optimism.

J. Edgar Hoover survived the attempts of several presidents to replace him as director of the FBI. There were many rumors that Hoover was homosexual, based on his close relationship with Clyde Tolson, an associate director of the bureau. Well after JFK's death, Hoover continued his practice of providing presidents with lurid classified files containing the personal indiscretions of high-ranking and influential individuals. Lyndon Johnson took full advantage of this practice. Soon after ascending to the presidency, he requested thick personal dossiers on each of "The Harvards": those members of the Kennedy administration who had once taken such great delight in taunting him. On an even larger scale, Johnson asked Hoover to dig up information on some twelve hundred real or imagined adversaries. J. Edgar Hoover, who like LBJ had felt personally humiliated by the Kennedys during JFK's time in office, was only too happy to comply. Lyndon Johnson returned the favor by issuing an executive order precluding Hoover from compulsory retirement, thus allowing the director to remain in charge of the FBI until his death in 1972 at the age of seventy-seven.

John Connally survived his Dallas wounds and went on to serve two terms as governor of Texas before returning to Washington to serve as Richard Nixon's secretary of the Treasury. He switched from the Democratic to the Republican Party, and ran for president in 1980. However, his campaign floundered badly, and he was forced to drop out after securing just one delegate. John Connally died of pulmonary fibrosis on June 15, 1993. He was seventy-six years old.

Marina Oswald never returned to the Soviet Union. She is still alive and has lived in Dallas for many years. She remarried, briefly, and had a son by her second marriage, which ended in divorce. Like her daughters,

June and Audrey (who now goes by the name Rachel Porter), the stigma of Lee Harvey Oswald has followed her since November 22, 1963. The girls even took the name of their stepfather, Porter, to avoid greater public scrutiny. Now and again Lee Harvey Oswald's family makes television appearances, but otherwise their lives are largely private.

In March of 1977 a young television reporter at WFAA in Dallas began looking into the Kennedy assassination. As part of his reporting, he sought an interview with the shadowy Russian college professor who had befriended the Oswalds upon their arrival in Dallas in 1962. The reporter traced George de Mohrenschildt to Palm Beach, Florida, and traveled there to confront him. At the time, de Mohrenschildt had been called to testify before a congressional committee looking into the events of November 1963. As the reporter knocked on the door of de Mohrenschildt's daughter's home, he heard the shotgun blast that marked the suicide of the Russian, assuring that his relationship with Lee Harvey Oswald would never be fully understood.

By the way, that reporter's name is Bill O'Reilly.

One footnote: A year earlier, de Mohrenschildt sent a letter to George H. W. Bush, then director of the CIA. In that letter, the Russian asked protection from people "following" him. That correspondence with Mr. Bush led to speculation that de Mohrenschildt had CIA ties—and also possessed undisclosed knowledge of the Kennedy assassination.

Another former director of the CIA, Allen Dulles, died of a severe case of the flu in 1969, at the age of seventy-five. To this day, conspiratorialists believe that Dulles was involved in the Kennedy assassination as payback for his firing in the wake of the botched Bay of Pigs invasion. Dulles also served on the Warren Commission, the panel that investigated JFK's shooting.

Sam Giancana, the Chicago mobster, was also thought by conspiracy theorists to be tied to the Kennedy assassination. Giancana was due to testify before a Senate panel investigating whether the CIA and the Mafia had any ties to the murder. Before he could testify, Giancana himself was murdered in his home on June 19, 1975. His assassin shot him in the back of the head, then rolled the body over and emptied the rest of the clip into Giancana's face. The killer was never caught.

Frank Sinatra became a Republican in the years after John Kennedy's Palm Springs snub and was a well-known supporter of President Ronald Reagan. But the singer remained largely silent on his feelings toward JFK. Not so **Peter Lawford**, the man John Kennedy forced to make the phone call telling Sinatra that the president would be staying elsewhere during his Palm Springs visit. In 1966, Lawford divorced JFK's sister Patricia and began making sordid accusations against the Kennedy family. Among them was that Marilyn Monroe had had an affair with Bobby Kennedy as well as JFK, and that Bobby was complicit in Monroe's death. Those charges came at a time when Lawford had lost his acting career to philandering, drinking, and drugs—and remain unproven. Peter Lawford died in 1984 from cardiac arrest brought on by liver failure. He was sixty-one years old.

Greta Garbo lived to the age of eighty-four, dying in New York City on April 15, 1990. She was a recluse to the end of her life, never marrying or having children, and always living alone. The legendary actress, however, was fond of taking long walks through the streets of New York, most often wearing a pair of oversize sunglasses—a habit that her admirer, Jackie Kennedy, would also assume. Garbo was very good with her money, and though she had been retired for nearly forty years at the time of her death, she left an estate to her niece worth more than $32 million.

It has been argued that **Camelot** was a myth concocted by Jackie Kennedy to burnish her husband's legacy. Whether or not the comparisons to Camelot were discussed in the Kennedy White House during the president's lifetime is unclear. But the comparisons are apt and, as Jackie had hoped, the story of Camelot shaped how her husband's presidency is remembered to this day.

John Fitzgerald Kennedy is buried on a slope near the former home of Robert E. Lee, in Arlington National Cemetery, the place he so admired just a few weeks before his death. He is one of only two presidents buried there—the other being William Howard Taft, who died in 1930.

Jackie Kennedy was insistent that her husband's funeral be as much like Abraham Lincoln's as possible. Professor James Robertson Jr., director of the Civil War Centennial Commission, and David Mearns from the Library of Congress were enlisted to research Lincoln's funeral in the short span between JFK's assassination and his burial. The East Room of the White House was transformed so that it looked almost exactly as it did when it held Lincoln's body in 1865. Also, the caisson and funeral procession through Washington, D.C., were copied from Lincoln's final journey.

John Kennedy's burial site at Arlington is lit by an eternal flame, at the suggestion of Jackie Kennedy. It burns at the center of a five-foot circular slab of Cape Cod granite. Jackie rests next to him, as do their two deceased infants, **Arabella** and **Patrick**. Television coverage of John Kennedy's funeral transformed Arlington from the burial place of soldiers and sailors into a popular tourist destination. To this day, no place in Arlington is more popular than the grave of John Fitzgerald Kennedy. A generation after his assassination, more than four million people a year still arrive at Arlington to pay their respects to the fallen president.

And also to the grand American vision that he represented.

Epilogue

We began this book associating John F. Kennedy with Abraham Lincoln. And so shall we end it.

On February 10, 1962, JFK wrote a letter to Washington lawyer Ralph E. Becker. The letter was to be read at a celebration of the hundredth anniversary of the Emancipation Proclamation. Throughout his presidency, John Kennedy often referenced Abraham Lincoln. There was a strong connection between the two men. The following letter is the best evidence that John Fitzgerald Kennedy and Abraham Lincoln were indeed kindred spirits.

TO: Ralph E. Becker, Toastmaster

It gives me great pleasure to send greetings to all
of you who are commemorating the 100th Anniversary
of the Emancipation Proclamation tonight. I wish
that I could have joined you.

Lincoln said about the Declaration of Independence
that it "gave liberty not alone to the people of this
country, but hope to all the world." It "gave promise that in due time the weights would be lifted from
the shoulders of all men, and that all should have an
equal chance."

The Emancipation Proclamation is even better described
by his words. Its importance has never been greater
than it is now -- the weights of slavery, lifted in this
country 100 years ago, have now been lifted almost
everywhere in the world. But it is a long slow march
to a world which recognizes freedom and equality as a
right basic to human life.

Our progress is marked, but it is not completed.
Lincoln's clarity of purpose and thought can serve to
strengthen all of us for the tasks still ahead.

John F. Kennedy

February 10, 1962

Sources

This book required both primary and secondary source research. Much of the primary material came from interviews and reporting that Bill O'Reilly has done over the years. In fact, he won a Dallas Press Club Award for his reporting on the JFK assassination while at WFAA-TV. Extensive new information was gleaned from a variety of law enforcement agents, in particular Richard Wiehl, the FBI agent assigned to investigate and debrief Marina Oswald after the shooting. We are grateful to Mr. Wiehl, who has never spoken before on the record about his findings.

The life and death of John Kennedy needs no embellishment. It stands alone as a riveting period in history. But since many of the events recounted in this book are so fantastic and also so horrific, and because so many of the details are rather intimate, it's important to remind the reader that *Killing Kennedy* is completely a work of nonfiction. It's all true. The actions of each individual and the events that took place really happened. The quotations are words people actually spoke. Those details are made possible in large part because JFK is a contemporary historical figure whose entire presidency was thoroughly documented by all manner of media.

This sheer volume of material available on the life and death of John F. Kennedy allowed for unexpected research delights when compiling the manuscript. Not only were there a number of first-person manuscripts that provided specific details about meetings, conversations, and events, but there is also extensive Internet video of JFK's speeches and television appearances, which brought his words and voice to life during each writing day. For readers, taking the time to find and watch these will add immeasurably to learning more about John Kennedy. The reader is directed, specifically, toward the 1963 Galway speech as an example of the president's wit, warmth, and presence.

To hear about life inside the Kennedy White House from Jackie herself, listen to *Jacqueline Kennedy: Historic Conversations on Life with John F. Kennedy*, a series of recordings she made not long after the assassination. It is remarkable to hear the candor with which the former First Lady speaks, particularly when she opens up about so many of the most famous and powerful figures in the world at that time. Like her husband, her wit, warmth, and sheer presence are palpable.

The authors owe a special debt to the team of Laurie Austin and Stacey Chandler at the Kennedy Library. No research request was too big or too small, and suffice it to say that it was quite a historical rush to receive, for instance, copies of John Kennedy's actual daily schedule, showing his precise location, the names of different people at various meetings, and the time each afternoon he slipped off to the pool or to "the Mansion." To read these schedules was to see the president's day come alive and gave a vivid feel of what life was like in the White House. When in Boston, a visit to the Kennedy Library is a must.

Special recognition must also go to William Manchester's *Death of a President*, which was written shortly after the assassination and built around first-person interviews with almost everyone who was with JFK in Dallas on November 22, 1963. Manchester's work was written with the complete cooperation of Jackie and the Kennedy family. The level of detail is fantastic for that very fact and proved invaluable as the ultimate answer to many questions when other resources conflicted with one another.

The backbone of this book are books, magazine articles, videos, the much-maligned but always fascinating Warren Commission Report, and visits to places such as Dallas, Washington, Galway, and the Texas Hill Country. The authors owe a debt of gratitude to the many brilliant researchers who have immersed themselves in the life and times of John Fitzgerald Kennedy. What follows is a detailed reference to sources. This list, however, is not exhaustive and includes only those works used for the heavy lifting of writing history.

Prologue: Arthur Schlesinger's *A Thousand Days*, Doris Kearns Goodwin's *The Fitzgeralds and the Kennedys*, Karen Price Hossell's *John F. Kennedy's Inaugural Speech*, and Thurston Clarke's *Ask Not: The Inauguration of John F. Kennedy and the Speech That Changed America*. Todd S. Purdum's February 2011 *Vanity Fair* piece on the inauguration was also very helpful, as were the National Archives database and the Warren Commission Report.

Chapter 1: John Hersey's 1944 *New Yorker* story about PT-109 provided the best account of the ordeal. Lance Morrow's *The Best Years of Their Lives*, which is a quick and fascinating read, nicely counterbalances Hersey's sometimes fawning version of events. Details about the Gold Star Mothers speech and the birth of the Irish Mafia can be found in William Manchester's *One Brief Shining Moment*.

Chapter 2: The White House Museum website offers a fine map of the entire building, along with its history in words and pictures. Also, Robert Dallek's writing on JFK's myriad medical woes was very helpful in our getting a handle on the many medications the president was required to take. The Kennedy Library's website is a great source of detail on life in the White House. Information on Jackie comes courtesy of Sally Bedell Smith's *Grace and Power*.

Chapter 3: William R. Fails's *Marines and Helicopters* details the evolution of presidential transportation, while Dallek's *An Unfinished Life* and Humberto Fontova's *Fidel: Hollywood's Favorite Tyrant* lend detail to the Castro atrocities. The weather comes courtesy of the Farmers' Almanac, while Manchester's *Brief Shining Moment* adds behind-the-scenes comments on the president's thoughts on the Bay of Pigs. Other notable resources: Dean Rusk's *As I Saw It*, Edward R. Drachman and Alan Shank's *Presidents and Foreign Policy*, Michael O'Brien's *John F. Kennedy: A Biography*, Thomas G. Paterson's *Kennedy's Quest for Victory*, Jim Rasenberger's *The Brilliant Disaster*, James Hilty's *Robert Kennedy*, Richard Mahoney's *Sons and Brothers*, and Richard Goodwin's excellent *Remembering America*.

Chapter 4: The reader is directed to go online and watch Jackie's excellent White House tour, particularly the body language between the president and First Lady at the end. Seymour Hersh's *The Dark Side of Camelot* was only too happy to spill the secrets of White House infidelities, while Sally Bedell Smith's

Grace and Power, Christopher Andersen's *Jack and Jackie*, Laurence Leamer's *The Kennedy Women*, and C. David Heymann's *A Woman Named Jackie* seem more intent on understanding the reasons why.

Chapter 5: The JFK Library and Jackie's own words in *Historic Conversations on Life with John F. Kennedy* speak to the topic of Camelot, as does Sally Bedell Smith's May 2004 *Vanity Fair* piece, "Private Camelot." Randy J. Taraborrelli's *The Secret Life of Marilyn Monroe*; *The Sinatra Files*, by Tom and Phil Kuntz; and the FBI's dossier on Sinatra add compelling detail to the goings-on in Palm Springs. Evan Thomas's *Robert Kennedy* provides insight into RFK. Hersh's *Dark Side of Camelot* was also invaluable. JFK's comments about the chase came from the *U.S. News and World Report* (May 9, 2004) interview with Sally Bedell Smith. The Gallup Poll's website offered information on approval ratings, while Sam and Chuck Giancana's *Double Cross* provided background on the various potential Mafia plots against Marilyn and the Kennedy brothers.

Chapter 6: The Kennedy Library's website has a feature that allows you to browse the *New York Times* by date. This provides much of the background information on the travels of the president, the atrocities in East Berlin, and the world's interest in matters such as Soviet cosmonauts and the revolutionary radio telephone. Robert Caro's *Passage of Power* was a treasure trove of information about the habits of Lyndon Johnson, particularly his travails as vice president. Details about life in the Deep South come from FBI reports documenting that period, while the story of Emmett Till came directly from his killers' *Look* magazine article, along with other sources that add more dimension, and from the *Ebony* magazine photograph showing his battered and flattened head. Dave Garrow's *Atlantic Monthly* piece of July/August 2002 documents the FBI's fascination with Martin Luther King Jr. FBI special agent Fain's recollection of Lee Harvey Oswald comes from Fain's Warren Commission testimony.

Chapter 7: Photographs of JFK's bedroom can be seen at www.whitehouse museum.org, and further detail can be found in Manchester's *Brief Shining Moment*. More White House history can be found at www.whitehouse.gov; Jackie Kennedy speaks a great deal about their life there in *Historic Conversations on Life with John F. Kennedy*. Specific conversations during the Cuban missile crisis can be found in *The Kennedy Tapes*, by Ernest May and Philip Zelikow, and in Ted Kennedy's *True Compass*. Also of note: Stern's *The Week the World Stood Still*; the archive file of Dean Rusk's meeting with Soviet foreign minister Gromyko; Charles Tustin Kamps's *The Cuban Missile Crisis*; *Jackie*,

Ethel, and Joan, by Randy J. Taraborrelli; *The Mind of Oswald*, by Diane Hollo-way; *Khrushchev*, by William Taubman; and *The Memoirs of Nikita Khrushchev*, by the late Soviet dictator. Robert Dallek's *Atlantic* story about Kennedy's medi-cal woes (December 2002) was also very helpful.

Chapter 8: Believe it or not, the *Mona Lisa*'s unveiling can be found on YouTube. Fascinating stuff. *Mona Lisa in Camelot*, by Margaret Leslie Davis, sheds light on this improbable chapter in our nation's history. The glossary of Manchester's *Death of a President* provides the Secret Service code names, while the Warren Commission Report includes a solid summary on the history of presidential assassination and the need for a Secret Service. The Secret Service's own website shows this, too. Much of the behind-the-scenes information about the various agents and their details can be found in Clint Hill's *Mrs. Kennedy and Me*, and in Gerald Blaine's *The Kennedy Detail*. Edward Klein's *All Too Human* was also very helpful.

Chapter 9: Caro provides more great detail on LBJ in *Passage to Power*. The Giancanas' *Double Cross* goes further into the Mafia conspiracies. These con-spiracies are not presented as facts in this book, but as theories—and *Double Cross* lays out these possibilities very nicely. Also of note in this chapter: Evan Thomas's *Bobby Kennedy*, Burton Hersh's *Bobby and J. Edgar*, Edward Klein's *All Too Human*, Jim Marrs's *Crossfire*, and the LBJ Library's website.

Chapter 10: The Winston Churchill website has a fine overview of this special day, while *Rethinking Camelot*, by Noam Chomsky, deals with the early days of Vietnam in graphic detail.

Chapter 11: Many details about the marchers came from *Washington Post* coverage the following day. Glenn Eskew's *But for Birmingham* and Diane McWhorter's *Carry Me Home* provide additional awesome detail. Shelley Tou-gas's *Birmingham 1963* speaks of how a single photograph changed so many minds. Seth Jacobs's *Cold War Mandarin* provides gruesome detail on the burn-ing of monks and the Diem regime. And once again, Manchester provides great behind-the-scenes glimpses of the Kennedy White House.

Chapter 12: Taylor Branch's *Parting the Waters*; Jessica McElrath's *Everything Martin Luther King, Jr. Book*; Marshall Frady's *Martin Luther King, Jr.: A Life*; Jackie Kennedy's *Conversations*; and *Newsweek*'s infamous January 19, 1998, issue were all valuable resources, as were Evan Thomas's *Robert Kennedy*, Robert Caro's *Passage to Power*, and Dianne Holloway's *The Mind of Oswald*. Clint Hill's *Mrs. Kennedy and Me* is a priceless peek into their relationship, and most helpful.

Chapter 13: Manchester, once again. And Hill. Klein's *All Too Human* and Leamer's *The Kennedy Men* provided insight as well.

Chapter 14: Dallek, *Unfinished Life,* and Thomas, *Robert Kennedy.* King's entire speech can be heard online at www.americanrhetoric.com.

Chapter 15: This interview between Cronkite and JFK is another Web gem, and worth the watch to see Kennedy's smooth knowledge about the many topics Cronkite throws at him and the way the two men relax so visibly when the formal filming is completed.

Chapter 16: Information from the JFK Library, *Death of a President, Passage of Power,* and the Warren Commission Report form the nucleus of this chapter. David Kaiser's *The Road to Dallas* was thoughtful and informative, and the FBI files on Aristotle Onassis provide fascinating background information.

Chapter 17: There are a number of websites devoted to Camp David. These are all well worth a look for a glimpse into such a private and exclusive compound. The information about Oswald comes from the Warren Commission, while Heymann's *A Woman Named Jackie* and the White House Museum website add great detail on the family residence dining room. Ben Bradlee's *Conversations with Kennedy* documents this special dinner. Donald Spoto's *JBKO* details the date of her last campaign appearance; Manchester provided details about her punctuation; and Heymann and Leamer document the letter from the yacht *Christina.*

Chapter 18: The bulk of this chapter comes from newspaper accounts and from Manchester. Bradlee's *Conversations* provides the "No profiles" quote.

Chapter 19: Special Agent Hosty's Warren Commission testimony provides the details about his visit to Ruth Paine. *The Kennedy White House: Family Life and Pictures, 1961–1963,* by Carl Sferrazza Anthony, provides the quotes about Arlington. It's interesting to note that Sergeant Clark also played taps at JFK's funeral.

Chapter 20: Barry Paris's *Garbo* and David Pitts's *Jack and Lem* speak well of this forgotten night in White House history. Thank you to Camille Reisfield of Ross, California, for writing to ask if the episode would be in the book, making the authors aware of this last-ever dinner party in Camelot.

Chapter 21: The Warren Commission and Kaiser's *Road to Dallas* provide unique insight into the days leading up to the assassination. There is still some question as to whether Oswald was actually the shooter whom Sterling Wood witnessed, as the owner of the shooting range swore he saw Oswald there on a completely different date. The fact that a lone man was seen firing a unique Italian rifle, however, is not in doubt.

Chapter 22: Hill, Manchester, Warren Commission testimony, and the White House Museum website.

Chapters 23 through 26: A wide range of websites and books were used to sift through the vast number of facts surrounding the assassination of John F. Kennedy. The timing, crowd descriptions, arrival scene, and all other aspects of the shooting and drive to Parkland Hospital are standard facts. However, the primary sources for specific conversations, private moments, and otherwise particular details are *Death of a President*, the Warren Commission, Clint Hill's fascinating *Mrs. Kennedy and Me*, Vincent Bugliosi's *Reclaiming History*, Dallek's writings on JFK's medical woes and on the assassination itself, and, of course, the Zapruder film. We watched it time after time after time to understand the sequence of events, and it never got less horrific—nor did the outcome ever change.

Chapter 27: Jackie's filmed newsreel can be found online, and her grief is still startlingly painful to watch. Any number of her biographers have briefly mentioned this taping. But it was hardly inconsequential. As with the night with Garbo, or that with the *Mona Lisa*, this event was unique and remarkable, and all too easily overlooked.

Acknowledgments

Super-agent Eric Simonoff continues to be amazingly perspicacious in both creative and business endeavors.

Makeda Wubneh, my assistant for more than twenty years, keeps all my enterprises running smoothly, not an easy task.

Also, much gratitude to my publisher Stephen Rubin, the best in the business, and to my boss at Fox News, Roger Ailes, a brilliant, fearless warrior.

—BILL O'REILLY

I would like to extend a debt of gratitude to all who made this book possible, including Steve Rubin, the rock-steady Gillian Blake, and Eric Simonoff. And, of course, much heartfelt love and thanks to Calene Dugard—muse, soul mate, and closet historian.

—MARTIN DUGARD

Index

Page numbers in *italics* refer to illustrations.

Killing Kennedy

Killing Kennedy

THE END OF CAMELOT

Bill O'Reilly

and

Martin Dugard

MACMILLAN

First published in 2012 in the USA by Henry Holt and Company, LLC

First published in Great Britain 2012 by Macmillan
an imprint of Pan Macmillan, a division of Macmillan Publishers Limited
Pan Macmillan, 20 New Wharf Road, London N1 9RR
Basingstoke and Oxford
Associated companies throughout the world
www.panmacmillan.com

ISBN 978-1-4472-3364-0

Visit www.panmacmillan.com to read more about all our books
and to buy them. You will also find features, author interviews and
news of any author events, and you can sign up for e-newsletters
so that you're always first to hear about our new releases.